# THE MUSE AS THERAPIST

# THE MUSE AS THERAPIST
## A New Poetic Paradigm for Psychotherapy

*On behalf of the United Kingdom Council for Psychotherapy by*

*Heward Wilkinson*

**KARNAC**

First published in 2009 by
Karnac Books Ltd
118 Finchley Road
London NW3 5HT

British Library Cataloguing in Publication Data

A C.I.P. for this book is available from the British Library

ISBN-13: 978-1-85575-595-6

Typeset by Vikatan Publishing Solutions (p) Ltd., Chennai, India

Printed in the UK by the MPG Books Group

www.karnacbooks.com

*To my wife Francis*
*Muse..*

We need another language that does not exist (outside poetry)—a language that is steeped in temporal dynamics. (Daniel Stern, *The Present Moment in Psychotherapy and Everyday Life*)

> Ah Sunflower, weary of time,
> Who countest the steps of the sun;
> Seeking after that sweet golden clime
> Where the traveller's journey is done;
>
> Where the Youth pined away with desire,
> And the pale virgin shrouded in snow,
> Arise from their graves, and aspire
> Where my Sunflower wishes to go!

The fool sees not the same tree that a wise man sees.

He who would do good to another must do it in Minute Particulars: general Good is the plea of the scoundrel, hypocrite, and flatterer, for Art and Science cannot exist but in minutely organized Particulars.

(William Blake)

# CONTENTS

# ACKNOWLEDGEMENTS

Acknowledgement of those who have been part of ones journey, as both influences and as catalysts, is a joy. There are many who have played a part, and yet are too many to be named, or about whom I have to be silent for other reasons. And, with such a late first book, there are some, named or unnamed, who are, alas, now … *precious friends hid in death's dateless night* (Shakespeare, *Sonnet* 30).

These catalysts include many of my students in one setting or another over the years who have been inspirational, provocative, and kind to me, and at the same time goads and thorns in my side, and necessary in their challenges. I wish particularly to acknowledge the members of my Scarborough Integrative Psychotherapy training group, Karen Davies-Hough, June Norris, Stephen Brindley, Sue Dennis, Carol Webster, Irena Kurowska. Those I have taught at the Minster Centre and at University College Cork who have impacted me are alas too numerous to name specifically.

I bear in my heart and mind the creative imprint of so many clients over the years, some of whom do know the influence they have had upon me, and some who do not know. To all of them I repeat with love the words Beethoven wrote upon the title page of his *Missa Solemnis*:

*Von Herzen—mögen es weider—zu Herzen gehen*
(From the heart—may it go again—to the heart).

Many people in the early days of UKCP, when it was even still the Rugby Psychotherapy Conference, and then the United Kingdom Standing Conference for Psychotherapy, played a huge part in enabling me to find myself. I wish specially to acknowledge Alan Lidmila, Dorothy Hamilton, Elspeth Morley, Michael Pokorny, Haya Oakley, and Deryck Dyne. The support of colleagues in the Humanistic and Integrative Section of UKCP, too numerous to mention, have been essential in the background of this book. And, scrapping with the catalytic culture and community of the Metanoia Doctorate, has been a major goad in enabling me to find the determination, and compel the articulation, to finish my book. From my days as a Nurse Tutor I wish to acknowledge the support and creative space I received from Terry Whyke, Roy Saunders, David Brendan McGinnity, and my friend Martin Gajos. From the depths of past relationships to revered teachers and icons, I wish to mention Pat Maguire, Lance Marshall, FR Leavis, Otto Klemperer, John Wisdom.

My mother Kathleen, father Cuthbert, and Elsa and Pip Whiston, gave grounding love which enabled me over the years to overcome my obstacles to the extent which I have done. Cherished Friends, Colleagues, and Elders, part of my inspiration over the years, include Brian Lake, Laura Donington, Ken and Mairi Evans, Mike Phillips, Robert Duffy, Deborah Bartlett, Irene Farmer, Jenny Corrigall, Kate Wilkinson, Sue Aylwin, Maggie Forbes, Janet Croft, Snezana Milenkovic, Ann Sayers, Mary Winspear, Steve Silverton, Ioan Waight, Patricia and Eduardo Pitchon, James Grotstein, Dan Dorman, Derek Portwood, Paul Barber, and Alice Maher.

The teamwork of UKCP and Karnac, among whom Pippa Weitz has been outstanding, created the opening which has given me this opportunity.

My beloved wife Francis, to whom this book is dedicated, has given me the love, the tolerance of my madnesses, the containment, and the sharp creative provocation, which has enabled me to find myself enough to complete this first book.

# ABOUT THE AUTHOR

**Heward Wilkinson**, BA (Cantab), MA (Lancaster), M Psych (Leeds), is Fellow of the United Kingdom Council for Psychotherapy (UKCP), currently Chair of its Humanistic and Integrative Psychotherapy Section, with a literary and theological background, out of which the thinking in *The Muse as Therapist* originated. Founding co-director of Scarborough Psychotherapy Training Institute, a Member Organisation of the UKCP, he was Senior Editor of the *International Journal of Psychotherapy*, the journal of the European Association for Psychotherapy, from 1994–2004; the author of many articles on psychotherapy from a standpoint of creative pluralism; and co-edited two books drawn from UKCP Professional Conferences: *Revolutionary Connections: Psychotherapy and Neuroscience*, and: *About a Body: Working with the Embodied Mind in Psychotherapy*.

# Discovering the Poetic Mystery at the Heart of Psychotherapy: An Unexpected Personal Journey

What this book explores and develops, is what I believe is a powerful and crucial analogy, between psychotherapy and poetry, which constitutes a new model or paradigm for psychotherapy.

Put in a brief sentence it says: Therapy is a form of poesis, and poesis in turn is therapeutic, or pertains to therapy.

I am concerned in this book with poetic process. I shall use the words "poetry", "poetic" (as a generic noun, like "dialogic"), and "poesis", and "poetic process" and variants in a mutually supplementary, contextually appropriate (I hope), way, because it is not simply poetry in the formal sense we are concerned with.

When we read the introductions others have written to their books we have the illusion of permanence; the introduction was always going to have been like that and, indeed, thus it has always been!

Writing this first one of mine myself, I now know very different. Various layers of this introduction, and indeed of this book, have been written at different times, as it has gradually shaped itself; it has created itself rather than being my creation, and is still doing so as I write. Indeed, I am not sure even now that I know what it is entirely! Some elements I am stitching together as seamlessly as possible with others, to be sure, but others just emerge as what ultimately makes sense of what I have previously written and what draws it together, but which I did not realise till then.

This autonomy of *writing* is at the heart of what this book is about. And so when I stand back from it, this sometimes seems to me a mad and strange book, something alien to me—and I am just the one who has written it!

However:

Though this be madness, yet there is method in 't. (*Hamlet*, II, 2)

As I approach its completion, the conception, which seemed so vast, has dwindled to life size or even to a kind of miniature! It begins to take on a life of its own in another way, that of the finished book, with all its imperfections, launched out on to its strange voyage into the world, to take its chance in a climate where, possibly, it will seem utterly obvious and platitudinous to some, and kind of impossible to others.

But it seems to begin to be a finite parcel of accomplishment, something I had hardly imagined possible when I began the writing of it.

For some, it will stretch the conception of a multidisciplinary framework so far as to be unapproachable. For others, its somewhat quirky trajectory may open doors; I hope so. My abiding fear is that it simply will not be understood, no one will "get it". I shall come back to why this is, and to what, if anything, I have done or can do, about this.

Chapter One presents the thesis with exemplifications, from the side of poetry and then from the side of psychotherapy.

Next Chapter Two presents an imagined sample psychotherapy session, nothing very special, but reasonably satisfactorily illustrative, which I comment on briefly in the light of this framework.

Chapter Three takes up the philosophy closest to this vision, that of Heidegger, and sets out to show that *it is as fully poesis as it is philosophy*, in the sense of this approach, in other words, that philosophy does not provide a foundation for this vision, but simply also articulates it in its own way. Implicit in this is a concept of a particularistic *a priori* or *a priori* of the particular, which pervades the whole book, and is most fully explored in Chapter Five.

Next in Chapter Four, we explore, in suitably multiplex fashion, a major example from literature. What unexpectedly became the passional centre of the book for me, comes here, a treatment of the Shakespeare Authorship question, which is derived from a psychotherapeutic-literary understanding of what we can reveal *about the author and his dilemma* from analysis of the work, *King Lear* being the main work chosen.

Thinking about Shakespeare, in sufficient depth, dissolves the traditional antithesis between text and world, in favour of a total *enactment* in which both the author, and we as enquirers, are inescapably implicated. The first part of the chapter gives the background, drawing on G Wilson Knight's (Wilson Knight, 1960) criticism, in relation to *Hamlet*, to bring the Authorship problem into view, with the specific possible solution involving the 17th Earl of Oxford. Even if that hypothesis were to fail, there is a great deal, of a literary-psychotherapeutic nature, about Shakespeare's writing, especially about the character of Edgar in *King Lear*, which would probably remain valid—perhaps just in the way someone like Wilson Knight remains valid even if one is an Oxfordian!

The final full chapter, Chapter Five, articulates the philosophy, and even, in a measure, the theology, presupposed in all this. It articulates the concept of poetic as enactment, taking passages from Daniel Stern's work as example. In a second part, it then goes on to integrate this with Kant's concept of synthetic imagination. This is related to a widened multi-modal concept of the self as a society, drawing on both the later Freud, and Karl Barth's modal conception of the Trinity in *Church Dogmatics*. This is all related to a Heideggerian analysis, as expression of the poesis of social-modal character of the self, of the modes of temporal awareness, past, present, and future.

An epilogue, Chapter Six, relates all this briefly to the state of psychotherapy, and its position in the politics of today, including a brief consideration of the role the United Kingdom Council for Psychotherapy (UKCP) has had in this evolution.

So, effectively, there are two chapters on Poetry and Therapy, two on the philosophy of Poesis, the second in two parts. Then there is one, also in two parts, on the application of the Poetry and Therapy concept to a major literary problem. The two two part chapters are those into which I have put most of myself, and I suppose they are also the most difficult and radical.

This is not only a new; at the same time it is an old model; it synthesises elements in a multiplicity of models, which have been written about in a variety of contexts; but I believe it sees them *as a whole* more than has been done before, and, in a sense, more simply.

As I have written it, it has seized hold of me in unexpected ways. The original plan remains intact in terms of its elements but the relative size of the elements has altered substantially!

Not to put too fine a point on it, a powerful poetic ghost has emerged in the space and possessed and taken over the organisational energy of the book. The ghost is Shakespeare; why he emerges or re-emerges for me in the form of a ghost will become acutely apparent; and how he is the pre-eminent illustration of the "psychotherapy is poetry" formula, likewise!

In the background, the framework for making sense of this analogy, and completing the articulation of a triad, is philosophy of existence (Heidegger, 1961, Mulhall, 2005). In the two chapters exploring this dimension I bring out the way in which philosophy of existence *develops an alternative account of the factual* from that of natural or social science, conventionally conceived. In short, it is the concept of factuality as significant—as significant totality.

These chapters are writing at the meta-level, and somewhat abstract; but my argument is that precisely that meta-level thought about psychotherapy is a dimension which is relevant to practice. More on this as we go on.

I suggest also how philosophy of existence is in turn reciprocally derivative with poetry and psychotherapy.

I do not believe this alternative account is ultimately at all at odds with natural and social science but complementary to them.

However, as conventionally conceived, they leave a giant gap, which it is the purpose of this book to fill!

I am expressing a wide-ranging vision within a relatively small compass, and the effects of compression on my style makes it hard to access what I am saying. I have done my best to, at any rate, indicate the key difficulties involved in this as I go along. But this book has stubbornly refused to be written in a way which oversimplifies the synthesis I am aiming at, or to turn out less radical than it is, though I have tried to explain the central concepts as best as I know. The problem is, the explanations make sense, when one has already had the "aha" of insight what the concept is, because it is an enactment.

Even as it is, some of my initial readers believe I have compromised my idiosyncratic style too much in the endeavour to make it accessible. On the other hand, others wonder, if this is what it's like *after* being simplified and clarified, what was it like before?!

In the process, the *breadth* of the book has diminished, as I have found myself exploring in depth certain major figures, without taking account explicitly of the whole range of those who are writing on these themes today.

*This book is simply an entrée, a sketch and a sample of something which will need to be developed on a much wider canvas—several canvases—in due course.*

Implicitly, the argument with a whole variety of relevant positions is there, but it is not worked through. My apparent neglect of many many such people is not as complete as it appears. An intensive treatment of certain fundamental themes is indeed here, which bears on the whole psychotherapy and literary field. But comprehensiveness has not been possible.

One example among many: I wanted to draw upon Eugene Gendlin's important work, which converges with mine in so many ways, but it has not proved possible; Daniel Stern, Immanuel Kant, and the later Freud, just hogged the space!

I ask the reader to allow, what I believe is its unique blend of insights, to gradually work upon you, and to trust that there is something there to "get". I believe it's worth the wait and effort if you do. I recommend reading it through without trying too hard to understand on a first reading, and then aiming at more precise understanding in a second reading.

I appreciate many will not have time for this. However, all the books I have wrestled with in writing this one are books which repay such efforts—the most striking contemporary example being Daniel Stern's *The Present Moment: In Psychotherapy and Everyday Life*, which I have now visited three times in four years, since my first review article on it in 2003 (Wilkinson, 2003b). And I wrestle with it more because I significantly disagree with it, yet am close enough to it for dialogue to be possible. Someone like my friend James Grotstein I have found too close to me for significant creative disagreement here, although my relation to him is partly sketched in the account (which is one illustration of the therapeutic dimension of my thesis) of the dream which was indirectly about him, that came to me in 2000, as the genesis of the vision of this book was getting underway.

My writing style is more abstract than my teaching style, because, when writing, I am aiming at accuracy and comprehensiveness, as well as immediate communication in a context. No doubt there is a compulsive and autistic element in this but I am also trying to ensure that, so to say, "justice is done" to the many sides of an issue, and to anticipate possible challenges as far as possible in what I write!

This book nevertheless remains a mere introductory snapshot in relation to the themes it is concerned with, and it is inevitable some of my comments and analyses will be one-sided and either unfair or at the very least overly cryptic. I can hardly avoid this altogether— but I remain open to correction! We all struggle with the tension between clarion calls of differentiation from those who represent opposite polarities from us—and then the watered down overqualified statements we emerge with when we realise there are no knock-down arguments!

My endeavour is essentially *to put all this out there* in an initial way; it will be possible to elaborate the several strands in books of their own once the background is established in this way.

I also of necessity assume a breadth of, not fully introduced, cross-reference which goes with the multi-disciplinary intention and ethos of my thinking.

This could only be avoided, if at all, if I had about ten times the space I do have! I apologise for the burden this may place upon the reader and in compensation I can only hope that the challenge and the substantial nourishment on offer, in this very concentrated fare, will outweigh the partial indigestibility of it!

Nested within the general framework and analogy, the book, secondly, develops a powerful, but I think fairly understandable, *three-aspect model, of both poetry and psychotherapy*, which synoptically overviews the whole range of the psychotherapies, and enables us to evoke the several simultaneous aspects which are continuously involved in our work.

In doing so I believe it gives the most elusive, but also most fundamental, aspects of psychotherapy a name, and a fully developed conceptual-philosophical foundation—perhaps for the first time—whilst relating them to and integrating them with, more familiar aspects.

Psychotherapy unfortunately remains a profession dominated intellectually and practically by the effects of the apprenticeship model of learning; it is intellectually immature as a consequence. As a result of this, it is but rarely a genuinely multidisplinary field. This has resulted in distortions, both of perspective and of policy. It *is* intrinsically a genuinely multidisciplinary field, but such a conception has but rarely emerged—and we need to find concepts which enable us to do justice to that.

Such is my endeavour in this book.

***

It represents the distillation of many years of my praxis in psychotherapy. And, before that, from twenty years praxis in psychiatric nursing—and, before that, again, in acquiring, at school and university, the basis for the intellectual-imaginative vision which, in its much more mature and developed form, I try to express in this contribution. It also embodies the distillation, for me, of the impact of an extraordinary journey both in association with, and in parallel with, the development of the United Kingdom Council for Psychotherapy (UKCP), since 1987, when Alan Lidmila and I, representing Yorkshire Association for Psychodynamic Psychotherapy, braved the great snow of '87 to travel the 250 miles from Yorkshire to Kent to investigate this thing called (then) "the Rugby Psychotherapy Conference", something which I also touch on in my final chapter.

In a manner of speaking, what I gradually discovered was, that reflection on the very essence of the process of psychotherapy *was the most fundamental influence for change* upon my praxis.

But by "reflection" I don't mean merely *ad hoc* on-going reflection on actual occurrences and interventions; I mean reflection *absolutely* on the fundamental nature of what I am doing. It was, in effect, philosophy with a bearing on praxis.

I found, over many years, that my reflections—both in supervision and in internal self-supervision—on the psychotherapeutic processes I participated in, gradually compelled me to articulate ever more penetrating, and general or fundamental, concepts, to make sense of what I found myself experiencing.

I found myself in the unusual situation that this deep level reflection seemed, for the most part, to be much more fundamental to my supervisory process, than actual commentary on what I had specifically done in my work, client situations, interventions, countertransference, and the rest. If I could articulate my thinking, the rest would mainly take care of itself. I was seeking another level of understanding, the nature of which for a long time I was not able to formulate.

For a long time during my own apprenticeship, I myself half felt this was something I should feel guilty about—a displacement or diversion from the "real" practical clinical task of supervision.

But gradually I began, more emphatically and less hesitantly, to grasp that it had a creative function. And I also found myself exploring affinities with, on the one hand, psychotherapeutic authors who also manifested a strong *philosophic* bent—such as (mentioning some but by no means all!) Ignacio Matte-Blanco, Wilfred Bion, Jacques Lacan, Daniel Stern, James Grotstein, Darlene Bregman-Ehrenberg, Louis Berger, and Freud himself—and, on the other, with philosophic authors who manifested a strong *psychotherapeutic* bent, such as Spinoza, Hegel, Nietzsche, Heidegger, Sartre, Robert Pirsig, and Jacques Derrida.

In a self-mythic and grandiose sense, I even began to present it to myself as that my "function on the planet" was to put labels on certain things which no one else had found words for ... .

These "certain things" are very elusive things, which it was very easy for individuals to feel to be sheer illusion, for a multitude of reasons.

These include:

the experience of profound inchoate obscurity in the psychotherapeutic process itself;

the way in which knowledge is doubly forbidden for many children; (the double veto of being required to know, but not to be able to know you know, and then, on the contrary, to have to truly believe there was nothing to be known; the paradoxes of theology, and of obedience to Big Brother in Orwell's *1984*, have nothing on this malign miracle of self-contradiction required of, and indeed *performed by*, the child!);

the elusiveness of sheer process, and experience, *as* process and experience;

and much much else.

It was also easy for individuals who struggled with these things to conclude, further, indeed, that this was, in them, stubbornness, and resistive non-adherence to the real tasks in hand, and which were expected of them.

These things, additionally, were again and again played out also in therapists' countertransferences, where the process was wont to be repeated, and would often, where a supervisor or examiner would fall into the trap, be condemned once more as distraction—or worse—from the "real" tasks in hand—such as:

clear formulations of the clients' problems or goals;

interpreting the transference;

identification and reinforcement of the client's real-time *contact* needs;

authentic recognition of the reality of the horrifically abusive character of their childhood experiences;

and similar things.

Now, it is not that these latter things are *not* real, but that these clients cannot reach them without something else first being recognised— namely *that the elusive character of their experience has a meaning as such, even if we cannot find it yet, and even if it is not in the least to be found where we expect it.*

It is not merely resistance, as is so often assumed. (Patently, there is an autobiographical element in this remark!)

Gradually, obscurely (the process in my own reflection—of course!— paralleled the original predicament of wordlessness) it dawned on me that, in articulating how to find words for *specific* predicaments, I was also gradually struggling to articulate a conception of *how wordlessness comes about as such*, in the human world, and of what it meant.

How was wordlessness (in whatever relation to *words and language* appertained to it) so much as *possible*?

With this Kantian-sounding question[1]—which I had by no means formulated as such at that point—latently and implicitly driving my enquiry, I began to enter more and more explicitly upon a process which gradually emerged into the open as **the endeavour to formulate a meta-concept of the psychotherapy field**.

As I progressed in this endeavour I found, somewhat to my surprise, that the more articulately I managed to think about *these* very general matters, the more my actual specific psychotherapy work opened up. This included the discovery of nuggets of rules of thumb and personal folk wisdom, which I began to incorporate in my teaching as well as in my praxis (the above concept of the double veto in childhood experience is just one which came to me in the course of this process).

*It was as if there were a subtle and unexpected interconnection, between the discovery of the widest and most general characteristics of the possibilities, or essential features, of psychotherapeutic experience and process, and the specifics of the process.*

It was as if the specifics were *always in some way already in touch* with very general and elusively all-pervasive features of the process. There is an analogy with the way in which, in Freud, the specific analyses of particular psychological predicaments are always in touch with a mapping of fundamental generalities with specific consequences.

It seemed almost as if Psychotherapy were a species of practical Philosophy!

In some way, in turn, this enabled me to create a space for evolution in my work.

### The emerging vision

A vision gradually emerged for me, in order to account for that common root, as (borrowing from Kant, 1964) we may put it, shared in and by this radical specificity, and the elusive universality implicit in it, of experience and psychotherapeutic experience. This is the vision which I want to articulate in this contribution.

I was previously in a position where I had a sense that I was "on to" something important, the sense of Psychotherapy as a species of Practical Philosophy was how I thought of it initially—but did not know how to say what it was, and therefore in a sense did not know what it was. I have gradually moved to one where I now feel confident of being able to name what it is that does conceptualise that common root of the specific and the elusive universal.

And now, instead, I feel a renewed immense apprehension as I approach the task of *communicating*, genuinely sharing my own understanding of, what I have named.

Previously I came nearest to articulating the total vision in my review article (*The Shadow of Freud*, 2003) on Daniel Stern's *The Present Moment: In Psychotherapy and Everyday Life*. But this was far too compressed, and also too generic a vision to be readily understood (c.f., e.g., Nissim-Sabat, 2005). In this contribution I have now found how to articulate what was merely implicit in that paper, especially in the remarks near the end indicating my total vision:

> Is this psychoanalysis? Freud wrote to Groddeck (Groddeck, 1988) that the defining features of psychoanalysis were transference, resistance, and the unconscious. In such work as we are now envisaging, upon a spectrum, transference oscillates with dialogue; resistance oscillates with play; and unconscious or non-conscious are part of a total spectrum, to which total access even in principle is contradictory, but which exerts its awesome pressure moment by moment in our work, wherein we both study the sacred "Holy Writ" of the "present moment"— but in the company of angels, of the whole encompassing "kosmos" of our human, animal, and cultural history brought to its head in this Kierkegaardian "instant", or the "Moment" of Nietzsche's "eternal return" (cf., Thus Spoke Zarathustra, part III, On the Vision and the Riddle, Nietzsche, 1883); and all of these are in continuity with what has been known as psychoanalysis; and constant and endless dynamic effects, in the fullest psychoanalytic sense (this is the core psychoanalytic discovery, not repression), play through all aspects of the process. And in the

light of this, also, the distinction between "active" and "verbal" psychotherapies becomes minor, by comparison with the vast processes of pattern-enactments and explorations, and pattern transcendings, in the work.

Then, in seminar discussions from around 2006, striving to explain myself, I found myself beginning to use the slogan of what seemed to me the obvious: therapy is poetry, poetry is therapy, and I suddenly found myself taking the equation seriously, and realising it was saying something which was not so obvious to everyone else. The rest was a matter of slotting it all into place, as best I could, as I have tried here to do. It is imperfect, and excessively compressed still, but I am clear about the fundamental step I am taking.

*⁂*

This contribution, then, firstly, attempts to go further than anyone, I believe, so far has done, *in finding form and conceptualisation for the aspects of the process of psychotherapy which are veiled*, for all sorts of reasons already partly touched upon, in silence. I emphasise, adequate form and conceptualisation, since many others, such as Bollas, Bion, Grotstein, Searles, Little, Ogden, Stern—and of course poets and writers like Eliot, Rilke, and Beckett—have recognised the phenomenon. Others have made the comparison with poetry; I do not know of anyone who has actually used the nature and essence of poetry to achieve the conceptualisation—unless it be Eliot himself, in *Four Quartets* (Eliot, 1944). I am open to correction here; like anyone else today my reading is severely limited by comparison with that which is available in one form or another.

In pursuing this analogy I am in a sense paying my homage to the huge catalytic effect Eliot's extraordinary work has had upon both my feeling and my thought since my schooldays onwards!

Since writing these remarks I have become aware of Don Coleman's (2005) work, *The Poetics of Psychoanalysis: Freudian Theory Meets Drama and Storytelling*, which I believe significantly converges with mine, but have not yet been able to read it. I wish to record this partial acknowledgement here, as a promissory note for a fuller response.

I hope this contribution will give a voice, and articulate a recognition, for many (as also those working with them) whose hiddenness is inaccessible to more positive, and definitiveness-claiming, accounts of the nature of psychotherapy.

One of the great sources of discussion of all this in psychoanalytic, and psychoanalysis-influenced approaches, is the poet John Keats' conceptualisation of "negative capability", from which Bion in particular has drawn (Bion, 1970). This is what Keats wrote to his brothers in 1817:

> I had not a dispute but a disquisition, with Dilke on various subjects; several things dove-tailed in my mind, and at once it struck me what quality went to form a Man of Achievement, especially in Literature, and which Shakespeare possessed so enormously—I mean *Negative Capability*, that is, when a man is capable of being in uncertainties, mysteries, doubts, without any irritable reaching after fact and reason -Coleridge, for instance, would let go by a fine isolated verisimilitude caught from the Penetralium of mystery, from being incapable of remaining content with half-knowledge. This pursued through volumes would perhaps take us no further than this, that with a great poet the sense of Beauty overcomes every other consideration, or rather obliterates all consideration. (Keats, 1817b/1947)

This contribution will, at what appears to be (but is not!) the other end of the spectrum, articulate, in the process of defining what wordlessness is about, the whole nature of what Lacan calls the symbolic—language in an extended sense—in a very straightforward and accessible way. It will seek to show that these dimensions of psychotherapeutic experience, (together with the third aspect, what I will refer to as *the relational field*), are *interdependent* in a profound way, that together they encompass nearly all of what needs to be encompassed in giving an account of the whole field, and that they have a common root.

The realisation I came to, which lit up in a lightning flash that puzzling affinity between the utterly specific and the elusively universal, was that there is another paradigm, equally at the heart of a certain kind of illumination of experience, but in a way which placed it, as it were, in tandem with the paradigm which is psychotherapy, namely *poetry*.

To be sure, we may have to here warily recall Freud's warning in *Beyond the Pleasure Principle* (1920/1984) against an elucidation involving an equation with two unknowns! Nevertheless, it is not as if poetry is totally unknown as a paradigm.

The account to be given *is not only intrinsic to psychotherapy as such, but equally to the nature of poetry and related forms of expression.*

*** 

My claim, then, is that we need an analogy to help us grasp the totality, the whole, of psychotherapy, something which offers a congruent parallel, a parallel which is, however, more readily intelligible or accessible—in one sense simply more *quotable* as such.

This analogy or parallel is poetry. (More widely, it is all the arts; but poetry, poesis, is most accessible for present purposes.) Poetry constitutes an available or accessible whole, which may be both analysed, and critically synthesized, in great depth and subtlety. And at its heart, at its ground, in the formative moments of inspiration and creation, is the same inchoate process from which my enquiry starts, into which I stumbled, in considering paradigmatic stuck moments in psychotherapy, and their releasement.

Both poetry and psychotherapy have a central or primal dimension, and involvement of the experience of the ground, which is the incommunicable or, perhaps, the *pre-communicable*—which I am calling "pre-communicability", and which was my starting point in all of this. But, for the full comprehension of what is implicit in that, we need two more dimensions.

Both psychotherapy and poetry have a dimension of *relation*—in a field of relationship—which I am calling "the relational field". (In relational and attachment-based, developmental, approaches—both psychoanalytic, and Humanistic-Integrative—these have been pretty fully explored.)

Finally, both have a potentially infinite dimension of *meaning*, of textuality, which reaches beyond any specific instance of meaning, and to which I allude as "text and context". This is the dimension, involving the capacity for metaphoric thinking, which Lacan calls the symbolic, Derrida "writing", which emerges in Piaget as the movement from concrete/animistic to formal mental operations (c.f., Searles, 1965), and which, in its form as the articulation of and into *metaphor*, Jaynes (1990, Wilkinson, 1999) regards as both what defines, and indeed creates, the transition from bicameral/hallucinatory forms of intentionality to consciousness-based ones.

This last dimension is the hermeneutic or interpretative dimension. It has the peculiarity that it is just as pervasive in Cognitive Psychotherapy as it is in Psychoanalysis!

We perhaps can make sense of this in that *it has a certain primacy, in one respect, within the network of analysis I am offering. For it is the dimension of meaning and intentionality which constitutes our humanness.*

This is certainly what Hamlet thinks, in a classic expression of the logic of the simultaneous human alienation which is likewise human uniqueness (I explore an analogous line of reasoning to this in discussing Heidegger):

> How all occasions do inform against me,
> And spur my dull revenge! What is a man,
> If his chief good and market of his time
> Be but to sleep and feed? a beast, no more.
> *Sure, he that made us with such large discourse,*
> *Looking before and after, gave us not*
> *That capability and god-like reason*
> *To fust in us unused.* Now, whether it be
> Bestial oblivion, or some craven scruple
> Of thinking too precisely on the event,
> A thought which, quarter'd, hath but one part wisdom
> And ever three parts coward, I do not know
> Why yet I live to say "This thing's to do;"
> Sith I have cause and will and strength and means
> To do't. Examples gross as earth exhort me:
>      (Shakespeare, *Hamlet*, IV, 4, my italics)

The awareness of the threeness of the dimensions of time Shakespeare invokes, in conjunction with what we would today call intentionality, connects with the three dimensions of psychotherapy and poetry which I am bringing in, in ways which will gradually become apparent, and which I explore in the chapter on enactment and poetry, where I touch on the "Trinitarian" implications of Freud's later metapsychology of "I", "It", and "Over-I".

*The dimension of meaning or intentionality—the hermeneutic dimension—is what enables us to recognise, against its background, the other two dimensions.* The other two dimensions bring out our community with the animal world; in them animals participate much more profoundly than they do in the hermeneutic dimension, though this is not altogether absent in them.

As far as the dimension of *relation* goes, there can, as is well-known, be mutual attachments, as great as any human attachments, between humans and animals.

And Buber, (1923/1958), for instance, has intimated that the exchange of beingness in a glance—what I am calling the *pre-communicable*, and which is, to be sure, related to the "It" used in a different sense from Buber's—can be as profound, for instance, with a cat, as with a person.

*In many ways, much of what I am saying, in this somewhat arcane form, here, relates to this very intimately private animal-precommunicable dimension of the body, of inchoate pre-verbal feelings and visceral processes, and so on.*

But *text and context*, the whole symbolic background and underpinning of intentionality and meaning, is arguably what makes us human and what makes this whole dialectic possible. To be sure, there is indeed also a context when two stags fight each other during the rut. And animal intelligence indeed becomes more remarkable the more we study it. Nevertheless, this dimension is still something of a criterion of how far a particular species—dolphins, whales, elephants, the higher apes, and so on—can parallel certain things central to human experience[1]. So it has a certain primacy in the analytic-methodological framework I am putting forward—but nevertheless only in certain respects.

But the three aspects take us far and wide. We have to embrace genuine multidisciplinary enquiry in psychotherapy to do them justice; "negative capability", the staying with, living with, uncertainty, *involves actual conceptual multi-facetedness*, not simply the inchoate sense of the unknown, though that is an essential dimension of it.

The three aspects are related to, but not the same as, such developmental conceptions as Daniel Stern's (1985) four senses of self, emergent, core, intersubjective, and verbal, and Piaget's (1952) analysis of the stages of mastery of cognitive operations, sensory-motor, pre-operational, concrete operational, and formal operational. The three aspects are a matrix which enables us to identify different simultaneous (and inseparable) "elements" in human experience, and in that sense bear to the developmental models somewhat the relation which the Kleinian concept of "positions" bears to the literal form of the Freud-Abraham concept of developmental stages. I return to the tensions of this relationship in the methodological chapter.

The three aspects are involved in detailed methodological analyses in the following pages. I use examples including from poetry, drama, the novel, psychotherapy, and from science fiction. There is a continuous stream of exemplification, from a multiplicity of discourses, in the book.

The book and the project develops the dialectical interface between the triad of psychotherapy, poetry, and philosophy, and the triad of the three aspects of psychotherapy and poetry, in ways which will gradually be unfolded, and it will use the triadic structure, in its turn, as a kind of methodological experiment.

I know that questions can be raised about the preoccupation with threes! (or indeed fours!) the book will test how far this can actually be taken, and whether it inclusively exemplifies the powerful explanatory reach I attribute to it.

It is not of course claimed that this is the only possible way of viewing the phenomena, just that it *is* a powerful and useful one!

*\*\*\**

There are many connections of this vision with a variety of traditions linked with the hermeneutic and phenomenological. My conception integrates and epitomises some diverse conceptions, in a striking convergence, and I mention a few of them now:

i. Derridean deconstruction, and his concepts of *difference* and of primary writing (this is the closest to what I am saying);
ii. the alchemical-symbolic tradition, with its Heraklitean preoccupation with the opposites, as explored in the later Jung, despite a certain unphenomenological hypostatisation of archetypal processes in Jung himself;
iii. the literary criticism and literary philosophy of DH Lawrence, FR Leavis, and J Middleton Murry's *Keats and Shakespeare*, which invoked a universalism of the specific (foreshadowed

by Coleridge and William Blake) in a better articulated way then ever before;

iv. Paul Ricoeur's developments of hermeneutic enquiry, and the hermeneutic interpretation of Freudian methodology;

v. Levi-Strauss's structural-anthropological analyses of myths;

vi. a major aspect, namely the pluralistic method of differentiation and then assimilative understanding (which looks back to Hegel, to be sure), of the dialectical theological methodology of Karl Barth;

vii. Robert Pirsig's "metaphysic of quality" (and related aspects of the pragmatism of William James and Richard Rorty, which even connect with certain aspects of Daniel Dennett's neo-Darwinism!);

viii. major elements in the phenomenological and existential-ontological traditions and in Nietzsche, and the later Wittgenstein;

ix. aspects of the work of the later Whitehead, and that of Michael Polanyi;

x. certain traditions in psychotherapy, particularly Gestalt;

xi. and the work of John Heron and Eugene Gendlin at the metaphysical boundaries of psychotherapy.

All these (together with earlier models—much of this ultimately comes out of the Romantic Movement in Germany and England, Hamann, Novalis, Schelling, Hegel, Blake, Coleridge and Keats being particularly crucial; some of this has been astutely documented by Sir Isaiah Berlin in *Three Critics of the Enlightenment: Vico, Hamann, Herder* (Berlin, 2000) )—appear to me, now, to clearly converge in this conception of *the fundamental epistemological-ontological importance of poetry-poesis as a paradigm,* in the light of which *psychotherapy emerges thoroughgoingly as a species of ad hoc or improvisatory poetry* (and also emerges in its proper location in relation to the post-Romantic tradition). I leave these in the background, of what I am offering, but they are there; this is not a gratuitous conception from out of the blue.

An increasing number of psychotherapy practitioners, members of doctorate courses, and authors in the psychotherapy field, are invoking poetry and the arts in their work. For instance, already many years ago Robert Hobson wrote *Forms of Feeling: the Heart of Psychotherapy* (1985), in which, drawing upon the work of Susanne Langer, and Winnicott's theory of transitional experience, he envisaged an understanding of psychotherapy in close connection with literature and symbolic communication of many kinds:

<http://www.guardian.co.uk/obituaries/story/ 0,3604,252220,00.html>

More recently Kate Maguire, erstwhile Head of the Doctoral Programme at Metanoia Institute, has explored the way in which survivors of extreme experiences resort to poetry or similar forms of communication when seeking to express themselves, when there is nothing else left (Maguire, 2001), and both Terry Waite and Brian Keenan, survivors of torture and solitary confinement in Lebanon, in different ways, addressing UKCP Conferences, also indirectly (by example and anecdote) confirmed this.

Again, Miller Mair has been pursuing similar themes of story and metaphor for many years (e.g.,):

<http://www.oikos.org/mairstory.htm>

And the Journal "Poetry Therapy", even though its concerns are somewhat different from mine, has been established for over twenty years:

<http://www.poetrytherapy.org/>

<http://www.tandf.co.uk/journals/titles/08893675.asp>

This whole trend of the poetic dimension of therapy and the therapeutic dimension of poetry might be considered, in the widest generality, as pointing towards thinking more about what psychotherapy *is* than what about it *does*. There has been a huge amount of valid, useful and substantial research work, both quantitative and qualitative, on what psychotherapy *does*. The bulk of the research work which has been done is about what it does, in one form or another.

It is part of my thesis that psychotherapy has implicitly integrated literary methodology (and also, less obviously, theological methodology) into its praxis.

This vision of psychotherapy will seek to establish a position which can do justice to the several unique features which psychotherapists have, variously, and with special emphases in one context or another, attributed to psychotherapy, but which have never been given a context which enables them to become intelligible in their own right.

The context is poetry.

Psychotherapy is a kind of poetry—an activity of the muses, an embodiment of inspiration, and a gift of the gods. But likewise poetry is a form of psychotherapy—to do with healing and release and expression of the soul. They come from a common root.

And I just this moment checked my Greek Mythology (yes, Google!) and, yes, Asclepios, god of medicine and healing, is the son of Apollo, god of poetry and the muses!

*Heward Wilkinson*
London, July 2007

## NOTES

1 Kant pioneered the concept of philosophical enquiry as *enquiry into the core or a priori preconditions which make certain kinds of experience*, such as the capacity for self-consciousness, *possible*, (Kant, 1964). Precisely what these statements mean is a complex matter, which will be touched on substantially again in this contribution.
2 See e.g., Gregory Bateson's (1979) poignant account of a dolphin's learning the meta-concept of "a new trick" in *Mind and Nature* (pp. 135ff.)

# Therapy is Poetry

## Introductory summary in three sentences

1. The structure of psychotherapeutic process is substantially an analogue of poetic.
2. Poetic process is substantially an analogue of psychotherapeutic.
3. Both, for their full articulation, lead into an ontology of human existence.

### 1. The parallel between psychotherapy and poetry

The conception, both psychotherapeutic and poetic, I want to explore, comes initially out of experiences as a practitioner, which will be familiar to many, in which one works with someone in a stuck space—and hangs in there with them, not doing very much, just enough to maintain the alliance, whilst the therapist struggles with their internal process (countertransference), and the client with whether they can cope with, either the oppression of their silence or confusion, or their impulse to speak, in the face of fear or shame. Then there dawns on one or other of us (it doesn't matter which) an insight, a shift, a releasement, and something moves in

1

the process. (If I were running a practitioner workshop, at this point I would invite participants to explore their own experience of such moments, or analogous moments.)

Then one wonders about whether one could explain it, (that is, the process), to an outsider—and one immediately realises that, unless someone has already had the experience, or something analogous, they won't "get" it. That is, they need a parallel "aha" to the one which occurred in the original situation!

I think it is, and can be quite well be, empirically established that such moments are "curative" or "mutative", by commonly and consensually accepted measures. But that kind of enquiry needs to be supplemented by one which tells us *what happened*.

What happened—that which psychotherapy *is*, as opposed to what it *does*—constitutes a whole which is beyond finite analysis, though one can do something with it if one has a transcript or, even better, a video of the interaction (or the recall memory of a Boswell or a Freud!)

That mode is familiar enough to assessors in psychotherapy, particularly within the Humanistic and Integrative cultures, but it usually is offered in a mode which *presupposes* the jargon and forms of analysis of the approach in question, and therefore does not offer an independent understanding of what is going on (c.f., Wilkinson, 1998).

So, we need an analogy to help us grasp that totality, that whole, something which offers a congruent parallel, a parallel which is, however, more readily intelligible or accessible.

This analogy or parallel is poetry. (More widely, it is all the arts; but poetry is most accessible for present purposes.) And in the end it turns out to be more than just an analogy.

Poetry constitutes an available or accessible whole, which may be analysed and critically synthesised in great depth and subtlety. And at its heart, at its ground, of its very essence, is the same inchoate process into which we have already stumbled, in considering such moments as alluded to above.

Both poetry and psychotherapy have a central or primal dimension, an involvement of the experience of the ground of the process, which is the incommunicable or, perhaps, the *pre-communicable*. This I call "pre-communicability", and it is my starting point above. But, for the full comprehension of what is implicit in that, we need two more dimensions.

Secondly, both psychotherapy and poetry further have a dimension of *relation*—in a field of relationship—which I call "the relational field". (In relational and attachment-based, developmental, approaches—both psychoanalytic, and Humanistic-Integrative—the dimensions of this have of course been pretty fully explored.)

Thirdly, both have a potentially infinite dimension of cross-referential *meaning*, of textuality, which reaches beyond any specific instance of meaning, and to which I allude as "text and context". This is the dimension, involving the capacity for metaphoric thinking, which Lacan calls the symbolic, Derrida "writing", the dimension which emerges in Piaget as the movement from concrete/animistic to formal mental operations (c.f., Searles, 1965), and which Jaynes (1990) regards as what defines the transition from bicameral/hallucinatory forms of intentionality to consciousness-based ones. (This dimension also provides a developmental criterion, which complicates the picture, but also holds out the prospect of solution to several problems, to which we shall return.)

I shall return to my brief account of this three-way structuring later, merely noting for now that, in its meta-level analysis and welding together of quite different "registers", it gives us space enough to avoid certain inveterate dogmatisms in psychotherapy, which tend to arise from an exclusive and over-concrete adherence to single monochrome theoretical frameworks. It also gives us, in a several aspected way, something like a criterion of completeness in psychotherapeutic work! In this it aspires to a comparable, and comparably testable, comprehensiveness as does John Heron's Six Category Intervention Analysis (Heron, 2001). As with his analysis, to which I have been indebted in developing this one, there can be other, quite different, lenses through which to view the field, which operate at other levels, and do not necessarily compete with this one.

So, therefore, there are:

1. existence or being ("pre-communicability");
2. relationality and intersubjectivity ("relational field");
3. the dimension of meaning, ("text and context").

(And, even at this point, we can detect a certain correspondence to Freud's "It", "I", and "Over-I" [Id, Ego, SuperEgo], Freud, 1923/1984, and gain a hint that this categorisation may have "structural" implications further down the line. We thus can also see a potential affinity with Lacan's "Real", "Imaginary", and "Symbolic", and there are also possible relations to the work of Fairbairn, Berne, and the Gestaltists.)

Because both the psychotherapy process or the poetry process are *wholes*—and indeed infinite wholes, encompassing the dimensions of both the actual and the possible, inextricably interfused—the kind of account which can be given of them is not primarily an empirical, factual, analysis, but an analysis such as is given by philosophy of existence (Heidegger, 1962). This does not contradict empirical accounts but complements and completes them. But philosophy of existence, in its turn, is nothing without poetry, without accounts of human reality, the human world, parallel or analogous to poetry, and drawing upon poetry.

In gaining a vantage point outside of psychotherapy as such we achieve a kind of *philosophical* or logical triangulation—indeed, a triangulation with respect to all three, psychotherapy, poetry, and philosophy. If this approach is valid, it may be startling what degree of illumination "of what we always knew", can be achieved with the cross-comparison.

In short, in psychotherapy and counselling, all along, what we have been doing is *creating poetry*—often low key, but none the less poetry for that—and poetic-dramatic narratives. To epitomise it: whilst for scientifically minded critics such as Köchele (2004) it is a *criticism*, that Freud presented his theories in novella form (a primitive unscientific phase, to be superseded as soon as possible), for me this is his masterstroke. Freud had indeed discovered the essential paradigm, serendipitously (c.f., Wilkinson, 2005a). But the consequence was that he could never found a science in the quantitative sense, much as, in one sense, he wished it, (and to this day psychoanalysis talks of its "scientific meetings", c.f., Ricoeur, 1970, Grunbaum, 1984).

Of course, if we were to adopt a wider concept of science, congruent with its meta-concept, then both philosophy and literary criticism will also be included as sciences, though then we also have to wrestle with the implications of pluralism, and the dissolving of neat criteria for the exclusion of pseudo-disciplines (c.f., Wilkinson, 2003a).

Accordingly, the methodology of appraisal we all inadvertently employ, in psychotherapy, is, whether or not we realise it, a species of *literary criticism*.

## 2. Poetry and psychotherapy

We can approach this analogy from either the end of poetry or that of psychotherapy. I think it is possible to show that a familiar kind of uncovering of, for instance, a dream with its associations, runs precisely parallel to the literary-critical and hermeneutic revealing of a poem. But I shall rather begin from the end of poetry, so as, after that, to throw a characteristic bit of psychotherapeutic elucidation into sharper relief, placing the familiar in an unfamiliar light, and thirdly an example from a very well-known piece of science fiction.

So I now introduce in more detail the consideration of poetry, with certain major points of comparison between poetry and psychotherapy (making the links with the three aspect model as I go along). All this will be articulated philosophically in Chapter 5, on poetry and objectivity, and I am just sketching it informally here.

1. A poem, like a psychotherapy session, firstly offers *a human whole*—an intentional whole, a whole organised around personhood, persons in relation ("relationship").
2. Secondly, a poem displays unaccountable or unexpected rhythmic shifts and movements in its process—sudden pauses and abrupt transitions. It has a "sloppy" element, in Daniel Stern's sense, (Stern 2004, Wilkinson, 2003c), and mimics the "sloppy", indeterminate, pre-rational/non-rational, chthonic, recalcitrant, aspect of human existence itself ("pre-communicability"). *Even when* it is quasi-logical in structure, as in Marvell's *To His Coy Mistress*, or TS Eliot's *Ash Wednesday*, this is making a trans-logical, enactive, communication.
3. Thirdly, it presents and enacts a patterned and scripted *human drama* ("text and context").
4. As such, fourthly, its human medium is primarily *emotion*, with the complex, temporally structured, implicitly history-ridden, intentionality of emotion; (it can indeed be argued that, historically, poetry *created*, and made possible, human emotion, c.f.,

Jaynes, 1990, Wilkinson, 1999, 2003c). In a not too stretched sense, emotion *is* poetry (and a theory of emotion is implicit in this—this involves all three aspects, ground, relation, and meaning, as we might name them in *this* context).

5. In the poem, fifthly, elements which may be displayed *bodily* (facial expressions and complexion shifts, gestures and movements, etc., whether or not worked with in a "body psychotherapy" way—"pre-communicability", "It") in a psychotherapy session, are *enacted* through rhythm, sounds of words, the intersection of meaning and sound, and so forth. This is the art of the poem in mimicking ("mimesis") and "replicating" life, and replicating (but in a Platonic mode) *individual-hood*, in the philosophical sense (Strawson, 1959, 1966, Wimsatt, 1967).

6. In the light of this essentially platonic implication, we can go on, sixthly, to note that the key to this whole matter, is that the truth of a poem (like that of any "platonic" identity) is primarily *disclosive*, or *aletheic* (Heidegger, 1962), not *assertoric* (this mainly takes us into "text and context", but also "precommunicability", and indeed all three aspects). In chapter 5. we shall analyse this under the heading of "enactment".

What this means is what emerges from the Greek term for truth, *a-letheia*, (literally "the taking away of Lethe", of forgetfulness)—that is, disclosure or unconcealment. It conveys a notion of truth in which *reflexive awareness is part and parcel of the whole disclosure*. It is participatory, not something separate, not simply factual correspondence; (this "participatory" aspect is, nevertheless, primarily where "pre-communicability" is located). It is enacted and embodied, in a host of ways, and therefore our primary mode of access to it is in the form of *disclosure*, not assertion corresponding to factual states of affairs (which is not to say assertion is not involved in the secondary elucidation of this). It is actual history and event, ("existence"), at least in the form of "repetition" (which is never purely repetition), not simply or primarily correspondence to fact, though factual assertion does secondarily correspond to it.

In this, it approximates to the condition of music (the word root is the same as that of "Muse"), the purest form of (platonic) enactment in time, but lacking the referential and mimetic element which poetry possesses. But music reveals its own truth in experience; it is pure lived disclosure of a created human possibility (platonic, essential, non-empirical), and as such illustrates the dynamic reality of the aletheic more vividly than any other paradigm.

Poetry, however, combines the aletheic and the representational in a unique and peculiar way. It *intersects* the realm of the representational and the ideal/aletheic in a way which transcends the empirical/a priori antithesis, which lies behind all scientific generalisation analysis of event and process. In a special sense a poem is what used to be called (following Hegel, c.f., Wimsatt, 1982) a *concrete universal*.

7. And a poem, seventhly, like a session, offers *a total network of interconnection*, textually ("meaning", "text and context"), which is an organic whole. This takes it into the realm of pure quality, pure infinity. This accordingly complements the proposition that a poem and a session/series of sessions can, as they can of course, have empirical effects, and accordingly it cannot be reduced to them. It has to be accounted for in its own terms, which are terms of *the wisdom of experienced judgement*.

Existence, relationship, meaning, the three dimensions: these, therefore, are all enacted in the poem, and the poem embodies an infinitude (Wilkinson, 2003b) in all three aspects[1].

### 3. Poetry and psychotherapy: Gerard Manley Hopkins (and Shakespeare's King Lear)

The examination of an actual poem illustrates all of this very graphically. As an example of my methodology, first with the focus on poetry, I begin with Gerard Manley Hopkins' poems, *No worst, there is none*, and *That Nature is a Heraclitean Fire and of the comfort of the Resurrection*. There are a whole cluster of issues in relation to what I am going to be saying here, in literary theory and debate. I cannot discuss these here; I merely note, for the sake of accuracy for anyone familiar with literary theory who wonders, that issues about the "intentional fallacy", the "affective fallacy", the "psychological reductive fallacy", the "pure form", or "pure text" fallacy, and so on, *are* in the background of what I am saying, and also the corresponding (if they are not, in fact, *the same* wolves in other clothing!) philosophical issues about intentionality, language, context, and so on (c.f., e.g., Wimsatt, 1982). These issues are touched on again in chapters four and five.

Now to illustrate all this.

In workshops I run on this theme, I set out to connect people's experience—and sensory evidence of this in their analysis of their process—of either stuckness in psychotherapy work, or moments of breakthrough/illumination (usually the two are connected), with parallels in the poems of the marvellous and original 19th century Roman Catholic poet, Gerard Manley Hopkins. Of course it is easier to convey when one is reading them out loud, and harder to convey on the written page.

A major technical innovator, who foreshadowed 20th century poetic innovations, Hopkins had pioneered, almost totally on his own, a new, immensely concrete and sensuous and rhythmic, poetic (which he called "Sprung Rhythm"), an intensification of the enactive-aletheic mode of poetic, full of grammatical compressions, and semantic and rhythmic improvisations, which ideally needs to be read out loud to convey its full power. Hopkins found in Duns Scotus, the mediaeval apostle of individuality, or individuation, "thisness", (also a key figure in Heidegger's early development of his own vision; Heidegger wrote his doctoral dissertation on a putative text of Duns Scotus'), a conceptualisation which released Hopkins' poetic, unique as it is, but a poetic nevertheless profoundly suited to emphasise the different kind of validity of literary methodology, as we shall see in a moment.

In 1885, Hopkins, no longer working as a priest, struggling, as Chair of Classics at University College Dublin, to teach concrete-minded Dubliners philosophy, and whose order, the Jesuits, had (not in ill-will, but incomprehension) a by no means adequate response to his poetry, and to the possibility of publication (his mature work was not published in his lifetime, I believe our only great English poet of whom this is true—except, perhaps, as we shall see later, Shakespeare), was in black despair.

Even his faith was taking the form of protest, in such poems (the so-called "terrible sonnets") as this:

No worst, there is none. Pitched past pitch of grief,
More pangs will, schooled at forepangs, wilder wring.
Comforter, where, where is your comforting?
Mary, mother of us, where is your relief?

My cries heave, herds-long; huddle in a main, a chief        5
Woe, world-sorrow; on an age-old anvil wince and sing—
Then lull, then leave off. Fury had shrieked "No ling-
ering! Let me be fell: force I must be brief".

O the mind, mind has mountains; cliffs of fall
Frightful, sheer, no-man-fathomed. Hold them cheap       10
May who ne'er hung there. Nor does long our small
Durance deal with that steep or deep. Here! creep,
Wretch, under a comfort serves in a whirlwind: all
Life death does end and each day dies with sleep.

If we simply considered, out of context, the magnificent lines:

O the mind, mind has mountains; cliffs of fall
Frightful, sheer, no-man-fathomed. Hold them cheap       10
May who ne'er hung there.

then we might think the poem is simply an evocation, expression, or description of feeling (and in that sense primarily "factual
correspondence").

But surrounding it, the aletheic disclosive-enactive aspect comes
out in the way it is saturated with many overwhelming elements of
*enactments and performatives* (Austin, 1975), such as prayerful voca-
tives addressed, variously, to the Holy Spirit, and the Virgin Mary,
and to himself, with voices from primitive visceral inner selfhoods

(Fury had shrieked "No ling-
ering! Let me be fell: force I must be brief".)

Grammatical rules are tortured to the limits of meaning, as with: *No
worst, there is none.*

This enactive element it is which (combining them) operates in the
realms of both *pre-communicability* and the *relational field*. This aspect

is retained in the condensed cross-referencing—this is the aspect of
*text and context*—of what follows.

As we explore the poem we become aware of a mass of images,
and, with them, allusions and resonances, biblical and Shakespearean
allusions, not all conscious, almost certainly, and allusions to human
situations, telescoped together in a mass of fused dreamlike conden-
sations (Hopkins' fusional poetic, like Joyce's poetic prose, might
almost be described as a technique for the intensification of the
dreamlike associative dimension of poetry).

> My cries heave, herds-long; huddle in a main, a chief          5
> Woe, world-sorrow; on an age-old anvil wince and sing—
> Then lull, then leave off. Fury had shrieked "No ling-
> ering! Let me be fell: force I must be brief".

In the line: *My cries heave, herds-long* there is introduced the theme
of herd animals, and, fast and furious, there successively implodes
into this allusion reference to storms, to "cries" fused in imagination
into, and as, animals caught in herds in a storm on the mountain-
side (the use of "fell", played against "fall" a couple of lines further
on, has multiple ambiguities, and the falling over the cliff invokes
the Gadarene swine, so that the "cries" becomes a stampede of pan-
icking pack animals, while "main", here an adjective, is simultaneously also, as a noun, an old word for "moor", as Hopkins the
Welsh-speaker would most probably have known), to horse-shoeing
and weapon-forging (the anvil), and to animal slaughter (and probably castration and the threat of suicide) in Fury's cry.

Heere the *enactive* component, and the *text and context* element are
inextricably intertwined, veritably coagulated together.

The ostensible believer in the Resurrection alludes to death as
oblivion in the final line, and hence implicitly again to suicide.

In this connection, the *cliffs of fall*

*Frightful, sheer, no-man-fathomed* also are almost certainly an allusion to the attempted suicide of Gloucester in Shakespeare's *King
Lear* (Act IV.Sc. 5):

> ["Come on, sir; here's the place: stand still. How fearful
> And dizzy 'tis, to cast one's eyes so low!
> The crows and choughs that wing the midway air

Show scarce so gross as beetles: half way down
Hangs one that gathers samphire, dreadful trade!
Methinks he seems no bigger than his head:
The fishermen, that walk upon the beach,
Appear like mice; and yond tall anchoring bark,
Diminish'd to her cock; her cock, a buoy
Almost too small for sight: the murmuring surge,
That on the unnumber'd idle pebbles chafes,
Cannot be heard so high. I'll look no more;
Lest my brain turn, and the deficient sight
Topple down headlong."]

I think the "wretch" in Hopkins' final line is also an echo of *King Lear*, where the word occurs incessantly (e.g., crucially, when Lear is about to go into the hut out of the storm, before encountering "poor Tom", III, 3, v. 25) and, once seen, there becomes evident a whole mass of allusions to *King Lear*. Shakespeare's mighty pagan/Christian opus of despair, nihilism, good and evil, and devoted sacrificial love, is indeed the fitting backcloth of this "terrible sonnet", one of several written at his blackest time around that period, when he was feeling utterly abandoned and hopeless, whilst working, very isolated, in Ireland. It also illustrates again the relevant "infinitude" in the mode of cross-referencing ("text and context").

But, now, it also turns out to illustrate the element of contextual falsifiability and of confirmability in literary methodology (and its parallel with the similar process of enquiry and disconfirmation in psychotherapy). For, armed now with the hypothesis of a powerful presence of *King Lear* in this poem, we can once more return to the first line in which grammar is put to torture, as we have seen:

No worst, there is none.

And we realize that in its extreme compression there is another echo of *King Lear*, an echo of the terrible moment in the play when Edgar encounters his now blinded father, and the following comes to pass (IV. Sc. 1) (note the already-mentioned recurrence of "wretch"!):

**EDGAR**
Yet better thus, and known to be contemn'd,
Than still contemn'd and flatter'd. To be worst,

The lowest and most dejected thing of fortune,
Stands still in esperance, lives not in fear:
The lamentable change is from the best;
The worst returns to laughter. Welcome, then,
Thou unsubstantial air that I embrace!
The wretch that thou hast blown unto the worst
Owes nothing to thy blasts. But who comes here?

Enter GLOUCESTER, led by an Old Man

My father, poorly led? World, world, O world!
But that thy strange mutations make us hate thee,
Life would not yield to age.

**Old Man**
O, my good lord, I have been your tenant, and
your father's tenant, these fourscore years.

**GLOUCESTER**
Away, get thee away; good friend, be gone:
Thy comforts can do me no good at all;
Thee they may hurt.

**Old Man**
Alack, sir, you cannot see your way.

**GLOUCESTER**
I have no way, and therefore want no eyes;
I stumbled when I saw: full oft 'tis seen,
Our means secure us, and our mere defects
Prove our commodities. O dear son Edgar,
The food of thy abused father's wrath!
Might I but live to see thee in my touch,
I'ld say I had eyes again!

**Old Man**
How now! Who's there?

**EDGAR**
[Aside] O gods! Who is't can say "I am at the worst"?
I am worse than e'er I was.

**Old Man**
'Tis poor mad Tom.

**EDGAR**
[Aside] And worse I may be yet: the worst is not
So long as we can say "This is the worst."

Of which, surely, the epitomisation, the drawing of the terrible logical conclusion, is Hopkins' grammatical reversal:

No worst, there is none.

Led by the word "comfort" we might then, further, turn to the scene
of Gloucester's blinding, and ask about the hidden presence in
Hopkins of the preoccupation with blinding, mentioned in several
other poems, but not overtly here (though I have referred already to
the possible allusion to castration, above). And "hung" and "whirlwind" also conjure up many further connections with *King Lear*. And
so on and on!

But at this point I shall desist—merely re-emphasising that there
*is* a method of enquiry here; it is not merely arbitrary; it has its own
canons of confirmation and disconfirmation, and use of evidence,
which duly reveal the three dimensions I am invoking. But these
canons are hermeneutic; they are "internal" to the "total situation"
(comprehending the possible as well as the actual, and therefore
"platonic", outwith the scope of merely empirical understanding)
realised in the poem. (It is not commonly noted that the psychoanalytic concept of the "total situation", e.g., Joseph, 1989, is inherently
"platonic", in this way.)

And arguably, even in as short a poem as this, the *inexhaustibility* of
the associations and allusions is a concept which can seriously be considered; at the very least, we can say there will never come a moment
when actually we know we have found all the meaning there is to
be found. And so the infinitude concept is confirmed again also. The
startling richness of meaning, and the unexpectedness of the connections, which is found to be implicit in such a poem, gives proof
of the fertility of the creative unconscious, which we may be inclined
to doubt as it is expressed in the fertility of sessional meanings and
in dreams; unveiling, in this manner, layers after layers in poetry,

reassures us that *those* findings are not as irrational or wishful, as they may be, and often are, considered to be (which does not exempt us from the task of developing the evidential aspects).

I have evoked this in such detail to convey the *cross-connective character* of poetry, text and context, the infinitude in its three forms, one of the central elements it shares with the process of psychotherapy. It illustrates likewise the hugely intense character of enactment, and disclosure through enactment, combining pre-communicability and the relational field, of which I have spoken.

It would now be possible to further go on to address the paradigmatic character of the awesome regenerative poem Hopkins wrote in 1888 (the year before his death) when he had regained the full energy of his faith, *in a way which drew from and incorporated the experience of his despair* (without denying it or repudiating it; *this* is the parallel with an approach to psychotherapy *which offers acceptance even more fundamentally than remedial "fixing"*[2]), in a poem which offers an experience of grace and self-healing, an experience expressed in this, one of the greatest of all Incarnational poems (we seem actually to hear the *Dies Irae*! the last trumpet sounding), which also drew in an striking way from Greek Herakleitian thought:

> That Nature is a Heraclitean Fire and of the comfort of the Resurrection

In the background of this late poem is probably the late Shakespearean counterpart to *King Lear*, *The Tempest*, as well as Hopkins' own earlier poem, his first in Sprung Rhythm, and his largest poem, *The Wreck of the Deutschland*. It digests the earlier despair without denying or effacing it:

> But quench her bonniest, dearest ' to her,
>     her clearest-selvèd spark                                  10
> Man, how fast his firedint, ' his mark on mind, is gone!
> Both are in an unfathomable, all is in an enormous dark
> Drowned.

But I shall not go into more detail here, merely noting the analogy in the evolution of the poetry, and the poet's heart, and in the cross-referencing between the poems, which parallels the evolution within, and the cross-referencing between, sessions in the process of psychotherapy. (I cannot resist inserting this wonderful poem in an footnote[3].)

### 4. Psychotherapy and poetry: A dream analysis of my own

When we turn to the evocation of the process of *psychotherapy*, we find that the comparison with poetry, and the analysis of poetry, can be pursued systematically.

As already indicated, I explored the infinity of psychotherapy in three aspects in my paper on James Grotstein of 2003 (Wilkinson, 2003a). To illustrate the parallel between poetry and psychotherapy, with an illustration which poses no ethical problems of consent, since it concerned myself, I shall draw further from this paper (with slight modifications), already referred to, on James Grotstein's work.

This is an extended analysis, which nevertheless brings out clearly that *the methodology for the analysis of personal emotional expression and communication in psychotherapeutic process is the same as that for the analysis of poetry.*

It will be clear enough in the text how the "Freudian infinite" ("text and context"), in this analysis, interplays with the "Hegelian infinite" (the "relational field"). It is characteristic of any particular communication to have an overt emphasis into one infinity dimension or another, with other dimensions less prominent but still latently there. Where, then, in this dream, and its uncovering, would be the dimension of the "Kantian infinite", of "existence", of "pre-communicability"? I shall return to this.

The (self-) analysis was of a dream I had after receiving a personal copy of James Grotstein's book, as a gift. The bulk of this, subject to minor adjustments, was written at the time—with an exception I shall come to below:

> "Now, when I, the present writer, first obtained my copy of Grotstein's book, I found myself dreaming a responsive "Freudianly infinite" dream—one ostensibly all about text, not subjectivities. Without uncovering all of its personal meaning of which I am aware—the censorship operates at several levels, as Freud found!—there is enough to illustrate the indefinite

textual infinity and reflexivity of the Freudian infinite, which
yet remains contextual."

A partial excursus into more personal material—but about which
there is no problem of consent!—is, then, unavoidable here, tran-
scribed from my extended notes made at the time. The rationale for
this is to emphasise the multi-layered reflexivity of the Freudian
mode of dreaming, its function, and its reduplication at level after
level, the Freudian infinity, of which this paper is itself, therefore,
a further manifestation. The interpretation and the censoring of the
interpretation are both part of the dream. And the dream, in its turn,
is part of a waking, and part-transferential, dialogue. The reference
to the subjectivities as the real correlate of the text is itself a floating
signifier, and constantly revisited, as one may in a literary work, as
one moves around in the text of memory. So, also, the Hegelian element is there in tandem with the textuality.

*Reflexivity of the dream*

"I am busily and steadily reading through Grotstein's dense
and rich text. It is highly "saturated", overdetermined, like the
work of Kant, Hegel, and Freud themselves. In the light of his
chapter on the dream, a fragment of one of mine (dreamt since I
began the book) makes an indirect comment/testimony on my
reading of the book.
    It was just a dream-fragment of a moment where I was trying
to gain access to my old, well-thumbed, much annotated, copy,
bought when I was at Cambridge in 1967, of *The Interpretation
of Dreams*, which in the dream had become buried in a pile of
leaves and branches and was dirty, wet, and slightly mouldy!! I
have recently got the new Oxford translation of the first edition;
also I have just recently found once more my copy of Schleiermacher's *Doctrine of Faith*, a treasured book, which I thought I
had lost. In the dream my "official" thought was that, as I had a
new copy of the first edition, I did not need to reclaim this one;
at the same time—more out of awareness—I felt sad and bereft!
So there is a theme about reclamation here!

As I have been reading the dream chapter I have found myself wrestling, in passing, with whether Grotstein's vision of the process of communication between the Dreamer who Dreams the Dream, and the Dreamer who Understands the Dream—with its echoes of Freud's model of the relation between the dream thoughts and the dream work, between the primary process and the secondary process, but also tapping into the whole debate which gradually emerged about the relation between psychotic and neurotic, pre-Oedipal and post-Oedipal, etc.,—all these resonances, all these signifiers—has not lost something of the haunting and teeming richness and saturatedness of Freud himself in *The Interpretation of Dreams*, even though, through its "reference back", it also accesses it. It is a guilty anxiety (for I am also identified with his shift of the emphasis) about a slight element of demythologization, or quasi-Jungian idealization, even though I feel less anxiety with his reconstruction, which so much reminds me of the remark (a remark made by Orme) Boswell quotes, about Johnson's *Journey to the Western Isles,* in *The Life of Johnson*—"There are in that book thoughts, which by long revolution in the great mind of Johnson, have been formed and polished like pebbles rolled in the ocean."—for every page is resonant with the depths of long meditations on these matters. But, increasingly, I am feeling that Freud needs reclaiming—warts and all—from the over-simplifiers, both pro and anti; as my review article on Totton's book (Wilkinson, 2000) suggests, Freud's own endless fertility and overdeterminedness is the most striking fact about him.

I am sure there is also an element of "envious attack"—or, more positively, of competitiveness—here too of course!

But there is also a motif of whether I may not myself have "buried" Freud in my own overcomplexifications, and also, that of nostalgia for a time when I was young and, however confused then, not having rolled my own thoughts around for so many years in Johnsonian fashion, was still not as "finished" as that "rolling around" implies. In my overprotection of the "overdeterminedness" of Freud there is a protection also of my own 19th century roots—my father was born in 1880, so I skipped a generation, as it were, and he was in the first motor vehicle (a Benz, before Mercedes!) to visit Stonehenge in 1895, the year of Freud's *Project for a Scientific Psychology* and of Oscar Wilde's imprisonment, the pre-First War world where the bulk of the world, as Jung said in the *Face to Face* interview with John Freeman, was still essentially mediaeval—and in my sense of Grotstein's Scottish roots and of his Scottish dream in this book, and his often traditional and archaic use of language I am feeling he also is, in that sense, a bridge, if not a throw-back, to that "ancestral time".

In Jungian terms there may also be an archetypal motif of "buried treasure" (my interest in Freud ran parallel with my obsession with Wagner's *The Ring* and Jung's preoccupation with Siegfried's retrieving of the Nibelung Hoard, and its bearing on Nietzsche's predicament!!)

(Incidentally, Grotstein's patient on p. 31–2 with the falcon and the snake put me in mind of Zarathustra's eagle and snake and therefore of Jung's massive commentary on all that in *The Seminar on Nietzsche's Zarathustra*.) There was a long period of my life when I was not as able, as I am now to reconnect with that enthusiasm and "getting carried away by my thoughts" of my youth. So this is the "reclamation" motif—the more I explore the more connections come up! There was a sense of the numinosity of the ancient—and this stirs in me also as I am reading this book.

This gives a sense of the depth of the level at which reading it is affecting me! Having read parts of it in "paper" form, it feels so different in book form—there is a mystery about "the book". There is also, I think, a "meta-level" self-commentary (Joycean/ Borgesian/Derrida-type reflexivity); this is a dream about a "book about dreams", in the context of a later "book about dreams", which comments on this original book about dreams, both books being about the "reclamation of the dream", and the dream itself is about the "burying of the book"/(treasure), in turn a long-term preoccupation of mine! There may also be something connected about the burying of my thoughts—in that, unlike Grotstein, I have published no books, only papers, and then by a kind of accident, and I often have a fantasy about being in effect like Coleridge whose influence through his conversation (Oscar Wilde and Johnson also come in here—I have always felt drawn to the great procrastinating talkers!) far outweighed his influence via his writings, despite the great value of his *On the constitution of Church and State*. So, the being cluttered under leaves and dirt has many resonances for me in connection with my use of my own (buried!) talent (c.f., the biblical resonance also here)—and with my identification with Freud (this is alluded to in my paper on *Phenomenological causality*, Wilkinson, 1998), and my thoughts about being connected with comparable breakthroughs! (Which is no longer possible.)

An ancient preoccupation of mine, naturally enough, then, is to make use of the fragmentary and to redeem it (Fellini's 8½, his film about an unfinished film, is an archetype of mine). Although *The Interpretation of Dreams* is a uniquely long book of Freud's, most of whose writings are effectively large paragraphs, monographs, fragments, his talent being for the fragmentary, as he wrote to Groddeck, I think, further, we can say that, belying its unique and exceptional length, the theme of *The Interpretation of Dreams* is still the Lacanian/Derridean one of the redemption of discards and fragments, which Lacan makes much of in relation to *The Interpretation of Dreams*—in this connection I can note that my dream memory was also a fragment. I think of *The dream of the botanical monograph*—that key envy dream of Freud's about a book or monograph!—in this connection, where his own "bookworm" propensities are a central element.

Thus, the reclamation of the discarded and fragmentary is a highly overdetermined and concentratedly "charged" theme for me. And in this demonstration of the endless interrelations embedded in this fragment there is an indication of the meta-reflexivity theme of the dream—a kind of "throw-away" of its very essence."

Later the realization dawned that, one layer of meaning was the recognition of the commitment to writing a book—which would be partly a response to this one of James Grotstein's. And with that movement we return of course to the Hegelian infinite of reciprocal mimetic intersubjectivity! It is worth saying that I have been uncannily influenced by James Grotstein in my own development, I experience minor synchroncities in connection with him, and that many elements of my own thinking interweave with his. For instance, his book gives a central role to Kant, about whose Scottish roots we have conversed; and in Chapter Five it will be seen that I, too, now return to Kant in a most emphatic way!

## Veiling/Unveiling

I now return to the question, where the dimension of existence and pre-communicability went in this dream? Surely the answer is, in Freudian vein, precisely in the contrast between the earthy concreteness of the *manifest* form of the dream, and the *latent* profusion, not to say prolixity (!), of hidden and reflexive meanings. This all relates to a famous and crucial, but never fully explored, footnote in *The Interpretation of Dreams*: "I had a feeling that the interpretation of this part of the dream was not carried far enough to make it possible to follow the whole of its concealed meaning. If I had pursued my comparison between the three women it would have taken me far afield.—*There is at least one spot in every dream where it is unplumbable—a navel, as it were, which is its point of contact with the unknown.*" (Freud, 1900/1999, my italics).

That footnote of Freud's would be my text, along with Jung's (1956) Foreward to the Fourth Swiss Edition of *Symbols of Transformation*, to enlist the two pioneers on behalf of the "infinite" dimension of my concept!

This veiling/unveiling contrast emerges as a major dimension of the element of "repression" which Freud discovered, which is associated with *concreteness*, and which therefore manifests itself in the opacity and "pre-communicability" of "primary process" work in psychotherapy, when psychotherapists are so prone to feel inadequate, as if they were wading in treacle or marshy swampland, a process involving the essential *hiddenness* of meaning in psychotherapy (transference and countertransference). Here, once again, we have a hint of the "text and context" dimension, the capacity for metaphor (Searles, 1965) as a developmental criterion, and a criterion of traumatic repression and developmental shock.

This hiddenness and veiling clearly *was* what the dream was communicating—as it turned out, in an almost infinite series of layered ways! In that, it is like the illustration Freud picks up in *The Interpretation of Dreams*, the Hans Christian Andersen story of *The Emperor's New Clothes*, which Derrida in his turn (Derrida, 1987) interprets as being *intrinsically* about veiling/unveiling. That is, to speak of veiling/unveiling is not an *interpretation* of the story, it is the *actual theme* of the story. And so here also.

And so, we both have a *confirmation* of the Derrida hypothesis in the symbolism of *this* dream, and an amazing revelation of how the *aletheic* actually works—not as a lifeless "something out there", but as something which teases and tantalises us with its seductive elusiveness, something (like the "Death of God" in Nietzsche's parable) *closer to us than we are to ourselves*, and yet having the creative elusive autonomy Groddeck attributed to the "It" (Groddeck, 1949). This Heidegger, in his turn, attributes to "Being", both of them, "It", and "Being" utterly transcending the personally human—yet subtly, ever so subtly, engaging with it. Such a gesture, of such subtlety, as this dream gave me, in this way, emphasises that the psyche or self is wise beyond compare; I am still discovering things about this dream five years later!

And I am also reminded that I am now writing the book I covertly envisaged in it!

In the subtle mutual reciprocity, yet dissociation, of aspects of the self here, we have an epitome of the kind of thing that led Freud to the later tripartite metapsychology, to which I return later.

The method of enquiry here, then, is essentially the same as that involved in thinking about the Hopkins poetry.

Clearly there can be others, and other methods in psychotherapy, than mine, but it seems plausible to say that they too would exhibit the parallelism—unless it could be shown that the parallelism is an artefact of the method!

## Unexpected illustration from Isaac Asimov

A third illustration, from a rather odd quarter, which recently caught my eye, and which may appeal to science fiction buffs (which shows that the parallelism applies equally to the novel as to poetry, c.f., Leavis, 1949, and also Chapter Four, below, on Shakespeare and Dickens), of what I am saying, comes from reflection on Isaac Asimov's *Robot, Foundation*, and *Empire* novels, particularly *Robots and Empire, The Robots of Dawn*, and David Brin's novelistic commentary upon it in *Foundation's Triumph*. This illustration particularly clearly brings out that *this conceptualisation is equally about the metaphoric-poetic transcending of the concrete, as it is about infinity in cross-referencing* (though these go together). This illustration is an epitomisation of the insight.

In *Robots and Empire* the two advanced robots R. Daneel Olivaw and R. Giskard Reventlov explore and act upon their discovery and formulation of a fourth Law of Robotics, which, as it takes precedence, where ascertainable, they dub the *Zeroth Law of Robotics*: http://www.anu.edu.au/people/Roger.Clarke/SOS/Asimov.html#Zeroth

The first three Laws of Robotics are basically in the form of obedience to rules, Categorical Imperatives in Kant's sense (Kant, 1997), obedience, in descending order, to the rules of "no harm to humans", "no disobedience to humans", and "no harm to robots". These rules are linear and, on the face of it, involve little in the way of interpretation and judgement, other than the recognitional judgement of deciding which rule applies and takes priority.

But there is already a loophole for interpretation in what constitutes "harm" to humans; in *The Robots of Dawn*, which precedes *Robots and Empire* in the order of events, Daneel convinces Giskard (ostensibly, since Giskard, who is telepathic, is possibly playing a part, testing Baley's resourcefulness) that Plainclothesman Elijah Baley will be more greatly "harmed" if he does not follow the dictates of his conscience, his sense of duty, and sense of identity, even though this will involve him in extreme phobic and physical discomfort and distress.

Here is the loophole that opens the way to recognising that "harm" may be constituted by an internalised, subjective, judgement of value, of qualitative well-being. It is but a small step to allowing that this may be constituted by a human person's perception of "harm to another", as being "harm to oneself", and thence to the perception of harm to humanity, and the destiny of humanity as a whole, as being harm to oneself. This is the Zeroth Law of Robotics.

Asimov attributes the original three laws to the significantly named Susan Calvin, his fictional robotics pioneer. Accordingly, in his fictional reinterpretation of Asimov's world in *Foundation's Triumph* (p. 82), David Brin writes ironically, but fittingly, of the three Laws as "the Calvinian Religion", and of the Zeroth Law as "the Giskardian Reformation". In these "sequel" novels, the drama and war of these reformations is played out primarily amongst the robots, though Hari Seldon, the pioneer of the "psychohistory" which is supposed to prevent the Galaxy descending into thirty thousand years of anarchy, is also heavily involved, and the novels look forward to the (very partial) return to human decision-making, involving Golan Trevise in *Foundation's Edge*. In the sense of Dostoievski's Grand Inquisitor, the robots of the Giskardian dispensation are a benignly motivated Inquisitorial Elite, serving humanity according to their own interpretation of its well-being, by protecting it from its inveterate (fallen, demonic) tendency to chaos, mutual destruction, and human sacrifice.

It also becomes clear, in the crux encounter between robot and human (the duel between the two robots and the embittered roboticist Vasilia Aliena) in *Robots and Empire*, that the corollary of this is that the robots now, ambivalently, regard themselves as *persons*, albeit Servant Persons (they have become—Asimov loved and admired PG Wodehouse!—a pan-Galactic Jeeves!), who are capable of genuine, not merely nominal, friendship, which—and not merely the as yet not fully formulated Zeroth Law!—is crucial in enabling Giskard to override his programming, and save Daneel from destruction by Vasilia, by rendering her unconscious, and wiping her memory of events, at the vital moment.

Now, it is in this sense of the Zeroth Law, that Asimov and his interpreters in effect take us into the realm of poesis, in the sense of my thesis. For, unlike the attempted linearity of the first three Laws of Robotics, *the Zeroth Law invokes the totality of human existence and personhood*. As such it brings in the principles of uncertainty, of negative capability, and of aesthetic polarities in the Herakleitian, and Jungian-alchemical, senses—all the ambiguity and light and shade of human existence—in ascertaining what makes for well-being in the realm of persons. They have to wrestle with the full implications of all of: embodiment and relationality and meaning.

The failure of Hari Seldon's attempted supplement to the Laws of Robotics—the science of psychohistory—when its exclusively statistical evaluation collides with the significance and influence of the unique individual, is time and again illustrated in the novels. In Elijah Baley's deathbed remarks, central to the formulation of the Zeroth Law by Deneel and Giskard, he significantly invokes the *aesthetic* metaphor of a tapestry (Asimov, 1994):

> The work of each individual contributes to a totality, and so becomes an undying part of the totality. That totality of human lives, past and present—and to come—forms a tapestry that

has been in existence now for many tens of thousands of years and has been growing more elaborate and, on the whole, more beautiful in all that time. Even the Spacers are an offshoot of the tapestry, and they, too, add to the elaborateness and beauty of the pattern. An individual life is one thread in the tapestry and what is one thread compared to the whole?

So, then, the Zeroth Law takes human and robotic—personal—value judgements out of the realm of the finite linear, and into the uncertain and ambiguous realm of the infinite and the poetic as I am invoking them. It is a graphic and unexpected, and so all the more compelling, illustration of the principles of interpretation I am invoking. What makes the world of Asimov's fictional drama so compelling is that it precisely takes us into this realm of the profoundest human dilemmas, and connectional poetic infinitudes, and many detailed illustrations could be given of that in commentary upon his *oeuvre*.

A poem, in sum, is the manifestation of a *person*, and, conversely, a person's self-expression, and total intentionality, reaches towards their "becoming a poem". *A poem is a paradigm of enacted intentionality*. To transcend the concrete and the linear, the goal of the narrative psychotherapies, at any rate, is by its nature to enter the realm of poetry, of totality and infinity, where meaning becomes infinite, and infinitely cross connected. *Poetry is therapy; therapy is poetry*.

The thesis is subject to its own kind of confirmation and falsifiability criteria, as I have partly illustrated. In terms of standard qualitative research classifications the nearest paradigms are hermeneutic and to a lesser extent phenomenological. One could at a pinch describe it as a fusion of hermeneutic and phenomenological methodology.

It still remains to place the work on what psychotherapy *is* upon a well-worked out basis. To achieve that will not of course settle discussions about what the true basis is, but it opens up the field to make that dialogue possible, and offers a crucial paradigm, which will locate the work of this significant network of explorations to which I have referred.

It will then be possible for all those, in many fields of psychotherapy, who have been reaching with partial clarity for such a foundation, to locate themselves, and become clear about the context they are working in, which will reduce confusion and liberate energy—and putting them explicitly in touch with the sources of their "inspiration"!

Inspiration, and reflection on inspiration, are not at all opposites, but are different phases or layers of the same fundamental poetic process, the process of transcending the concrete and the literalness of meaning. Against the background of this poetic awareness, *literalness of meaning is revealed as a restrictive paradigm, not an elementary building block*, as something which has to be accounted for in terms of the wider paradigm, not vice versa. This methodological difference of starting point or primary assumption is the fundamental argument[4]! To map the most fundamental character of what psychotherapy is will establish the field in a more secure way.

We will now follow this intuition through chapters: exemplifying therapy in this light; considering how to integrate philosophy of existence, its closest neighbour, within this vision; bringing this poetic-psychotherapeutic vision to bear on the gigantic enigma of the Shakespeare Authorship question; and developing the philosophy of poesis (in poetry, psychotherapy, and even philosophy) as enactment.

## Notes

1 As well as corresponding to the three dimensions outlined above, these three aspects correspond to the three "infinites" of psychoanalysis, which I discussed in my review article on James Grotstein's *Who is the Dreamer Who Dreams the Dream?* (Grotstein, 2000, Wilkinson, 2003b):
    To resummarise: The Kantian infinite is the metaphor of an infinity behind any and all experience, an infinity of the unknowable. ["pre-communicability"]
    The Hegelian infinite is the metaphor of a mirror infinity of mutually reflecting, or mutually alienating (but still, in that sense, negatively mutually mirrored), centres of subjectivity, implicit in experience. ["relational field"]
    And the Freudian infinite is an infinite of cross-referencing, and mirroring, reduplication in a textual sense, transcending the immediacy of experience, a textual sliding away from any possible metaphor, model, or located centre of subjectivity, with various degrees of mutual suppression, censorship, and forced disguise, or partial revelation, which form the substance—a textual model—of what is meant by "repression". ["text and context"] (Wilkinson, 2003b, p. 164).

2 In this conception of psychotherapy as acceptance, besides many well-known references such as Biesser (1970), I am much indebted to discussions with my colleague Stephen Silverton, who is exploring all of this under the metaphor of "Heartbreak Hotel" (Presley).

3 **That Nature is a Heraclitean Fire and of the comfort of the Resurrection**

CLOUD-PUFFBALL, torn tufts, tossed pillows ' flaunt forth, then chevy on an air-built thoroughfare: heaven-roysterers, in gay-gangs '
they throng; they glitter in marches.
Down roughcast, down dazzling whitewash, ' wherever an elm arches,
Shivelights and shadowtackle in long ' lashes lace, lance, and pair.
Delightfully the bright wind boisterous ' ropes,
       wrestles, beats earth bare                                            5
Of yestertempest's creases; in pool and rut peel parches
Squandering ooze to squeezed ' dough, crust, dust; stanches, starches
Squadroned masks and manmarks ' treadmire toil there
Footfretted in it. Million-fuelèd, ' nature's bonfire burns on.
But quench her bonniest, dearest ' to her, her clearest-selvèd spark   10
Man, how fast his firedint, ' his mark on mind, is gone!
Both are in an unfathomable, all is in an enormous dark
Drowned. O pity and indig ' nation! Manshape, that shone
Sheer off, disseveral, a star, ' death blots black out; nor mark
       Is any of him at all so stark                                         15
But vastness blurs and time ' beats level. Enough! the Resurrection,
A heart's-clarion! Away grief's gasping, ' joyless days, dejection.
       Across my foundering deck shone
A beacon, an eternal beam. ' Flesh fade, and mortal trash
Fall to the residuary worm; ' world's wildfire, leave but ash:       20
       In a flash, at a trumpet crash,
I am all at once what Christ is, ' since he was what I am, and
This Jack, joke, poor potsherd, ' patch, matchwood, immortal diamond,
       Is immortal diamond.

4 Are there fundamental building blocks which are simple or linear in form? Or are there simply headings for the analysis of an irreducible cross-referential, incarnate, complexity? This is the fundamental difference which I tried to tease out in another way in my paper on Daniel Stern's *The Present Moment* and which is also, I believe, the root of my puzzling dispute with Marilyn Missim-Sabat:
http://hewardwilkinson.co.uk/SternReview.pdf
http://mentalhelp.net/poc/view_doc.php?id=2540&type=book&cn=28

# CHAPTER TWO

# A Therapeutic Dialogue

**A** 1: So, how do we begin then?

**B** 1: *I am wondering where your sense that you need me to tell you comes from? Is it a matter of genuine ignorance how these processes go, or is it that you would feel safer, or more out of the limelight—or something—if I took on the responsibility of that?*

**A** 2: Well, I would feel a bit less exposed. I feel very peculiar, being here. But if you were selling me a gadget you would expect to have to explain to me how it worked and what it was for, and so on. Why shouldn't I enquire?

**B** 2: *I absolutely support your right to enquire, and certainly the comparison is valid. Yet there are also peculiar elements about this type of work. To the extent that I am now beginning to explain to you, to anticipate something of how it unfolds, I am shouldering some of the burden of responsibility here. I imagine you already feel some relief.*

**A** 3: I feel less exposed. I feel more settled and comfortable. I also feel you have recognised my legitimate anxiety and that makes me feel better.

**B** 3: *So what would have happened if I had stayed silent for a little and let you struggle with it?*

**A 4:**　Well I think I would have been angry with you. Is that allowed? Goodness! I would have felt deserted and abandoned by you.

**B 4:**　*If you are angry with me that is fine though I am not trying to provoke you. But notice how already such very powerful feelings are coming up—and notice how my taking on some of the responsibility immediately settles you into a more secure relation to what is happening.*

*And I might feel—if I were to let my own power complex surge!— that you have subtly manipulated me into being bland and safe, and not exposing you to the full intensity of the work.*

**A 5:**　Goodness, this is fiery stuff. I didn't think your feelings came into it like that—that feels pretty scary.

**B 5:**　*Well, whether we like it or not, we are, after all, two human beings who have never met before, even if we are in an official setting called therapy, and we are like dogs on the sidewalk—we are eyeing each other up and having a sniff!*

**A 6:**　Wow! (laughs) This is way out man!

**B 6:**　*Yes I realise all this is beginning to sound a bit bizarre! I shall track back in a moment and anchor it a trifle more—as you say, that is a legitimate demand. But before I do lets notice that it is indeed powerful, fiery, hot stuff, we are getting straight into it, and I have to make sure you are safe in the process, but we do need to get into it!*

*A bit more explanation: my form of therapy is of the kind that does not start from the idea that the therapist leads the work, but that the client does. So I don't set the agenda or the method—except to the extent that I try to leave a space. This space for things to happen in my experience means that such a type of therapy will quite quickly get into deep areas. This I believe is about the fact that this approach unmoors and uncouples a person from the normal boundaries of the ways relationships are conducted in roles. Like teacher, nurse, doctor, minister, father, mother, lawyer, judge, trainer, and so on and so on.*

*And this immediately opens up that feeling of vertigo and of being over deep water without any protection which I imagine you have been feeling from time to time here.*

**A 7:**　Right on!

**B 7:**   *And now I am noticing that I am doing all the talking! How do you feel about that?*

**A 8:**   Well I was starting to wonder who is the client here … (laughs)

**B 8:**   [*is impishly tempted to ask "well, who is the client?" but feels this would be going too far, clocks his impulse to impishness in response to this client for later examination, and retreats—somewhat—to the more conventional … .*] (laughs) *Well I suppose we'd better assume you are!*

**A 9:**   (also laughs) For a moment there I was wondering if you'd be paying me!

**B 9:**   *No flies on you then?! But now we seem to be being swept over by a wave of laughter—we do seem reluctant to start!*

**A 10:**  So how do we begin then? (both laugh at this return to the beginning—and they sit back and look at each other. Long pause.)

(taking the plunge) I've been having an affair and now my wife's found out. We're living apart now and she said she won't entertain my coming back unless I get some therapy. I don't want to lose her—so here I am!

**B 10:**  *So does that mean you are here because you have been sent?*

**A 11:**  I don't think so—maybe initially but not now I *am* here. A bit of me is quite excited.

**B 11:**  *Can I risk saying what popped up for me then?*

**A 12:**  No problem. Be my guest.

**B 12:**  (*tempted by the facetious again—to release his mild irritation at the ostensible hyper-cooperativeness of A. And—slipping into diagnostic mode—wondering what is behind that …*) *You are too kind* (smiling).

*Well what came to me was that you were now feeling you had out-smarted your wife again—because you got a sense that you could be naughty here, whereas she's thinking you are going to have to be very responsible … . My hunch is—its a bit like the affair all over again! Of course I may be way off beam here, I am really pushing the boat out I guess …*

**A 13:**  No! No! You're not off beam at all—I *am* feeling as if I can be naughty here, somehow. That's really peculiar feeling—we're only minutes into this and already I feel as if I can tell you my most stealthy secrets. What's all that about, for God's sake?

**B** 13:    *So—some more secrets to come eh?*

**A** 14:    Only just beginning, man! Only just beginning!

**B** 14:    *So I guess for a start off your girlfriend likes you naughty and your wife doesn't?*

**A** 15:    Cheeky! [*B. is aware of how very camp this is all now feeling—what is going on? Beginning to entertain some speculations about his family situation ... .*] Well, I thought my wife liked me naughty as well—and she actually did at the beginning! She was wild as hell sexually—but what I didn't realise was that she was jealous. As this dawned on me—she would get really rattled if I looked with any interest at all at another woman—I began to feel trapped and my sexual energy started to withdraw into myself. Usual thing—if we were out and had a bit of time to relax and got a bit drunk some of the old fire would return, but this got less and less effective and I began to realise that I was really on my own.

**B** 15:    [*with a somewhat depressed feeling that he is going to sound very conventional, but feeling he must ask to halt the flood of self-absorption a little*] *You don't think there may have been another common element?—that your wife wanted more intimacy and commitment than you were prepared to offer after the first enthusiasm began to wane? Perhaps if your wife had felt more secure at that level she would have been less jealous?*

**A** 16:    Yes that's what she said, that's what she still is saying, that's what her bloody therapist is saying (she's a fucking woman, yes you bet) ... I am afraid it just sends a chill down my spine though ... I just am such a hedonist and nothing else makes much sense to me ...

**B** 16:    [*persisting stubbornly and with a feeling of futility but at a loss—getting the danger signals about the other therapist, and wondering what this is about, but still an instinct pressing him to persist*] *Are you really saying you simply can't give your wife what she needs? I know that sounds very strong—and I am not being judgemental, but I am wondering if you are just two very different animals in the end of the day ... What stopped you leaving?*

**A 17:**    She wants to bloody own me. She's a ruddy control freak. She's just got hold of a few ideas from therapy and so on, you know—and she wants to run my life.

**B 17:**    *And part of you lets her!*

**A 18:**    What do you mean?

**B 18:**    *Well its pretty obvious you wouldn't be with such a powerful woman without **something** keeping you there? What's with this "powerful women" business Jason?*

**A 19:**    (Silent for a good time at first …) I feel confused. I feel *torn apart* by my need for women.

**B 19:**    *Wow that's a strong thing to say … (He is starting to feel the need to enquire into the family background—but immediately feels hesitant because the process of what is happening seems so powerful and he does not want to interrupt it. He decides to wait.) So what's that confusion like?*

**A 20:**    Its like I am a mass of contradictions—I love women and yet I hate them and I am terrified of them. I feel dominated by them—and yet I cannot resist getting them to respond to me. Inside its like there is a tiny little boy who is just terrified—and absolutely does not know what to do. I feel helpless. That wonderful promise women have—and then suddenly there is a whole different side to them one never suspected!

**B 20:**    *It sounds like you don't really accept the "different side" of them as part of them?*

**A 21:**    Well yes also I do—its also part of the wonder of them that they are so quixotic and unpredictable, so overwhelming.

**B 21:**    *But at the very start there's just sheer sheer sweet excitement? Yes?*

**A 22:**    Yes—that magical moment when desire sweeps through one—through both of us—and one begins to fall in love …

**B 22:**    *But when the crocodile in woman grips one tight then it is another matter …*

**A 23:**    God! That's a strong way of putting it—but yes, that's about right. It reminds me of that Kipling *Just So Story* about the elephant getting his trunk …

**B 23:**    *Always struck me there was something pretty phallic about that story! Professor Sigmund Freud of Vienna would have had a field*

*day with that one!* [*He becomes aware that we are right in the midst of castration anxiety with that—and wonders if he can risk interpreting it. In the light, again, of the earlier reference to his wife's therapist, he decides to take the longer route.*]
*Now! This may sound like a real change of topic—but its not really.* **Do you think of therapy as feminine or as masculine?**

**A** 24:    Wow! Strange question!

**B** 24:    *I was thinking, with what you said about your wife's therapist you might be thinking of it as feminine?*

**A** 25:    Well yes I suppose I would have—but now, I am amazed so soon into this, it seems as if we are making therapy feel quite different, this feels quite different from anything I ever expected. I suppose I expected basically to be ticked off and told what to do.

**B** 25:    *Is that what you always expect from authority?*

**A** 26:    More female authority than male. Of course I have encountered some real bastards of males in authority—but quite a few with whom I could be real buddies also.

**B** 26:    *That's quite a polarity there!*

**A** 27:    Quite a what?

**B** 27:    *Sorry—jargon. Occupational hazard! Or even our occupation! I mean quite an extreme contrast—between your images of authority in men—and in women!* [*He is constantly struggling with a sense that the huge web of interconnections he is aware of is not available in any way yet to this curiosity-driven, yet somewhat concrete, man—yet he has a vivid sense that this man's psychology is nevertheless touching right into that whole network of interconnections ... What a temptation to pursue the path opened up by the Kipling story, for instance ... How to handle this?*]

**A** 28:    I suppose I always have a secret sense that men gang together against women, that there's a freemasonry ...

**B** 28:    *So both your image of women in authority—and of men together with one another—seems to be being lived out by your experience, respectively, of your wife's therapist—and, apparently, now—as far as we can tell in this short time!—with me as your own! Its amazing how that happens!*

**A 29:**  How what happens?

**B 29:**  *How what happens outside the consulting room gets repeated in it!*

**A 30:**  I don't think I am getting this. Once again I have the sense that you are bringing yourself into this pretty centrally and I don't see how that works. Can you put me in the picture a bit more?

**B 30:**  *OK! The idea is, in simple terms, that each of us human beings has built up a character based upon character traits—that is, in fact, on patterns of action, and feeling, and ways of organising our world, and protecting ourselves, and so on. Now the essential idea is that, since these are very fixed patterns, we will apply this wherever we are—so if we apply it in our general life, and then we come into therapy, we will pretty well automatically apply it there also. Follow so far? Therapists call this "process".*

**A 31:**  Yes I get it.

**B 31:**  *But where it gets quite striking and dramatic is, that its sometimes almost **as if life itself** organises around our patterns. So for instance your wife seems to have—at least as you perceive it (maybe you are wrong or being too simple?)—a therapist who absolutely fits your image of women in authority. And now you meet me—who seems absolutely to fit in some way into your pattern of expectation of men as buddies. Now this could be just your perception—as I hinted already!—but even on that model its quite striking.*

**A 32:**  So what about all that stuff about therapists being professional and neutral and so on?

**B 32:**  *[Tempted again to react with a "well you weren't demanding neutrality a moment ago!" but resisting the temptation—but clocking it for later examination.] Well it's all about how one uses these patterns—but not in denying them, not behaving as if they did not exist in all of us. My job is to be aware of them as they occur and bring them into awareness so that they can, if need be, be modified by contact with a wider network of connections—so that some of their oversimplifyings can be dissolved a bit.*
*But now I feel as if I am taking on all the responsibility again—and some of this just comes with an "aha" as we go along.*

**A 33:**  But at least you are trying to take care of me—I always felt more of that from my father, than my mother, you know.

**B** 33:    *What went wrong?*

**A** 34:    Who said anything went wrong? O shit, better tell you—my father died when I was thirteen and when I went to the grammar school I had to cope all on my own.

**B** 34:    *Why the hesitation in telling me?*

**A** 35:    Oh you know—stiff upper lip and all that! Had to learn not to show my pain to survive at the school. Mother was depressed for three years and I was propping her up. Monica was only six when he died, so she was part of the burden.

**B** 35:    *Monica?*

**A** 36:    Oh, my younger sister.
           Mother was not much available for me anyway even before that—she wanted to get the eye of the world too much. She was a kind of dream for me. She was trying to be an actress you know. She had dreams of being a film star.

**B** 36:    *Dad?*

**A** 37:    He was steady and loyal and always supported her ambitions.

**B** 37:    *Did she support him?*

**A** 38:    Looking back, I can see he was disparately in love with her and he never ceased to be—but she used him basically.

**B** 38:    *And what about you?*

**A** 39:    What do you mean, what about me?

**B** 39:    *Were you in love with her also and did she also use you?*

**A** 40:    Don't be ridiculous!

**B** 40:    [*Aware of feeling quite competitive and aggressive.*] *Its not so absurd! You already gave me half of it just now, when you said you had to prop her up after your father died. Isn't that what he used to do for her before he died, as you just indicated?*

**A** 41:    God you are relentless! Feels like you are trying to impale me with your insights.

**B** 41:    [*Wondering if that too parallels something—but refraining. But wondering where the hidden powerful male is … .*] *Sorry! I do get a bit carried away—got the bit between my teeth.*

**A** 42:    Funny though—part of me likes it. Wish my father had been a bit more forceful like you. [*Long pause. A. has tears in his eyes.*]

**B** 42:    *You loved him very much …*

**A 43:**    [*Weeps uncontrollably now*] Why did he go? why did you leave us dad? God I haven't wept like this for years!

Wow! I don't think I ever was able to grieve for him. I don't think I have ever really grieved for him. I remember standing at his funeral and just feeling numb. I knew mum was falling apart. She never dreamt of acknowledging how much she depended on him—never faced it! I had to hold it together.

**B 43:**    *Did you have any support from anyone?*

**A 44:**    There were a couple of my mum's sisters but they were no use—just mouthed platitudes and got away as quick as they could. My uncle—my father's brother—he was an alcoholic. He was a womaniser; he was always liable to let the side down. Couldn't rely on him.

**B 44:**    *I am aware you are still feeling the tumult of this. But nevertheless, can I ask an awkward question?*

**A 45:**    I am all right. I feel a sense of release. Its all right.

**B 45.**    *Not doing the stiff upper lip bit again?*

**A 46:**    I don't think so. What was your question?

**B 46:**    *Might not your wife say something the same of you?*

**A 47:**    As?

**B 47:**    *As you said of your uncle? That he was a womaniser and always liable to let the side down and you couldn't rely on him.*

**A 48:**    She might well—yes I suppose she would.

**B 48:**    *So whats the difference between you and your uncle?*

**A 49:**    Well, I am not an alcoholic for a start.

**B 49:**    *Is that an essential difference?*

**A 50:**    I *have* supported her. She's not so totally sorted as she likes to make out, you know! She falls apart in total panic periodically you know!

**B 50:**    *So in some ways its more like your father in relation to your mother, not your uncle?*

**A 51:**    Yes.

**B 51:**    *And is it like you are the steady one, and she is the wild one—at another level—then?*

**A 52:**    She just goes berserk sometimes.

**B 52:**    *So there's something hollow about this wild hedonist image of yours? Yet you both collude to create it?*

**A** 53:   What do you mean?

**B** 53:   *If I am to judge by the way you have portrayed yourself, and also by the way she portrays you in sending you for therapy, you would seem both to be in agreement that you are the wild one—she the sensible one. She's the one who can manage intimacy and you cannot resist straying. But I don't think its as simple as that in reality.*

**A** 54:   What do you mean?

**B** 54:   *I think a deeper—less obvious—element in her portrayal of you is she is secretly portraying you as weak—as not able to stand up to her, not able to master her. On the public relations front it may suit her to portray you as the Don Juan and the betrayer etc.—but hiddenly she is portraying you as like your father, not able to stand up to your mother. [This is all very well—but B. feels himself in deep waters with the complexity of all this. He decides to push onwards—feeling sure it will gradually clear of itself.] Do you think there is anything in that?*

**A** 55:   One of the things she called me when I was unable to choose between her and Helga was spineless! And there have been many quarrels over the years when she has called me names for indecision.

**B** 55:   *So the powerful woman is also the tempestuous woman—who wants you to take charge? And—losing your father when you did, and perhaps also him being the man he was—you never mastered that. You always felt like a little boy inside.*

**A** 56:   (Reflective.) God, I suppose I am almost a sort of gigolo— you know, I really did learn to please women with sex very early on. But then I was submissive to them.

**B** 56:   *What do you mean? How did that happen?*

**A** 57:   Well at the grammar school I was a shy boy and was bullied a bit—not terribly badly, but quite enough to drive me to keep myself very much to myself, apart from one pal William. When I was about fifteen I used to spend a lot of time at his place and stay over quite often. It got me away from mum. Well William had an older sister, Lou, about 24, who was big, quite plump, but really nice and friendly. I secretly fancied her—she was really sexy and comfortable feeling. One day William had to go round to one of his aunts to go out to a show which for some reason Lou and me could neither of us go to, and his mother was out somewhere (she was always out somewhere!)—I got up to go, but Lou said why not stay and have some tea, and then after that she suggested we watch a film. I was excited and I couldn't resist—well she came and sat with me on the settee and I think we watched a video of *Tom Jones*, God knows how she had such an old film but she did. Well that is quite a sexy film! We found ourselves snuggling up and she put her arm round me and I was so excited, I felt her large breasts near me, and her perfume was everywhere and I put my arm round her shoulders and then she turned to me and began to kiss me. God my heart was racing and she seemed pretty excited too. "Have you ever done it?" she asked me and I said "no". "Want me to show you?" Well who was I to turn that down and we went up to the bedroom—and to cut a long story short she did show me, very gently, and it was fantastic, and we did it twice—I came a bit quick the first time but the second time I was more relaxed and we made love for a long time and I could tell I really pleased her, and she told me I had given her a huge lot of pleasure and that's how it started. We did it on and off for the next two years and then I went to University and by the time I came back she was married. We have never spoken about it since—I rather lost touch with William though not altogether (God it was a bit difficult with William after that! But I did keep silent.)—but occasionally when we have been together in the same room she's given me a kind of winking smile which shows me she has not forgotten! And certainly *I* never have!

**B** 57:    *You don't feel she abused you!?*

**A** 58:    Oh no—not at all! I may have been young but I was not naïve, I was old beyond my years in some ways, and I was totally up for it just as much as she was. I knew what I was doing—and I also know that if I had said no she would have accepted that. She said later she checked to be sure it was what I wanted and there was no question in her mind it was. And it certainly was!

**B** 58:    *OK. But don't you think, in a sense—with your mother unable to give you adequate maternal support—to have this unconditional*

*sexual offer from a much older woman who therefore protected you
from all the anxiety of the first time—don't you think this may
have given you a sense of women as much less fierce and real and
of the real world than in fact they are. Don't you think it may have
given you a kind of forged passport to heterosexual relationships,
so to speak? Did it not make the confusion of sex and depending
on someone as a maternal figure all the more difficult? So that
you never really got to know the demandingness of sex which has
caused you so many problems later?*

**A 59:**    I never thought about it like that. (Long pause—he bows his head.) So later, you think, when I got to know Melissa ...

**B 59:**    *Your wife?*

**A 60:**    Sorry—yes. When I got to know Melissa, who was very powerful and swept me off my feet really, you think I saw her as all-caring and maternal like Lou? I kind of surrendered to her.

**B 60:**    *Just wondering. (He is experiencing a strong submissive element in A. whose voice has become very small ...)*

**A 61:**    (Helpless tone of voice.) What should I do?

**B 61:**    *Are you putting me in the position of the helpful caring mother?*

**A 62:**    (Tone of voice changes sharply.) God—I suppose I am! (*With acute curiosity*) Is **that** what you mean by that thing of, if it happens out there it happens in here?

**B 62:**    *You got it!*

**A 63:**    (*Still more curious.*) So am I turning you successively into my father and then my mother maybe and then Lou—and so on ...?

**B 63:**    *I prefer to think its more of a kind of working hypothesis, derived from their past, that people explore on-goingly—but it is still lived and experienced, its not just abstract. You might say you tested the hypothesis of maternal care (which you did get with Lou) with Melissa and it was found wanting!*

**A 64:**    (Conspiratorial again) You can say that again! (laughs)

**B 64:**    *But was it entirely?*

**A 65:**    No of course it wasn't! In the early days there were times when Melissa and me used to lie on the riverbank in the summer and she used to cradle my head and rock me and I felt as if I were completely safe—in paradise. And we would make love and it was like nothing I had experienced since Lou. She took me right into her—she swallowed me up, but I *wanted* to be swallowed up. And it was like I had found the centre of the world. She was more powerful than Lou—who was very easy going in a way—and that made me feel safer. Lou by comparison was just a boy's adventure—this was something else, this was *Tristan and Isolde.*

**B 65:**  *This is a very deep love you are talking about.*

**A 66:**  I had a lot of adventures before Melissa but this was something else. I must have been with ten or fifteen women before I got involved with her. Women were drawn to me because from Lou I had derived confidence and experience—I knew what to do, women liked that. I didn't pretend to be faithful—I let them know what kind of being I was, I rejoiced in it and mostly so did they. I knew by instinct with most of them that it wasn't going to be more than a fling and I was perfectly honest—but they liked it. I think in a way I kept my image of Lou intact by only seducing women who weren't really going to touch my heart and evoke my passion.

**B 66:**  *So what did go wrong with Melissa? Or* **has it actually?** *Is this just part of your dance with her?*

**A 67:**  God! I wonder? We do have this very strange way with each other.

**B 67:**  *And what part do I play?*

**A 68:**  What do you mean?

**B 68:**  *Well, you have this strange dance—this oddly exciting war and simultaneous passion—with your wife, its almost like one of these internet psychological quest contests, and she out-manouevres you by forcing you to come to this therapy as a condition of your having any chance of going back home. And now, suddenly, here you are in clover, with me hypnotised by your adventures so you can go back and say what a wonderful time you are having in therapy— and how helpful it is, and all the time you are feeling that nothing is forbidden you here, which is just the feeling you want in your relationship anyway …*

**A 70:**   How do you mean, hypnotised?

**B 70:**   *You have me absolutely fascinated with your story and the dance of parallel psychic tendencies it displays—don't you know you have?*

**A 71:**   But I hadn't realised …

**B 71:**   *Sure of that? Isn't this the way you seduce your women—by telling them stories? And you are really telling me you don't know when you have got them in the palm of your hand?*

**A 72:**   OK! touché.

**B 72:**   *And don't you do it with men too?*

**A 73:**   You think I'm gay?

**B 73:**   *No. (He thinks he has jumped too quickly with this "no" but goes on anyway …) A bit camp maybe … . And there's something about how you relate to men, how you feel safer with them. But I think you still seduce them, (He decides to go for it …) I think you seduce everybody, I think that's what you do.*

**A 74:**   You don't mean literally?

**B 74:**   *No I mean in the way you connect and communicate with people—I think you fascinate them and then bring out the protector in them, like you did with Lou, and then with Melissa, and like you are with me …*

**A 75:**   God I feel like some kind of monster now … always out for number one …

**B 75:**   *What does that feel like?*

**A 76:**   I suddenly realise I feel quite elated and powerful from it … . God! I must be a bit of a bastard …

**B 76:**   *And how does **that** make you feel?*

**A 77:**   Excited! Excited! Why's that? What's that all about?

**B 77:**   *What if it makes you realise your power?*

**A 78:**   I'm potent, I feel potent, I feel I can take it or leave it whatever Melissa does, wow, wow, wowee, what's all that about?

**B 78:**   *Why are you so astounded at your own power?*

**A 79:**   I just never realised, I just never realised … . Three quarters of an hour with you and everything changes, what's that about, what's your secret man?

**B 79:**   *There's no secret, you're the secret, I'm the secret, life is the secret, it just happens if you let it … . If you are free to follow your nose*

*you find it, or rather you have already found it, you already were*
*powerful, it was just a question of finding it, it just comes together*
*all of a sudden …*

**A** 80: It just came up didn't it? But you weren't rattled by it all, that's also vital to it …

**B** 80: *Its being in this free space, its being able to dance your dance, touch your own crystal …*

**A** 81: Sounds a bit way out …

**B** 81: *Well more prosaically, you stumbled into it, we stumbled into it … . When it shifted round to your seducing me, then your seducing everybody, then the man to man bit, following on from your recalling how powerful your relation with Melissa was and is, I think it just came to a head, reached critical mass, something shifted. That's how it works you know.*

**A** 82: Well it amazes me I have to say … I am still a bit stunned …

**B** 82: *Well, when I feel nothing seems to be going on I don't give up, I just wait openly and keep things going along, and when something crystallises I just accept it as a gift from the universe, so to speak, as well … . Whether it seems barren or when it seems fertile. I think it just kind of follows invisible patterns, like iron filings in the path of a magnet. That's why the "inside the therapy/outside the therapy" mirroring happens so readily, also.*

**A** 83: I'll have a lot of reflecting to do from all this … .

**B** 83: *Some loose ends there are, I feel. What about Helga, you haven't talked about her, and also, perhaps more important, I think there is a link to be made in relation to your father and the experience you have had with me.*

**A** 84: Helga! I feel now that will all sort itself out, I am somehow not worried about it any more, I don't mean that Melissa wont give me a hard time, but I am not *terrified* any more.

**B** 84: *Got your manhood back?*

**A** 85: Yes—or just *got* it! And I feel I am different with my father now. You have given me that, it feels different. I can see him as he is or rather was, but also feel his strength. I think I was kind of being my mother in a funny sort of way. Now I have got him back and I feel stronger.—How do you learn this stuff?

**B** 85: *How long have you got …?*

This piece of imagined work—which I am aware as I wrote it of many echoes which I did not try to exclude, from Yalom, for instance, and Asimov, and also people I have known, as well as autobiographical elements—is certainly no great shakes as an imagined piece of work. And of course it is artificially much more rapid in its progress, and its abrupt and oversimplified ending, than would normally happen in life, though these things do happen.

But I hope it is fluent enough simply to suggest what I want to suggest, that the descent into the melting pot, and resulting transformation which it illustrates, is pretty commonplace in the work both of analysis based therapists (Freudian and Jungian, both) and humanistic and integrative therapists—all kinds of narrative-based practitioners. I am not saying my types of *intervention* are to everyone's taste, just that the *process* is in common (c.f., e.g., Rowan, 2001).

Obviously, my point is that this is precisely the "poesis" this book is talking about!

Programmatically-based practitioners may initiate a different kind of process, though I suspect they too will have a dimension of their work which is actually like this also.

But by limiting the extent to which they will allow the dimension of the pre-communicable to take hold, they limit the measure of the poesic unfolding which is possible in the work.

This will not mean they cannot do other things, and very important things, maybe better. There are real choices to be made in our work.

Certain very advanced forms of hypno-psychotherapy, for instance, those influenced by Milton Erickson, do access and use the pre-communicable, perhaps even in a particular programmatic way of their own.

How far there can be programmatic framings *which actually incorporate the pre-communicable,* in that sense, is a very important question, but outside the scope of this book.

Unless this book, too, should turn out to be a systematisation of the pre-communicable!

I leave that question to my readers!

CHAPTER THREE

# Poetry or Existence?—Poetry Dialogues with Philosophy Dialogues with Poetry

W hy Heidegger?
I now want to test the proposition that *philosophy of existence itself* is also, in a sense, defined by not knowing, (and so by poetic multi-facetedness in the relevant sense).

As I have already indicated, I am linking the model based in poetry to *philosophy of existence*. Philosophy of existence was pioneered by Martin Heidegger more than any other single person. In summary, philosophy of existence places *the human experience and enactment of being*—becoming as a self-aware process—at the centre of its concept of things, as a conduit to the nature of existence itself. For human existence, existence is an issue and something which is always at stake.

I have repeatedly appealed, especially in relation to *pre-communicability*, to Keats's (1817b/1947) conception of *negative capability*. Now, *a multi-faceted approach to the nature of existence* is the actual specific form that "negative capability" takes, if it is not to turn out to be just some vague appeal to ineffability. When the multi-faceted approach is expressed in poetry, and in the poetic character of therapy—taking into account the infinitude of cross-connection, working at the level of the unknown—the form it concretely takes has to be multi-discplinary. This is when its implicit character as unknown, as pre-communicability, passes through, and emerges through, text and context, and on into explicit relatedness, that is, the threefold nature of poetic exploration.

Keats' concept, I believe, developed, takes us, then, into genuine multi-disciplinary enquiry:

> I had not a dispute but a disquisition, with Dilke on various subjects; several things dove-tailed in my mind, and at once it struck me what quality went to form a Man of Achievement, especially in Literature, and which Shakespeare possessed so enormously—I mean *Negative Capability*, that is, when a man is capable of being in uncertainties, mysteries, doubts, without any irritable reaching after fact and reason—Coleridge, for instance, would let go by a fine isolated verisimilitude caught from the Penetralium of mystery, from being incapable of remaining content with half-knowledge. This pursued through volumes would perhaps take us no further than this, that with a great poet the sense of Beauty overcomes every other consideration, or rather obliterates all consideration. [Keats, 1817b/1947, my italics]

Only this appeal to the multi-faceted nature of knowledge precludes the three aspect model being lop-sidedly and reductively assimilated to one of its parts: nowadays, commonly the relational field (understood reductively in terms of developmental theory in both psychoanalytic, and humanistic and integrative, approaches). But in this the *threefold* character of: *pre-communicability* (negative capability); the *relational field*; and *text and context* (the infinitude of cross-connection), may be lost. This again applies to other viable models of the diversity, such as John Heron's 6 Category Intervention Analysis model (Heron, 2001). Most modalities have a tendency to such lopsidedness—or, like psychoanalysis, a tendency to split into a multitude of single lopsided emphases, which then have to make heroic attempts to reassimilate what was excluded (for a more detailed discussion, c.f., e.g., Wilkinson, 2000).

So I now want to test the proposition that *philosophy of existence itself* is also, in a sense, defined by not knowing, (and so by poetic multi-facetedness in the relevant sense). This will involve a somewhat extended detour through some fairly "philosophical" philosophy, in which it may seem I have left therapy behind—but it eventually leads us back to the fundamentals I am concerned with in this book!

This is perhaps the knottiest part of this book: Heidegger in, what? twenty pages or so!? Patient expository work, once again, is needed—but patience is something negative capability does require of us, whether as psychotherapists, poets, critics—or even expositors of Heidegger! This book is, unfortunately, enacting very vividly my sense that to understand where we are in psychotherapy today we just do have to put a substantial amount of other understanding in place as well. But I do not think it can be helped.

I want to show how the attempt to define a single centre for psychotherapy or psychology of the mind breaks down *even here*, and that it just goes on moving on round the hermeneutic circle, to embrace all dimensions in in its interconnections!

In what follows, then, I draw upon Heidegger (1889–1976), who I believe opened up, and explores more profoundly than anyone else, the question of existence, or Being (*Sein*), as he calls it. I am referring to it as *philosophy of existence*, because I think this more accurately and emphatically conveys what he is concerned with, for us in the Anglo-American world. It refers to existence both in the sense of the existence of physical things, and in the sense of personal or human existence. This means existence not only in the sense of actuality, what actually, contingently, exists, but also in the sense in which numbers and ideas and parts of speech may also be said to exist— that is, it means *all forms of existence*, existence as incorporating and as transcending all the categories and modalities, forms, of existence (c.f., Strawson, 1959, part II).

By considering Heidegger we can see whether one very influential attempt to give a non-reductive account of human existence actually fully works.

Heidegger, at the same time, gives us living, and very full, examples of the *"a priori of the particular"*, which replaces empirical knowledge in phenomenology and philosophy of existence, and which I have dealt with in several parts of this book, though there are also very subtle tensions in respect of this which we shall also explore. As I shall try to show, I do think he succumbs to the drive to offer positive knowledge, which does not quite go the whole way to developing an alternative non-reductive account.

Pursuing the logic of "negative capability", I note that, in his profound explorations, which constantly and never-endingly seem to take us right up to the very edge of the mystery of existence, Heidegger again and again leaves the matter in suspense. It is never quite finished. So the attempt to ascertain "what is going on here", is, in our expanded non-reductionist sense, a psychotherapeutic enquiry.

It is not at all that Heidegger never accomplishes anything; he is one of the hardest working and most indefatigable of all philosophers, whose total production, including seminars and lecture series, still in the process of publication, must run eventually into forty or fifty books, and who has produced masterly summations, and radically renewed formulations, of the insights of most of his major predecessors, particularly Plato and Aristotle and the Pre-Socratics, Aquinas, Duns Scotus, Suarez, Descartes, Leibniz, Kant, Schelling, Hegel, Nietzsche—and so on and on!

I shall, for the most part, not pursue his commentaries upon the poets, and upon artists. I am concerned to bring out how there is a poetic even at the heart of what appears to be an autonomous placing of other domains of understanding on a philosophical-ontological basis which is claimed to be more primary than anything else, and therefore to bring out that it is simply *equi-primary*.

I shall also not try to fathom here the implications of his getting caught for a while (some would say longer, but I am now (I have not always been, c.f., Wilkinson, 1999, 2000) with those who feel he did indeed draw back from it, and in the profoundest fashion, c.f., Young, 2003) in the Nazi fascination and the Nazi movement. Almost anything one may say in respect of this is an oversimplification, and I shall have to leave it at that, but it is impossible not to mention it (c.f., e.g., Derrida, 1991, Farias, 1989).

Where occasion arises to make comment, which might make partial sense of that getting caught of his, below, I have taken it.

To return to the theme of uncompleteability, in almost every work, most famously, but not only, *Being and Time* (Heidegger, 1962), the work breaks off and remains a torso (though less so than is often assumed with regard to *Being and Time*; as Mulhall, 2005, for instance points out, the promised later parts of *Being and Time* are all presented *somewhere*—just in a different form from that originally projected). Unlike Wittgenstein's brief paragraphs in the *Philosophical Investigations* (Wittgenstein, 1967), each "paragraph" is gigantic—but, like Wittgenstein's, they remain as paragraphs, unfinished.

My question is, in the light of the "negative capability" concept, is, is this an accidental character, *or does it reflect something intrinsic uncovered in Heidegger's insight into the philosophy of existence, an uncompleteability, perhaps, into which his philosophy takes us*? And which may, as hiddenness, unthoughts and uncompleteability, in the terms of this book, have something to do with pre-communicability.

To approach this, I begin with an attempt at what is, in relation to the immense panorama of his book, a very condensed summary, focusing on the early part of the book, which I shall then try to evidence from his analyses.

Now, in what follows, for anyone not familiar with Heidegger, it may seem we are just banally concerned with people working in workshops and on farms, and driving cars about, and so on, all situations where people are involved with using equipment. But the relevance of this—the paradoxical flip over by which it takes on poetic, and hence on my argument psychotherapeutic, significance—I believe becomes apparent in due course!

Here, then, I shall gradually move towards trying to substantiate some such statement as the following, which could be claimed as a synopsis of Heidegger's analysis of man, which is, *faut de mieux*, like Freud's, a "Fall" analysis—certainly in *Being and Time*:

*Man is the animal who becomes alienated from his world, through the developments of his **technology**, which **also** expresses his unique relationship with his world; and **thereby** develops an awareness of death, being, and nothingness.*

Now, it can be argued that in the extraordinary, the stunning, analysis of "Zeug" ("equipment") early on in *Being and Time* we have the whole Heideggerian philosophy in epitome. "Zeug" means: "tools", "equipment", "gear", "tackle", "utensils", "instruments", etc;—note the Freudian and masculinist resonance which Heidegger does not pick up, but which would further and elementally confirm his analysis, by taking it into the most intimate aspects of the *Dasein*'s—human existence's—relation to our own, and each others', body! This, the first section, where the full analysis finally gets under way, after the introduction, of *Being and Time* (1962, III §§14–24, *The Worldhood of the World*, §§16 and 18, especially), and leading into the analysis of the Worldhood of the World, seems to present the whole Heideggerian philosophy in its seed-germ.

Though this is contrary to Mulhall's analysis (Mulhall, 2005), which—in a very accessible and non-reductive introduction to *Being and Time!*—places great emphasis on the second part of *Being and Time*, upon the exploration of being-toward-death, and original temporality, as entailing a *transformation* and destabilisation of all the insights of the first part, I shall argue that even these, as he admits, are implicit embryonically in these early pages of the great work.

The difference is perhaps one of emphasis; neither emphasis is incorrect; but I think the emphasis which I am laying does bring out the extraordinary *totality of vision* which underlies Heidegger's highly layered exposition, and which makes it so profoundly relevant to psychotherapy—however gradual its unfolding in other ways.

Of course, there is much else which slowly unfolds in *Being and Time*, and its sequel writings, work which evinces an ever deepening unfolding of the recognition of *the inner emotional basis of our experience of the world*—in anxiety, guilt, care, anticipation of death, resoluteness, and so on, with their characteristic temporality, which he construes as the *horizon* on which an understanding of existence is *projected*.

But the analysis of equipment and worldhood puts in place the *carrying out*, in living, and, above all, in work, of that emotional base; it puts in place the way in which our emotions are manifest when we are *absolutely immersed* in our world, in the way Keats evokes in a passage in one of his greatest letters. This is a passage which, in its reference to animality, is deeply—and earlier in the letter explicitly—indebted to the "man is but a poor forked animal" passage in Shakespeare's *King Lear*, explored elsewhere; characteristically Heidegger does not engage with the animal dimension, and this becomes significant later:

> The greater part of Men make their way with the same instinc-
> tiveness, the same unwandering eye from their purposes, the

same animal eagerness as the Hawk. The Hawk wants a Mate, so does the Man—look at them both they set about it and procure one in the same manner. They want both a nest and they both set about one in the same manner—The noble animal Man for his amusement smokes his pipe—the Hawk balances about the Clouds—that is the only difference of their leisures. This it is that makes the Amusement of Life—to a speculative Mind. I go among the Fields and catch a glimpse of a Stoat or a fieldmouse peeping out of the withered grass—the creature hath a purpose and its eyes are bright with it. I go amongst the buildings of a city and I see a Man hurrying along—to what? the Creature has a purpose and his eyes are bright with it. [Keats, 1819a/1947]

In this passage of Keats, with its emphasis upon *purpose* (or intentionality, as, following Brentano and Husserl, we should now say) immersed in the world or in life, we glimpse what Heidegger is after when he tries to evoke the primordial character of Being-in-the-World. He offers, in relation to Husserl's work (e.g., 1977), a vastly expanded concept of intentionality.

I shall first attempt to expound the conception he is unfolding, and then go on to discuss just what it implies and what to make of it. [In all of the following I normally quote verbatim from the Robinson and MacQuarrie translation of *Being and Time* (Heidegger, 1927/1967), with the exception that I italicise the central concepts of *Being-in-the-World* and *Dasein* all the way through, and I italicise or emphasise certain key passages—I have marked where I do this. The German words and phrases presented are ones which are included in the original by Robinson and MacQuarrie, as explanatory, and as pointers to Heidegger's unique idioms, in the way he uses the German language.]

Heidegger writes, for instance, in a famous, and key, passage:

In dealings such as this, where something is put to use, our concern subordinates itself to the "in-order-to" which is constitutive for the equipment we are employing at the time; *the less we just stare at the hammer-Thing, and the more we seize hold of it and use it, the more primordial does our relationship to it become* [my italics], and the more unveiledly is it encountered as that which it is—as equipment. [Heidegger, 1927/1967, p. 98]

I shall explore what that "primordial relation" is and signifies, what its implications are, later. But here we can first see and note that Heidegger is implying, as it were, that there is a *natural alienation from ourselves* (that is, from our reflective, interior, selves) in what I am designating as this animal immersion in the world (or vice versa, an alienation *from* our animal selves, for the matter of that, depending on starting point, as we shall see), which is intensified, and, in a manner, set in concrete, by our latterly developing mastery of technology.

This mastery of technology simultaneously *reveals* us to ourselves in the full potentiality of what we are (which is only dormant in animals), and yet irretrievably *veils* us from ourselves, at the very same time, and in the very same process. This revealing-concealing conception is at the heart of Heidegger's concept of truth as *aletheia*, unconcealment, as we have already seen earlier in this book.

Now, my experience is that people tend either to "get" Heidegger or they do not (some people may have had an "aha" which enables them to move from one to the other!) The Anglo-American conceptual world, in particular, sees him through spectacles, and a kind of vision, that is fundamentally foreign to his, and is indeed what he is essentially trying to overturn. I try to make this comprehensible later.

Interestingly, nevertheless, Gilbert Ryle, the highly Anglo-American author of *The Concept of Mind*, the state of the art anti-Cartesian account of logical behaviourism (1963), who one might have assumed would take a quite different position, was highly affirming of *Being and Time* in a review of it he wrote in *Mind* in 1929, and he actually studied in that year with Husserl, and with Heidegger himself in Freiburg (Amie L. Thomasson, 2002). But Heidegger, too, was highly critical of Descartes' analysis of the world.

However, not all will be convinced! the best I can do is to expound Heidegger and the implications of his analyses as well as I can, and hope and trust that people will "get" it as best they can.

Now, for him, technology, *by evoking implicitly the full symbolic context of our being*, enables our being to dawn upon us, as it cannot dawn upon animals.

But this recognition of the symbolic dimension, as we shall see, and in line with my poetry-based analysis, is the Achilles heel of

Heidegger's attempted comprehensiveness in *Being and Time*. As such it also constitutes the notorious hinge between his earlier and later philosophy, which is not so much a difference in fundamental aim and value system, but simply in his understanding of how the recognitions unfold themselves. In the later philosophy what in essence happens is that the dimension of "poetry", as we are here envisaging it, *becomes irreducible*. He is able to make explicit his seeing of something which was already there in *Being and Time*, but not fully named; we shall find hints of this later.

In this symbolic context there becomes available to us the phenomenon of "the World", which is precisely the symbolic *context of contexts* in which our use of equipment takes place, and to which it implicitly refers:

> Taken strictly, there "is" no such thing as *an* equipment. To the Being of any equipment there always belongs a totality of equipment, in which it can be this equipment that it is. Equipment is essentially "something in-order-to … . ["etwas um-zu …"]. A totality of equipment is constituted by various ways of the "in-order-to", such as serviceability, conduciveness, usability, manipulability. [Heidegger, 1927/1967, p. 97]

This conception of a *totality* is gradually developed in these passages, in order to evoke the character of *Being-in-the-World*. In these excerpts I am presenting here, however dense and sometimes lengthy they are, only a glimpse is afforded of the cumulative brilliance and detailed profusion of Heidegger's analyses:

> The ready-to-hand [the "handy", or handiness of equipment, its availability for use for us] is not grasped theoretically at all, nor is it itself the sort of thing that circumspection ["umsicht"— "around-sight", participant overviewing—there is no ready English translation] takes proximally as a circumspective theme. The peculiarity of what is proximally ready-to-hand is that, in its readiness-to-hand, it must, as it were, withdraw [zuruckzuziehen] in order to be ready-to-hand quite authentically. That with which our everyday dealings proximally dwell is not the tools themselves [die Werkzeugeselbst]. On

the contrary, that with which we concern ourselves primarily *is the work*—that which is to be produced at the time; and this is accordingly ready-to-hand too. *The work bears with it that referential totality within which the equipment is encountered.* [my italics] The work to be produced, as the "towards-which" of such things as the hammer, the plane, and the needle, likewise has the kind of Being that belongs to equipment. The shoe that is to be produced is for wearing (footgear) [Schuhzeug]; the clock is manufactured for telling the time. The work which we chiefly encounter in our concernful dealings—the work that is to be found when one is "at work" on something [das in Arbeit befindliche]—has a usability which belongs to it essentially; in this usability it lets us encounter already the "towards-which" for which it is usable. A work that someone has ordered [das bestellte Werk] *is* only by reason of its use and the assignment-context of entities which is discovered in using. [Heidegger, 1927/1967, p. 99]

He leads this analysis onwards to the discovery of "Nature" it/her self, *as a thing and realm of use* (quoted below), and gradually opens the way to the recognition of the "Worlding" process in which all this is to be discovered and unveiled.

The first examples, in which he argues this "Worlding" character is exposed, are situations in which equipment breaks down, is unsuitable, or is unavailable—those maddening encounters with the intractability and "diabolical malice" of inanimate matter with which we are all so familiar, in life and in comedy (one wishes he had shown more sense of humour in his writing!), and which Robert Pirsig evokes so vividly in the "gumption-traps" section of *Zen and the Art of Motorcycle Maintenance* (Pirsig, 1974):

The structure of the Being of what is ready-to-hand as equipment is determined by references or assignments. In a peculiar and obvious manner, the "Things" which are closest to us are "in themselves" ["An-sich"] and they are encountered as "in themselves" in the concern which makes use of them without noticing them explicitly—the concern which can come up against something unusable.

[Inserted comment: here he is invoking that "primordial relation" to the hammer, for instance, invoked above. This is not a matter of primitiveness; I am in just as primordial a relation to this, year by year more advanced, computer and its keyboard as I am using it; and the "primordial relation" includes the implicit symbolic totality. What is essential to that "primordial relation" is that *I am absorbed in what I am writing, and have forgotten I am using a keyboard even as I am using it*. In very fluent forms of self-reflection, to be sure, I am aware of my absorption even while I am absorbed, but the awareness, even so, *is not at all at the same level as the absorption*. I shall return to the implication of this.]

> When equipment cannot be used, this implies that the constitutive assignment of the "in-order-to" to a "towards-this" has been disturbed. The assignments themselves are not observed; they are, rather, "there" when we concernfully submit ourselves to them [Sichstellen unter sie]. But *when an assignment has been disturbed*—when something is unusable for some purpose—then the assignment becomes explicit. Even now, of course, it has not become explicit as an ontological structure; but it has become explicit ontically for the circumspection which comes up against the damaging of the tool. When an assignment to some particular "towards-this" has been thus circumspectively aroused, we catch sight of the particular "towards-this" itself, and along with it everything connected with the work—the whole "workshop"—as that wherein concern always dwells. *The context of equipment is lit up, not as something never seen before, but as a totality constantly sighted beforehand as circumspection. With this totality, however, the world announces itself.* [Final set of italics mine] [Heidegger, 1927/1967, p. 105]

If my computer breaks down—this computer through which I am engrossedly absorbed in the "towards-which" of writing this book—suddenly I am aware of its useless sitting there in the whole context of my study, and I am likely to get up and wander around, suddenly aware of the whole room and the whole house, and perhaps go off to the kitchen to make a cup of tea, and prepare to use the phone to ring the relevant Computer Helpline; suddenly the whole range of resources I am turned towards widens. (As regards the displacements, as I *also* am likely to do if I get stuck in the writing itself!)

Now imagine that the electricity goes off altogether, the kettle will not work, and so on. In wartime (Baghdad at the present time, for instance) this is, and would be, a frequent occurrence. Now the house itself is reduced to being a mere shelter from the elements, something which a bomb may destroy at any moment, and ceases to be something around and within which I seamlessly wrap my life.

Anyone who has ever been in a vehicle crash knows from immediate experience the almost stunningly instantaneous transition—from a state-of-the-art usably seamless extension of ourselves, into a tangled mess of useless and cumbersome metal, in which we sit looking round at an "unfeeling world" about us!

Heidegger is saying that that "seamless wrapping around my life", in which we are normally unreflectingly immersed, with its network or totality of involvements and background assumptions, is our *Being-in-the-World*, and that this implicit totality will be revealed, sometimes in an extremely uncanny way, when it is radically disturbed.

Elsewhere (Heidegger, 1981) Heidegger illustrates this poignantly in quotation from Rilke's description of the life maintained in torn down houses in *The Notebooks of Malte Laurids Brigge* (Rilke, 1992):

> But the most unforgettable were the walls themselves. The tenacious life of these rooms refused to let itself be trampled down. It was still there; it clung to the nails that had remained; it stood on the handsbreadth remnant of the floor; it had crept together there among the onsets of the corners where there was still a tiny bit of interior space. You could see that it was in the paint, which it had changed slowly year by year: from blue to an unpleasant green; from green to gray; and from yellow to an old decaying white which was now rotting away. But it was also in the fresher places which had been preserved behind mirrors, pictures, and cupboards; for it had drawn and redrawn their contours and had also been in these hidden places, with the spiders and the dust, which now lay bare … [etc.]

In this paradoxical life of the decayed and part-demolished—which we also experience in a peculiar way in our preoccupations with both ruins, and even ancient corpses, such as mummies, and peat bog corpses; and perhaps there is also an analogy with viewing a corpse in Rilke's evocation of the houses!—Heidegger is saying that the *totality* character through which we constitute the World, our World, our *Being-in-the-World*, comes into vivid life and we are enabled to catch a glimpse of what it involves, which we normally take for granted. We also get a very sharp inkling of this when we witness theatrical, or quasi-theatrical, presentations, drama or opera or film, and become utterly absorbed and engrossed in their created "world"—genres to which we adapt so readily, and at such an early age! Or, again, we get an inkling of it when some fictional author, who creates a perhaps minimalised, yet utterly distinctive world, like Jane Austen or PG Wodehouse, enables us to access or enter their world with a stunning economy of brushstrokes!

Similarly, it is the symbolically evoked *absence* of the *expected* totality character of a context—and the stark presence of an alternative one!—that Shelley evokes in his famous poem, *Ozymandias*:

> I met a traveller from an antique land,
> Who said— "Two vast and trunkless legs of stone
> Stand in the desart ... . Near them, on the sand,
> Half sunk a shattered visage lies, whose frown,
> And wrinkled lip, and sneer of cold command,
> Tell that its sculptor well those passions read
> Which yet survive, stamped on these lifeless things,
> The hand that mocked them, and the heart that fed;
> And on the pedestal, these words appear:
> My name is Ozymandias, King of Kings,
> Look on my Works, ye Mighty, and despair!
> Nothing beside remains. Round the decay
> Of that colossal Wreck, boundless and bare
> The lone and level sands stretch far away." (Shelley, 1818/1999)

And of course here again, as with ruins and peat corpses, we get a glimpse of the link with the Heideggeian preoccupation with death, as complete annihilation!

But Heidegger wants to go further, in a more "behavioural", or conceptual-reflexive, sense. He is also concerned to show how we exploit the character of *Being-in-the-World*, and at the same time illuminate it, for our own purposes, when we, as it were, actually lift it *structurally* into view, in the being of *signs* and *indications*. He thinks it has a *structural reflexivity* of its own built into it.

He illustrates this with the example of traffic indicators on cars, and the general statement about signs he makes is this:

> Signs of the kind we have described let what is ready-to-hand be encountered; more precisely, they let some context of it become accessible in such a way that our concernful dealings take on an orientation and hold it secure. A sign is not a Thing which stands to another Thing in the relationship of indicating; it is rather *an item of equipment which explicitly raises a totality of equipment into our circumspection so that together with it the worldly character of the ready-to-hand announces itself.* In a symptom or a warning-signal, "what is coming" "indicates itself", but not in the sense of something merely occurring, which comes as an addition to what is already present-at-hand; "what is coming" is the sort of thing which we are ready for, or which we "weren't ready for" if we have been attending to something else. In signs of something that has happened already, what has come to pass and run its course becomes circumspectively accessible. *A sign to mark something indicates what one is "at" at any time. Signs always indicate primarily "wherein" one lives, where ones concern dwells, what sort of involvement there is with something.* [Last set of italics mine] [Heidegger, 1927/1967, pp. 110–11]

*Now, by contrast with other signs, language is, in a sense, the apotheosis of the sign* **as** *sign, in which sign transcends context into something else.*

And this brings out, by the contrast, the normal rootedness of signs in a *given* context, and as revealing key elements of that context—which is what he is trying to evoke. One gets an inkling of how *this too* seamlessly becomes part (in the very nature of the case this is hard to prevent, and so his attempt to evoke it from an example *within* the framework itself is paradoxical!) of our *Being-in-the-World*, again, by the contrast with a deficient form or example of it—when we are trying to master the system of signs in a foreign country with whose language and road-conventions we are unfamiliar.

Thus, as the English, who so rarely have a fluent grasp of other European languages, and who are furthermore used to driving on the "wrong" side of the road, issue forth in our cars from a Continental European port or entrance, we English suddenly are confronted with an alien "world" in which the most elementary tasks of "road management" suddenly become daunting. Even sign systems which are familiar suddenly become foreign again as we descend into incompetence and bewilderment—and are faced with a monstrous environment in which we are aliens!

So here now is the long, but illuminating passage, immediately preceding the one I have just quoted, in which Heidegger expounds how signs, as such, become a particular form in which equipment becomes sign-equipment:

> What do we mean when we say that a sign "indicates"? We can answer this only by determining what kind of dealing is appropriate with equipment for indicating. And we must do this in such a way that the readiness-to-hand of that equipment is genuinely grasped. What is the appropriate way of having-to-do with signs? Going back to our example of the arrow [*for us today the arrow indicator is superseded, and for us it is currently a flashing light, but the principle is not altered*], we must say that the kind of behaving (Being) which corresponds to the sign we encounter, is either to "give way" or to "stand still" *vis-à-vis* the car with the arrow. Giving way, as taking a direction, belongs essentially to Dasein's *Being-in-the-World*. Dasein is always somehow directed [ausgerichtet] and on its way; standing and waiting are only limiting cases of this directional "on-its-way". The sign addresses itself to a *Being-in-the-World* which is essentially "spatial". The sign is *not* authentically "grasped" ["erfasst"] if we just stare at it and identify it as an indicator-Thing which occurs. Even if we turn our glance in the direction which the arrow indicates and look at something present-at-hand in the region indicated, even then the sign is not authentically encountered. *Such a sign addresses itself to the circumspection of our concernful dealings and it does so in such a way that the circumspection*

*which goes along with it, following where it points, brings into an explicit "survey" whatever aroundness the environment may have at the time.* [My italics] This circumspective survey does not *grasp* the ready-to-hand; what it achieves is rather an orientation within our environment. There is also another way in which we can experience equipment; we may encounter the arrow simply as equipment that belongs to the car. We can do this without discovering what character it specifically has as equipment: what the arrow is to indicate and how it is to do so, may remain completely undetermined; yet what we are encountering is not a mere Thing. The experiencing of a Thing requires a *definiteness* of its own [ihre eigene *Bestimmheit*], and must be contrasted with coming across a manifold of equipments, which may often be quite indefinite, even when one comes across it as especially close. [Heidegger, 1927/1967, p. 110]

"The sign addresses itself to a *Being-in-the-World* which is essentially "spatial"."

Heidegger is drawing attention to the way in which, in using signs, like traffic lights and traffic indicators, when a car in front of us signals to turn, and we suddenly become aware of "the road up into the country to the right" they are turned towards, for example, we operate in a *contextualised* spatiality. We always do; but this kind of situation calls it into view. It is also, as I have just implied, situational, and situationality is the human, which is what Heidegger is working his way towards.

So, at last, now, I am in a position to introduce Heidegger's initial comprehensive formulation of the *Being-in-the-World* conception. It is a lengthy quotation, but will repay with its illumination of what he is after saying:

To say that the Being of the ready-to-hand has the structure of assignment or reference means that it has in itself the character of *having been assigned or referred* [Verwiesenheit]. An entity is discovered when it has been assigned or referred to something, and referred as that entity which it is. *With* any such entity there is an involvement which it has *in* something. The character of Being which belongs to the ready-to-hand is just such an *involvement*. If something has an involvement, this implies letting it be involved in something. The relationship of the "with ... In ... ." shall be indicated by the term "assignment" or "reference".

When an entity within-the-world has been proximally freed for its Being, that Being is its "involvement". With any such entity as entity, there is some involvement. The fact that it has such an involvement is *ontologically* definitive for the Being of such an entity, and is not an ontical assertion about it. That in which it is involved is the "towards-which" of serviceability and the "for-which" of useability. With the "towards-which" of serviceability there can again be an involvement: with this thing, for instance, which is ready-to-hand, and which we accordingly call a "hammer", there is an involvement in hammering; with hammering there is an involvement in making something fast; with making something fast, there is an involvement in protection against bad weather; and this protection "is" for the sake of [um-willen] providing shelter for Dasein—that is to say, for the sake of a possibility of Dasein's Being. Whenever something ready-to-hand has an involvement with it, *what* involvement this is, has in each case been outlined in advance in terms of the totality of such involvements. In a workshop, for example, the totality of involvements which is constitutive for the ready-to-hand, is "earlier" than any single item of equipment: so too for the farmstead with all its utensils and outlying lands. **But the totality of involvements itself goes back ultimately to a "towards-which" in which there is *no* further involvement: this "towards-which" is not an entity with the kind of Being which belongs to what is ready-to-hand within a world; it is rather an entity whose being is defined as *Being-in-the-World*, and to whose state of Being, worldhood itself belongs.** [my emphasis] This primary "towards-which" is not just another "towards-which" as something in which an involvement is possible. The primary "towards-which" is a "for-the-sake-of-which". But the "for-the-sake-of" always pertains to the Being of *Dasein*, for which, in its Being, that very Being is essentially an *issue*. **We have thus indicated the interconnection by which the**

> structure of an involvement leads to Dasein's very Being as
> the sole authentic "for-the-sake-of-which"; for the present,
> however, we shall pursue this no further. [my emphasis]
> [Heidegger, 1927/1967, p. 114–116]

The key passage here is:

> "But the totality of involvements itself goes back ultimately to a
> "towards-which" in which there is *no* further involvement: this
> "towards-which" is not an entity with the kind of Being which
> belongs to what is ready-to-hand within a world; it is rather
> an entity whose being is defined as *Being-in-the-World*, and to
> whose state of Being, worldhood itself belongs."

Now, what is the relationship between the "primordial relation",
mentioned earlier, involved in hammering, for instance, and this,
more reflexive, recognition of the nature of *Being-in-the-World* as the
" "towards-which" in which there is *no* further involvement"?

I must now take a detour into epistemology. We now return to
the issue of the difficulty of what Heidegger is attempting to an
Anglo-American ear or eye! For what Heidegger is attempting to
evoke is something which is considered impossible, contradictory
(or meaningless) within the Anglo-American philosophical framework—either within its empiricist-pragmatist-positivist strand, or
its linguistic philosophy realist strand. My remarks here must, of
necessity, be brief and summary dogmatic interpretations; I have not
the space to provide the direct analyses which would vindicate the
positions I am taking.

With that proviso, I would argue that, on the one hand, in *phe-
nomenalistic empiricism* it is ultimately considered impossible to
refute scepticism and sceptical arguments (Hume, 2000, offers the
classic and incomparable exposition); the best that can be done is
to map the order of verifications within an empiricist framework
(the classic expositor of *this* is AJ Ayer in many works, e.g., particularly, Ayer, 1954), and I believe that this is even the position in
which both Kant and Husserl, remarkable as their creative versions
of transcendental idealism are, eventually find themselves (Kant,
1998, Husserl, 1977).

Likewise, on the other hand, I would argue that *linguistic philosophy*, including the later Wittgenstein, ultimately (with the proviso mentioned below) takes up a realist commonsense position, in which the existence of the "external world", the world beyond perception (the linguistic philosophers would say that is a misnomer, but I do not myself think it is avoidable), is simply *given* without question or without need of argument.

Wittgenstein and the Wittgensteinians, as well as PF Strawson, believe they have a different position on this from that of GE Moore's defence of commonsense beliefs (e.g., Wittgenstein, 1969, §§6, and 39, Strawson, 1959, 1966, Moore, 1959).

But I believe that, for instance, the Wittgensteinian position (1969) in "On Certainty" that fundamental beliefs are *without foundation*, *neither* defensible *nor* assailable, either goes forward to Moore and commonsense, or backwards again to Hume or Berkeley, scepticism or phenomenalism. Or else it goes forward to the *a priori*. But in that case it belongs within the realm of what I am arguing. On the former postulate, it rests upon the assumption that the status of sense-data or appearances *can remain undefined*, and therefore that there is no question of an *inference—a priori* or any other; there would be only sheer givenness of the world of commonsense (for this argument in implicit form, c.f., Austin, 1962b). Similar arguments apply to related positions and versions.

If, then this is all so, we have either to retreat to a *subjectivism*, or idealism, in which objectivity is inferred or constructed from the phenomenal experience of the self or the subject, or advance to an *objectivism*, or realism, in which the world, as other than the self or subject, is conceived of as simply given unambiguously to our knowledge without further ado.

*Heidegger's position attempts to define something that fundamentally refuses these alternatives.* What of the validity of this?

Now, while accepting that there is always something disturbing, and indeed also provincial, about Heidegger's Germano-centricity, one may reasonably ask whether an English or American philosopher could remotely have written *Being and Time*, and one may find an almost archetypal English/German difference between Strawson's and Heidegger's respective commentaries on Kant's *Critique of Pure Reason* (Strawson, 1966, Heidegger, 1990a), with Heidegger canonising Kant's doctrine of "imaginative synthesis" (see the poetry and objectivity chapter, below), whilst Strawson completely excises (or exorcises!) it! (Even Coleridge, the most "transcendental" of the English authors, only found himself philosophically through immersion in German thought, particularly Kant and Schelling.)

*Being-in-the-World* is conceived of as something which is rooted in the selfhood of *Dasein* as prior to anything which, as part of the ready-to-handness of bits of the physical world, is constituted by an involvement in some context. But its *Being-in-the-World* is a *whole* in which the *"in-the-World"* is just as primordial as its *"Being-"* and indeed its interpersonal dimension, *"Being-With"*. For Heidegger the two elements cannot be separated. Once more the *conjunction* of the two elements is vividly caught by Keats in the passage previously quoted:

> I go among the Fields and catch a glimpse of a Stoat or a field-mouse peeping out of the withered grass—the creature hath a purpose and its eyes are bright with it. I go amongst the buildings of a city and I see a Man hurrying along—to what? the Creature has a purpose and his eyes are bright with it. [Keats, 1819a/1947]

He is indicating the immersion in purpose which characterizes the primordial relationship Heidegger is considering. To invoke this he, almost by reflex, makes the comparison with the non-reflective immediacy and aliveness of the *animal's* absorption (from earlier in the quoted passage):

> The greater part of Men make their way with the same instinctiveness, the same unwandering eye from their purposes, the same animal eagerness as the Hawk. [Keats, 1819a/1947]

Heidegger equally considers the "towards-which" which is *Being-in-the-World* is most manifest when it takes the form of immersion in a total context. Think of sporting teams, and their spectators, immersed passionately in a competitive game! Heidegger would say that their relationship with *the ball*, as a piece of equipment, is primordial—and what it is directed *towards* is "scoring a goal" or "hitting a boundary", as a form of "defeating the other team"; the ball as ball is not in question at that moment (though it may instantly become so). It is:

the peculiarity of what is proximally ready-to-hand …
that, in its readiness-to-hand, it must, as it were, withdraw [zuruckzuziehen] in order to be ready-to-hand quite
authentically. That with which our everyday dealings proximally dwell is not the tools themselves [die Werkzeugeselbst].
On the contrary, that with which we concern ourselves primarily is *the work*—that which is to be produced at the time; and
this is accordingly ready-to-hand too. [p. 99]

Or the outcomes towards which the sporting contest is directed:
scoring a goal, striking a boundary, etc.

In other words, our *Being-in-the-World* is most manifest in
immersed relationships in which we have temporarily "lost ourselves". In terms of the three-aspect model this starts in the dimension of pre-communicability, but implicitly embraces the others.
The totality of the context of involvements of which I have spoken
refers onwards to the *Being-in-the-World* of the Being whose Being
is not an involvement:

> *Dasein's* very Being as the sole authentic "for-the-sake-of-which"
> [p. 117]
> But the "for-the-sake-of" always pertains to the Being of *Dasein*,
> for which, in its Being, that very Being is essentially an *issue*.
> [p. 116]

So he is saying that *Being-in-the-World* simultaneously is grounded in
*Dasein's* own characteristic "existential" (non-Thinglike) Being, *and
that* it primordially reveals, or uncovers, *in-the-World* realities, in the
form initially and primarily of the ready-to-hand, characterised by
the involvements *Dasein* invests in it.

The Anglo-American tradition, as I have described it, would consider this a contradiction; something is either in the objective realm
or the subjective realm, but there is no intrinsic marriage between
them (that of course *is* the epistemological problem!), whereas for
Heidegger they are inextricably entwined together.

Now, here there is perhaps an important ambiguity in Heidegger.
In respect of this type of immersion in *Being-in-the-World* he believes
that certain concerns, being-towards-death for instance, which may

become available to *Dasein*, in the resoluteness in which I become aware of my being-towards-death (the "impossible possibility" of my annihilation), are suppressed and displaced, are merely *latently* available for more reflective awareness on *Dasein's* part, and that the immersion is therefore *inauthentic*.

But, as mentioned earlier, as a value criterion, the authentic-inauthentic dichotomy is actually one which is pulled this way and that by a number of competing or complementary criteria-aspects—such as spontaneity and reflectiveness.

Not only are there many ways of being (some of which have a lively influence on Heidegger!) which actually celebrate unreflective immersion in activity as an *authentic* way of being (Gestalt being an approach within psychotherapy which illustrates this, and, in literature, Tolstoy's celebration, following the Gospels' "be not anxious; take no thought for the morrow", Mt. 6.34, of the spontaneous work, and unreflective wisdom of being, of the life of the peasants). There are also major elements in Heidegger himself which suggest that he sees this unreflective immersion as something to celebrate.

Something around the deeply unresolved tension of this, and related ambiguities, his hunger for an unreflecting certainty of immediate connection with the world, combined unresolvedly with a desire to, wisely and in an authoritarian way, "stand above" it (there is a strange peremptory yet self-pitying "note" which he recognisably slips into, when this element comes to the fore in his writing), may perhaps be connected with what got him temporarily caught in the Nazi hypnosis.

Firstly, there are many elements in both his biography, and his work, which indicate a deep reverence for, and deference to, the way of life of the countryfolk, such as his wonderful and poignant comments, great poetry in its own right, on Van Gogh's painting of a peasant woman's shoes, in *In the Origin of the Work of Art*:

> From the dark opening of the worn insides of the shoes the toilsome tread of the worker stares forth. In the stiffly rugged heaviness of the shoes there is the accumulated tenacity of her slow trudge through the far-spreading and ever-uniform furrows of the field swept by a raw wind. On the leather lie the dampness and richness of the soil. Under the soles stretches the

loneliness of the field-path as evening falls. In the shoes vibrates the silent call of the earth, its quiet gift of the ripening grain and its unexplained self-refusal in the fallow desolation of the wintry field. This equipment is pervaded by uncomplaining worry as to the certainty of bread, the wordless joy of having once more withstood want, the trembling before the impending childbed and shivering at the surrounding menace of death. [Heidegger, 2001]

And a good deal of this mode is already in *Being and Time* also. Thus, his already mentioned evocation of "Nature", (in which the "expressive"dimension of nature is not separated out from the "equipmental"—something which the later Heidegger does differentiate), as something which cannot be accounted for by a purely speculative or observational stance, graphically, in its shift of emphasis, carries something of the force of it:

> Here, however, "Nature" is not to be understood as that which is just present-at-hand, nor as the *power of Nature*. The wood is a forest of timber, the mountain a quarry of rock; the river is water-power, the wind is wind "in the sails". As the "environment" is discovered, the "Nature" thus discovered is encountered too. If its kind of Being as ready-to-hand is disregarded, this "Nature" itself can be discovered and defined simply in its pure presence-at-hand. *But when this happens, the Nature which "stirs and strives", which assails and enthralls us as landscape, remains hidden. The botanist's plants are not the flowers of the hedgerow; the "source" which the geographer establishes for a river is not the "springhead in the dale".* [Heidegger, 1927/1967, p. 100, last set of italic mine]

In this passage we can see Heidegger shift from the "purely technical", quasi-industrial, view of technology, in which the mountain is a quarry of rock, in the first part of the passage, to the reverential stance, almost Wordsworthian in its resonances, with the tendency towards pure expressiveness, of the last part, whose spirit leads on to so much in his later writings. (In them it perhaps enabled him to liberate himself from his Nazism—though, to be sure, not his

Germano-Greek-centricity ...) There are, for instance, the Van Gogh description, his evocations of poets like Hölderlin and Trakl, and his fascination with the revelation of truth as *aletheia* in the simplicities of Greek temples, which eventually led him to take his only visit to Greece, in 1962, his touching account of which has only recently been published (Heidegger, 2005).

But, now, the problem with *Being and Time* is that there is an inextricable entanglement between specific cultural and value-based analyses, and analyses which claim the complete generality of an ontological account. What is the relationship between these? We have already seen the oscillation between the mountain as a quarry for rock and "the springhead in the dale", which reflects Heidegger's profound ambivalence about technology;—but also it is a conflation of separate ontological elements as well.

In this context, let us briefly look a little more closely at the implication of Heidegger's rapturous investment in the ancient Greek world.

Part of what made the ancient Greeks, so greatly admired by Heidegger, temporarily supreme, despite their far inferior levels of population, in the Mediterranean area, and then, in the person of Alexander the Great, supreme in European Asia as far as India, was their immense and intense technological drive, with which we can couple their even more intense drive to develop forms of political and social organisation. Mining and metal manufacturing were immense industries in the ancient Mediterranean and European world, and are the background of the Greeks' successful war-mongering and imperialism.

It is a matter of dispute (e.g., Finley, 1999) how far the Greeks' technology, and their forms of economy, against the background of their differentiation of themselves from the great theocracies of Asia, and North Africa, Persia, Babylon, and Egypt, were on the way to the development of science, and also to capitalistic forms of finance, but undoubtedly elements which made for advance at this time, and later, were being developed.

In other words, the Greece so profoundly admired and invoked by Heidegger was *also* in the grip of technical advance, even though neither technology nor money, undoubtedly, were differentiated out, and, as it were, secularised, to the extent with which we have become familiar.

Heidegger, in his accounts in *Being and Time*, is oscillating between an account of a *secularised* technology and economy, and what we may call, for want of a subtler term, a *sacred* one; and to a very substantial extent his releasing of himself from Nazism, which he rightly came to associate with the development and exploitation of secular technology, coincides with the emergence of a much clearer grasp of the character of mass secular technology and economy in the modern world, which affects all the economies and political systems in the modern world indifferently (Heidegger, 1982, 1992, Young, 2003, Wilkinson, 2000).

But the conception he falls back upon is one in which, as with FR Leavis (e.g., Leavis, 1962), whilst ostensibly not denying the reality of secularisation in this sense, an idealised pre-industrial agrarian economy and technology is nevertheless partly invoked as the paradigm against which the modern is measured. In a fairly Hegelian way, he, certainly, alongside of this, does somewhat abstractly envisage that the taking of secular technology (which he considers dependent upon the march of ultimate cultural thought-framing, "Enframing", as he refers to it, 1982) *to its extremes* may release what can save us—maybe save us from it (Heidegger, 1982).

And at the ontological level, also, if we now return to the "primordial relation" (p. 98) with the hammer, already quoted, Heidegger has actually grasped something which is *essentially beyond* the conflict between "secular" and "sacred" technology. It applies equally to the tribesman carving a sacred totemic carving, to the shoemaker in mediaeval Nuremburg working at his last, and to the computer geek gripped by the internet; it applies equally to an Irish monk, in the 8th or 9th century, transcribing the Gospels in an illuminated manuscript, and to someone on the London Underground reading the latest Stephen King thriller.

The value differentiations, with which Heidegger is increasingly preoccupied, which enable us to recognise Van Gogh's painting as a masterwork, and the "world" of his peasant woman, as being evoked by Heidegger as one of deep human distinction and value, are predicated *upon the basis* of something even more elementary about the relation with tools and artefacts, which must be described first. In *Being and Time* this is his aim, but it is entangled with value issues, in a way which prevents certain aspects of the wider context being clearly seen.

I now come to the nub of this. He is invoking the "primordial relation" in a way which forces us to see the embodied human-physical totality of *Being-in-the-World* as a relational whole. *The relationality of the involvement of the ready-to-hand of the hammer, for instance, is something which cannot be split into its parts.* The readiness-to-hand of the hammer is something intrinsic to it in its relation to human being, *Dasein*. And this is correct, as far as it goes.

But the train does not carry all the way to the buffers! *For he analyses it exclusively from the side of the human, without taking into account the position of the physical realities.* The hammer is something which is, at the same time, *as* something intrinsically related to human being, culture and context relative, dependent on what Wittgenstein would call the *institutions* of contextual practices (such as money; or particular forms of worship, in the case of the bread and wine of the Catholic mass; or Western musical form in the case of a violin; or computer-use in the early 21st century in the case of my computer; and so on, and on).

*This* dimension of the cultural contextualisation of equipment, to which I shall return, is something which is both necessary ("*a priori*") and *necessarily particular*, as Heidegger emphasises in many elements of *Being and Time*. Whilst it is founded upon the "primordial relation", it *necessarily carries it into the all-pervasive particularity of the realm of the symbolic*, which constitutes it an *a priori of the particular* of unique scope, and so inextricably interwoven with the concrete and contingent, that we require a new development of the concept of the *a priori*. I return to this.

But the hammer also has a dimension ("physics", let us call it) which is *not* culture relative—except in the very broadest sense in which physics itself is culture relative. So is there a reciprocity with this aspect of the hammer? The question one wants to put to him is this: can he do justice to the *reciprocity* of the relation, or will he not have, in the last analysis, though taking it much further than anyone else, to postulate a residual objectivism, at the heart of his analysis, in his idea of *the human unveiling of the hammerhood of the hammer*? Does there not have to be, in the extreme primal quality of this immersion, a tacit never fully expressed *reciprocal* element which gives Heidegger's marvellous sense of the uncanny immediacy its force?

If he does not postulate a reciprocity, will he not, in the last analysis, be embracing precisely what he wished to avoid, namely the postulate of an objective "in-itself" of physical things, like Kant's "things-in-themselves", on top of which, then, inexplicably, a layering of human subjectivity is added?

And does he not, to avoid this, have to embrace once more two Greek recognitions he wished to surpass or reinterpret—Plato's eternity of the ideas, and therefore, of truth, and a development of Aristotle's potentiality (dunamis) of physical things, and therefore their power to be in *potential* relation to the human and the human world, even when that is only actualised in particular human contexts? [In his commentary (1931/1995) on Aristotle's account of *dunamis* and *energeia* Heidegger is sympathetic to the latter doctrine, but does not address the issue of reciprocity.]

Otherwise reality is something which "exists", even when there is no truth in the sense of *aletheia*, so that *aletheiaic* truth, paradoxically against its essence, becomes so to say a subjective paste-on to reality (since on Heidegger's model, Newton's Laws, for instance, only "exist" when there is *Dasein*, Heidegger, 1962, p. 269), and the old Cartesian-Kantian dualism, in a yet new variation, returns once more:

> Through Newton the laws became true; and, with them, entities became accessible in themselves to *Dasein*. Once entities have been uncovered, they show themselves precisely as entities which beforehand already were. Such uncovering is the kind of Being which belongs to "truth". [Heidegger, 1927/1967, p. 269]

Here is none of the inherent ambiguity of veiling/unveiling which elsewhere, as we have seen, appertains to his concept of truth as *aletheia*. This is pure *unveiling* only, which perhaps even collapses back into truth as assertion.

In short, Heidegger, however magnificently he evokes certain structures of human experience, in his particular development of the phenomenological method, *is* in the end in the same position as the Anglo-American realists, and the later Wittgenstein, of postulating an "in-itself", which is then wondrously revealed in its "as it is" through the rich *aletheiaic* forms of access to it which *Dasein* possesses. But this does not at all account for how the "in-itself", for its part, acquires a relation to *us*.

Alfred North Whitehead, the modern Leibniz, the only major British philosopher to grasp the nettle of the relation of causality and perception, and hence to mount an effective challenge to Hume's scepticism, in the process, of necessity, also grasps the nettle of the reciprocity of the human and the physical (in *Process and Reality*, 1929/1979, Whitehead, 1979). He argues that *presentational immediacy*, the visual mode of perception, from which as a model, even if not explicitly, all the sceptical problems arise, must be supplemented by, and integrated with, the *causal* mode of perception, which he calls the mode of *causal efficacy*, and is illustrated vividly by, for instance, our experience of sitting down on a drawing pin, or a hot stove, or diving into very cold water, but in general in our whole experience of embodiment.

Clearly the whole mode of readiness-to-hand in Heidegger would come under this latter heading, (except that Whitehead would consider it a *symbolic mode* process, that is, one which combines aspects of both modes). And Whitehead believes that the primitive experience of the impact of the physical world upon functionally physical, not merely visual-presentational, aspects of ourselves—such as body parts, or eyeballs, and hands—involved in such "causal efficacy" points towards a universal process of causal reciprocity, in which all beings-in-process, or "actual entities", as he calls them, participate. *The simple corollary for him is that all being is reciprocally represented in the being of every other being, and there is no inherent "in-itself-hood" without relation, in any mode of being.* The question of existence becomes straightforwardly the question of reciprocity—not something more mysterious or recondite. And reciprocity includes the symbolic, the textual reciprocity of cross-referencing. The "objecthood" analogy is in many ways even more radically dissolved in Whitehead than it is in Heidegger or Wittgenstein.

We have no space to, and we do not have to, explore the immensely complex metaphysic (1929/1979) in which Whitehead develops this assumption, and which of necessity goes beyond phenomenology to inference; it is enough that such an analysis exists and *is possible*.

From this, it would therefore also follow from Whitehead's analysis that Heidegger, like Kant, and like Husserl, despite his best and magnificent efforts, remains caught in the framework of analysis derived from "presentational immediacy", the visual-aesthetic mapping of experience. His version of phenomenology in *Being and Time*, ostensibly released from Husserl's "presentational immediacy" invocation of the Cartesian epoché, in fact still remains within its ambience, and never allows him to consider what lies "on the other side" of phenomena.

What remains prodigious and extraordinary about it is the marvellous dense detail of revealing of so many human situations we normally pass over unnoticed. For this profound "not noticing" he constructs as explanation the whole conception to which I have alluded, of the contrast between inauthentic Being immersed in, or fallen into, "the one" or "the they" ("Das Man"), and authentic Being which is characterised by the capacity for individualised conscience, and resolute acceptance of "ones" Being-towards-death.

But it is much more plausible to hold that the possibility of immersed involvement appertains to our animal ("causal efficacy") level of being, which is not a product of human herd modes of Being, they being, if anything, secondary to it, and it being utterly neutral in terms of authenticity (the whole analysis of which must be reconstructed on a more complex basis). Heidegger's equivocal stance in relation to our animal nature (Derrida, 1987/1989) can be disentangled.

I now return to my initial formulation of Heidegger's account:

*Man is the animal who becomes alienated from his world, through the developments of his **technology**, which also expresses his unique relationship with his world, and **thereby** develops an awareness of death, being, and nothingness.*

In effect, Heidegger articulates a *two-level analysis*; at the animal level we are simply immersed in our world, as Keats evokes, and this has a primary character which undercuts that of the being of equipment, and which therefore actually undercuts the comprehensiveness of the alienating role he attributes to the "they". But, through technology, *techne*, we acquire the "later" possibility of self-reflection, though it is, through our symbolic grasp, seamlessly "read back", in its totality contextualisation, into our apprehension of being immersed in the ready-to-hand. And this is why I say the second Division of *Being and Time* is latent in the first. It is latent in the ambiguity in readiness-to-hand we have explored. (I shall return to the question which emerges from the relational-reciprocal analysis, of temporality as the horizon of being, in the chapter about Trinitarian understandings and the later Freudian metapsychology.)

In our construction and use of tools and signs, *we become able to discover our world as alien to us*, in the discovery of the incessant threat, that our mastery of the world, and our re-immersion in it as tool-users and sign-users, may break down. In discovering the world as alien to us, we each become exposed to our inescapable Being-towards-death, and to the existential necessity to constantly reconstitute our world, and thus we go on to discover reflexivity, and the possibility of symbolic reduplication of the world, for instance, in scientific theory and philosophy.

So, our "primordial relation" to hammering and any other immersed activity with equipment—source of extreme nostalgia in our aspiration to envisage it as something characterised by total spontaneous concentration—*is nevertheless haunted by the permanent possibility of its own destablisation, and deferment/deferral* (this is where Derrida takes off from Heidegger). Heidegger indeed indicates this in his moving evocation of Van Gogh's portrayal of the peasant woman's shoes, already quoted. Thus also, the "mechanical" and "mass-produced" character of post-industrial technology was always latent in all technology, and in being human.

But, therefore, Van Gogh's peasant woman's shoes *are not primarily referential-equipmental; they are symbolic-expressive*. It is always *possible* even for an actual tool, and even more for any form of sign or symbol, to either lose, or transform, its meaning. The anthropological indications are that sign use is more fundamental than tool use (which chimpanzees also possess) in the emergence of the awareness of death and of the ritualisation of existence (c.f., e.g., Jaynes, 1990, Durkheim, 2001, Levi-Strauss, 1966). And the inherently self-transforming *bricolage* (c.f., *Introduction*, above, and Levi-Strauss, 1966) of symbolisation is inescapable.

This means, on the one hand, an indefinite *widening* of the process of contextualisation beyond the ostensible "immediate" reference (c.f., Derrida's analysis in *Limited Inc*, Derrida, 1988, and c.f., Shelley, 1818/1999, above), which can also include, and bracket within itself, contextual "narrowings" of it (which are, in fact, really specialised elaborations, the "narrowing" being an illusion of art), as in the fictional contexts I have mentioned above.

On the other hand—and precisely because we can liberate the full implication of sign and symbol, which point beyond themselves indefinitely, and in an indefinitely large number of ways and categories—we are free to explore the metaphysics of what is *beyond phenomena*, through both the philosophy, and the science, of the fundamental constituents of both matter and brain—and as well, of course, mind!

This process begins with such simple phenomena, and inferences from them, which Hume adduces in his chapter *Of Scepticism concerning the senses* (Hume, 2000), as for instance producing double vision by pressing on ones eyeball!

This shows us immediately that *what we see at any time* is an optically caused hallucination, and that our assumption of an external world, as the basis of it, goes beyond appearances. This is something which Hume ridicules, on the basis of the assumption of the primacy of presentational immediacy, *even though it is he who has called attention to these "causal efficacy" types of experiment*, which immediately take us beyond (visual) phenomena (as perception, in its "causal efficacy" dependency, inherently does):

> But as no beings are ever present to the mind but perceptions; it follows that we may observe a conjunction or a relation of cause and effect between different perceptions, but can never observe it between perceptions and objects. 'Tis impossible, therefore, that from the existence or any of the qualities of the former, we can ever form any conclusion concerning the existence of the latter, or ever satisfy our reason in this particular.
> [Hume, 2000, Book I, part iv, section 2]

Crucial to this process, therefore, is the permission to make inferences and move beyond appearances or phenomena ("perceptions", in Hume's terminology), or purely linguistic conceptions, but combining this with a kind of Wittgensteinian willingness to wrestle with the particularities of each problem. In this spirit the vexed problems, which are commonly glossed over, of resolving the dualistic dilemma, can be tackled, not in a formulaic way, but in a way which teases out how inferential enquiry into levels of existence can be undertaken.

I take this a bit further in discussing Daniel Stern's recent work, in the chapter on poetry and objectivity.

Here and now, I turn once more to the other aspect of this, the indefinite *widening* of contextualisation and sign and symbol. Here we come back, at last, to the nature of the *"a priori of the particular"* once more. And I can illustrate it all with yet another, but ironical, possible variant of readiness-to-hand!

The perennial incompleteness of the involvements of our *Being-in-the-World* can be illustrated vividly and ironically by the way in which, if we are reading *Being and Time* **itself**, with its dense evocation of a whole immense suggestive world of philosophical and anthropological insight, what we experience in the book, as a book, a deeply enigmatic book, is *the elusive character of the readiness-to-hand of text*, which, unlike a tool or piece of equipment, *carries its implicit infinity directly within it*, as it were, rather than in its context.

Wittgenstein writes of such awareness (awareness of not just his books but of his overall thought and teaching, *an actual possibility* for him, whereas its status is different for us after his death):

> I am showing my pupils details of an immense landscape which
> they cannot possibly know their way around. [Wittgenstein,
> 1980, p. 56]

Now, all the above analyses are attempts at philosophical *classifications*, which permit also *discriminations*, such as the already discussed discrimination of levels as between the "primordial relation" involved in hammering, and the symbolic-reflexive stepping back which enables the context-totality involved in readiness-to-hand as a whole to be seen, as *Being-in-the-world*. And these then, through the apprehension of alienation in our *Being-in-the-world*, permit the apprehension of such dimensions as temporality, and being-towards-death (conceived of unequivocally as annihilation by Heidegger), as latent possibilities of self-reflection embedded within the totality mode of *Being-in-the-world*.

So these enquiries are analogous to the *a priori* explorations of categories since Aristotle.

At the same time, the example of reading a book or a poem reveals, at the level of the sign and symbol, an infinitude of relations implicit in *this particular form* of the ready-to-hand as text and context. And of course it can reflexively include backwards, so to say, the "philosophical *a priori*" dimension, that level of generality, just as "philosophy" can take on literary form, as in Eliot, Proust, and Pirsig.

What we then grasp—most vividly in this particular illustration of it—is that *within each category also* there is an *a priori of the specific* which nevertheless remains an *a priori*, and of course many shadings between them. That is, within the category, there is a detailed development of the dimension of meaning and understanding which belongs to it.

We have been confused by empiricism's or positivism's exclusive emphasis upon the contingent and the factual as that which could have been otherwise. We are all involuntary disciples of Dickens's Mr Gradgrind in *Hard Times*:

> The One Thing Needful
>
> "Now! what I want is, Facts. Teach these boys and girls nothing but Facts. Facts alone are wanted in life. Plant nothing else, and root out everything else. You can only form the minds of reasoning animals upon Facts: nothing else will ever be of any service to them. This is the principle on which I bring up my own children, and this is the principle on which I bring up these children. Stick to Facts, sir!" (Dickens, 1854/1994)

But what this omits is not only the dimension of classification, which is either prior to fact, or alternates and interfuses with fact, and is not reducible to it—which would be the most extreme empiricism, only to be embraced in flight from the inexplicable terror of reverting to being a Platonist again (c.f., Quine, 1951/1961)!—*but also the dimension of creation.*

Voluntary creation, which is involved in the temporal, in the irreversibility of event—such as the articulation, in speaking a sentence, of the meanest novel sentence which has not been created before (c.f., Wilkinson, 1998)—creates a pattern, a meaning, a Platonic entity! This was Chomsky's starting point for his structural linguistics as well (Chomsky, 1957). Patterning, as Gregory Bateson, like Freud, understood (Bateson, 1979, Freud, 1920/1984), is at the heart of all existence—as it is at the heart of all psychotherapeutic process ("transference" being simply a *subset* of this). The pattern, whilst embedded in the recognition of event, immediately and inherently also transcends the contingency of event and becomes a trace, a record, a meme, an iteration (Derrida, 1988), a replication, a *replicator*. In the poetry and objectivity chapter I explore the tensions which arise from this double-aspect, for Daniel Stern, for instance, in respect of his analysis of "present moments" (Stern, 2004)

And my mappings of the three dimensions/aspects, and their interrelations, are also an *articulation* of structure of existence, and human existence; they can only be laid bare and articulated, not reduced to any simpler framework. They are a structural pattern-ing, in a broad sense of structure, and hence bear the analogy to Freud's later, itself non-reductively articulated, metapsychological analysis of structure they do, as we shall explore in a later chapter. And they consequently invoke all the cross-disciplinary enquiries which they do invoke—literary, the fine arts, philosophy, theology, and so on!

We have seen that they have more general aspects, which might be labelled "philosophy", and more specific ones, which might be labelled "poetry". *But the whole skein of concept and pattern here, whether general or specific, is a priori. A*nd its interaction with the domain of the factual is immensely complex. Again, I shall return to this in more detail in the next chapter.

We have seen that, under the impact of a closer enquiry, the claim to philosophical generality, which is central to Heidegger's view of his "ontological" analyses as being distinguished from specific scien-tific enquiries, of *Being and Time* partly, but not wholly, destabilises. Conversely, we saw in the Rilke passage that the forms which *Being-in-the-World* takes are highly local and idiosyncratic, though not the less Platonic in the sense envisaged here. *Above all, the enquiry* **process** *implicates the a priori through and through, whatever view we ultimately take of it.*

I shall end by illustrating such an idiosyncratic form, which leads us on to the fuller analysis of the *a priori* in the chapter on theory and method, with an extraordinary poem, one of the "Lucy" poems, of

Wordsworth's, in which his entire *Being-in-the-World* mutates irreversibly in the face of death:

> A slumber did my spirit seal;
> I had no human fears;
> She seemed a thing that could not feel
> The touch of earthly years.
>
> No motion has she now, no force;
> She neither hears nor sees;
> Rolled round in earth's diurnal course,
> With rocks, and stones, and trees. (Wordsworth, 1799/2004)

About this poem there is critical disagreement as to whether the first stanza is before or after the girl's or woman's death—and whether, like Mahler's *Kindertotenleider*, there is a *projective* element in the poem, being about a feared, rather than an actual, event.

But there is absolutely no doubt that the second stanza is apprehended as subsequent, and therefore that it records a form of *Being-in-the-World*, as a world which is now completely pervaded by the death and loss of her, who has become part of the earth—but part of the earth conceived both astronomically (earth's rotation) and yet also humanly—"diurnal course" implies *human* time.

In Heidegger's phrase, this death has become elementally part of his "ownmost" experience.

And here we glimpse the truth that *the infinite unique particularity of experience* is part of the Platonic essence, the *a priori* of human reality. Heidegger in the end, like Nietzsche, leads us back to Leibniz and Blake:

> Thus, although each created Monad represents the whole universe, it represents more distinctly the body which specially pertains to it, and of which it is the entelechy; and as this body expresses the whole universe through the connexion of all matter in the plenum, the soul also represents the whole universe in representing this body, which belongs to it in a special way. (Leibniz, 1714/1998)
>
> The fool sees not the same tree that a wise man sees.

He who would do good to another must do it in Minute
Particulars: general Good is the plea of the scoundrel, hypocrite,
and flatterer, for Art and Science cannot exist but in minutely
organized Particulars. (William Blake, 1977)

In the theory and method chapter we see in more detail how the
*a priori* of these Minute Particulars emerges in the fine grain of
psychotherapeutically informed exploration of human personal
phenomenology.

In this chapter I have sought to show how the aspiration to generality even of philosophy of existence itself, is drawn back again to
the Minute Particulars, and the poetic cross-connectedness of reality
and the human.

Before we turn onwards to the putting in place of the philosophical background to this, exploration of another substantial example
comes first. In the next chapter I apply literary-psychotherapeutic
method to one of the greatest unsolved riddles of history, the
Shakespeare Authorship question itself.

# CHAPTER FOUR

# Reality, Existence, and the Shakespeare Authorship Question: *King Lear, Little Dorrit,* and the Man Who Was Shakespeare

*Part I*
*"The courtier's, soldier's, scholar's, eye, tongue, sword;*
*The expectancy and rose of the fair state"*

[Note: all biblical quotations in what follows are from the Geneva Bible of 1560/1599, which would have been the Bible both Edward de Vere, 17th Earl of Oxford, and William Shakespeare of Stratford, would have known.]

I think I could probably say that it was principally through absorbing Shakespeare in my school days that I developed the way of apprehending his world, that led me first into psychiatric nursing and then into psychotherapy. Shakespeare firstly gave me an inner view of madness—in *Hamlet, King Lear,* and *Macbeth.* Secondly, it was through Shakespeare above all, understood with the help of John Keats (later Tolstoy supplemented this at age 17) that I *gained a sense of the possibility of a universal understanding of persons,* the possibility of a universal psychology.

It remains through Shakespeare above all that I find a corrective to over-narrow and over-technical views of human psychology, and who pointed me in the direction of poetry as the paradigm to understand persons. And it is now, thus, that I return to him, and draw upon him as a corrective, but now having acquired some element of the universal psychology towards which he led me!

In the process I have myself enacted elements of the poetic process which I am writing about in this book.

In the course of writing of this chapter Shakespeare has forced himself into the central place in this book, for many reasons, and I shall start by talking a little about that.

I began with the intention of writing about the Shakespeare authorship in terms of the relation of *King Lear* and Dickens' *Little Dorrit*; this is still part of the chapter, but only as the rounding off of what actually took the process over, and which, no more than the links between Hopkins and Shakespeare's *King Lear* in Chapter 1, had I in the least anticipated.

Instead, I found myself beginning from the problem of the strange status of Edgar in *King Lear*, and found myself discovering or at least hypothesising things about this crucial, but extraordinarily hidden, character which were utterly new to me. I was led to them because they connected very deeply, on the one hand, with the psychology of the authorship issue, which is my thematic illustration and enactment in this chapter in terms of the purpose of the book, along with the alchemical-hermetic universality of the Shakespearean vision of the supreme Renaissance author. On the other they made intelligible to me why I myself became so possessed both by this theme, and by the authorship issue in general. The fundamental process uncovered is the fascinating Freudian theme (Freud, 1939/1967) of *the return of the repressed*—a vast repression now nearly four centuries old and counting, but of which the author, in an extraordinary way, gives us the means—if we can take them up!—to unravel it! The result is a very long chapter, the thematic centre of the book, the rest of which is now organised around it, as a multi-faceted configuration setting this one off, and which now has the most of me in it. I shall try to touch on this *en passant* as I go along.

It is central to all this that it still remains uncertain *who Shakespeare was*!

So, now, could a psychotherapeutic revelation of the hidden heart of a supreme author expressed in his work, actually help us to settle the dispute as to who he is?

And can we take account of the total communication of an author, in their existential historical context, without addressing the evidential relationship between the work and the life?

And, if, conversely, we take adequate account of the life, can this help us to interpret and explore the work?

These questions addressed to literature are somewhat analogous to the old questions, in psychoanalysis and psychotherapy, questions of a triangulating character, about the location of therapeutic change: firstly, in the person's current life and context; secondly, in their past and history; and, thirdly, in the transferential/repatterning process of the therapeutic encounter, and of course in the dialectical interplay of all of these (Malan, 1979/1995).

As this chapter works initially in terms of literary assumptions, which will be familiar enough in general terms to any literary readers, I shall intersperse it with comments attempting to explain to my psychotherapist and counsellor readers "what is going on", in psychotherapeutic terms.

Effectively, my aim is to conduct a partly psychotherapeutic enquiry, a test case piece of psychotherapeutic detective work (with psychic interior descent and identification work), into the works of Shakespeare, to see what we can infer about the author, on the hypothesis that he was not William Shakespeare of Stratford, that he was, in fact, Edward de Vere, 17th Earl of Oxford.

The issues here would be straightforward enough—but for the fact that it is still the case that few people outside certain, fairly unorthodox, literary circles actually realise there is a live issue here, let alone what it opens up if we pursue it.

The evidence in this question is deeply circumstantial, and many people have, therefore, developed lines of circumstantial enquiry in terms of postulates.

For instance, the pioneer of the Oxfordian hypothesis, JT Looney (an unfortunate name in England—and Oxfordians have retaliated against Stratfordian ridicule by using Shagsper, Shaksper, and variants for the Stratford candidate; we should, I think, none of us, stoop to such rhetorical devices), having concluded that William Shakespeare of Stratford could not be the author, he postulated that we could infer from the plays and poems, and their presupposed forms of practical knowledge, and commonest discernable strands of opinion and belief, a comprehensive set of characteristics which he deduced would *uniquely* fit one person.

By these means he was led to Oxford—the case being made more authentic by the fact that Oxford was hitherto unknown to him (Looney, 1920).

Likewise Diana Price's important recent book (2001), *Shakespeare's Unorthodox Biography*, examining the credentials of William Shakespeare of Stratford, develops a set of criteria by which an author can be validly evidenced as an author with contemporary materials, such as the difference between a letter which includes a personal reference to a writer (implying that the writer knew the writer as a writer personally) as opposed to an impersonal one (such as one praising the works of such an author). The bulk of Oxfordian reasoning is based upon making direct, or more subtle, factual connections between allusions in the plays and poems and events etc of Oxford's life.

In this essay I wish to use a different kind of circumstantial postulate, one which infers something about the *character of the author* from *the creative psychological character found in the work*. This is different from Looney's seeking to identify the external personal characteristics of the author, and has not to my knowledge been often used systematically by Oxfordian authors, though often enough *en passant* (Berney, 2007, who pursues enquiry into the significance of Autolycus, in *A Winter's Tale*, in a way very close to mine here into the character of Edgar in *King Lear*, is a significant exception to this).

So this would be applying literary critical method systematically to the authorship question, in a way which draws as fully as possible (but not reductively, as most psychotherapeutic method has previously been) from a psychotherapeutic dimension of insight.

The questions I began with are connected. By means including an in depth consideration of *King Lear* and of the relationship between *King Lear*, and Dickens's *Little Dorrit*, I want to open up three avenues of exploration, with potential promise of validity, simultaneously, in this chapter. I unfortunately have to leave some matters fairly speculative and hypothetical in virtue of the limits to what I can get in to this chapter in this book.

In what follows I shall assume the reader has familiarised themselves with at least the story of these works—and preferably re-read at least *King Lear*!

So, first, then, I want to use psychotherapeutic method in the context of a major literary dispute, the Shakespeare Authorship question—and to demonstrate that it can helpfully be so used. I want to move things forward in respect of the authorship dispute—and offer a model for related disputes.

As I have said, not everyone realises there *is* a dispute here; the orthodox position of the authorship of William Shakespeare of Stratford is that there is no doubt about the authorship of Shakespeare's works. But there have been dissenting voices about this since at least the later 17th Century, and now hundreds, perhaps thousands, of books exist promoting a variety of (apparently up to 80) candidates (Ogburn, 1988).

Secondly, I want to shed new light on *King Lear* as such; working with the assumption of the 17th Earl of Oxford's authorship of the plays and poems, I shall try to show that new doors open on the play if we use that assumption.

And, thirdly, in the converse direction, I want to make the extraordinary power and creativity—and the powerful *methodology of insight* involved in it—of great literature available for psychotherapy, psychotherapy which sometimes persists in using an unduly narrow experiential and cultural base for its explorations.

All this can and must be done simultaneously. This has a circular aspect, but it is cumulative. We do sometimes validly conclude, on the basis of circumstantial evidence and evidence from character, that someone has, for instance, committed a crime, without a direct piece of incriminating evidence, and such evidence is mainly cumulative. In psychotherapy, also, we validate interpretations through a process of cumulative dialogical detective work, both through a process of elimination, and through inferring interpretative constructions. It is rarely decisive at any given point, but may cumulatively give rise to conviction without inappropriate dependence on suggestion and information giving. The process of an interpretative critical process, making contextual judgements in relation to a poem, as I have been pursuing in previous chapters, is similarly rarely absolutely conclusive. But it develops cumulative conviction.

It is an odd kind of hypothetical *a priori* reasoning, but such is our process in such contexts as law, art criticism, and even linguistic philosophy (which Austin, 1961, called "linguistic phenomenology").

As in other chapters, my main fear is that the complexity of what I am opening up will overwhelm my readers. This is the longest chapter in the book, and contains, in my own view, the most ground-breaking material.

I am aware that I have to introduce or presuppose, in relation to the above, three different frameworks of knowledge simultaneously, and that this is asking a great deal, especially in the context of a very difficult issue in literary-psychotherapeutic judgement. I have to introduce a *literary-critical* framework. I have to introduce a framework of non-reductive *psychotherapeutic enquiry into literature.* And I have to introduce *literary-psychotherapeutic enquiry*, to shed light upon the nature of psychotherapy in a wider context.

In the end, this is a combined enquiry with multiple elements, which is not reducible to any of them, and its success will be justified by what it opens up and illuminates. I am not assuming that my arguments in this chapter are final, but they may deepen the non-quantitative probability in question here.

Each dimension introduces elements which are unique to it. Yet it also follows from the thesis of this book that it will turn out we are pursuing very similar types of enquiry in all three dimensions.

That the exploration of great literature naturally takes the form of a kind of psychotherapy is evident from John Keats' great poem about *King Lear*, a remarkable piece of testimony from our most Shakespearean poet, of Shakespeare's successors, in which the purgatorial character of the play is understood in terms we would think of as psychotherapeutic, and in which, also, an ancient English, possibly Druidic, understanding of the play is also hinted at, something which, (refocused in terms of the Arthurian heritage, and in which the author, hiddenly, turns out to be summoning very ancient "Albionic" resonances indeed), turns out much more important than I ever realised:

### On Sitting Down To Read *King Lear* Once Again

O golden tongued Romance, with serene lute!
Fair plumed Syren, Queen of far-away!
Leave melodizing on this wintry day,
Shut up thine olden pages, and be mute:
Adieu! for once again the fierce dispute

> Betwixt damnation and impassion'd clay
> Must I burn through; once more humbly assay
> The bitter-sweet of this Shakespearian fruit.
> Chief Poet! and ye clouds of Albion,
> Begetters of our deep eternal theme!
> When through the old oak Forest I am gone,
> Let me not wander in a barren dream,
> But when I am consumed in the fire,
> Give me new Phoenix wings to fly at my desire
> (Keats, 1818/1977)

Thus, then, we begin with a notorious literary-critical debate, the Shakespeare authorship question. I have already indicated, but now declare an interest directly: I am one of those who is of the view that Edward de Vere, 17th Earl of Oxford, was the main author of the works.

I am greatly indebted to many contributions on the Oxfordian website, *The Shakespeare Fellowship*: http://www.shakespearefellowship.org/

I am secondly much indebted to Mark Alexander's collection of Oxfordian materials, and writings, *The Shakespeare Authorship Source Page*: http://www.sourcetext.com/sourcebook/index.htm

And I am very highly indebted to Nina Green's rich collection of relevant texts of and relating to Oxford, *The Oxford Authorship Site*: http://www.oxford-shakespeare.com/

Nina Green's own forum, *Phaeton*, for debate of Oxfordian matters is an invaluable resource, offering a model of pluralistic rational argument, in which strengths in opponents' positions are recognised, as well as weaknesses and myths in a variety of Oxfordian arguments, and debate is carried on with respect. Finally very many of the linkages I make here I owe in some form to Ogburn's seminal work, (Ogburn, 1988) which was what opened the Oxfordian hypothesis, as for so many others, for me some 15 years or so ago.

Now, a great deal of the theoretical argument, about whether William Shakespeare of Stratford wrote the works of "Shakespeare", or whether Edward de Vere, for example (Freud's preferred candidate, now the front running alternative candidate), did, appears to hinge upon (or perhaps, conversely, to dictate) what we understand about the relation of works of literature, and of art, to their creators.

Though this is a literary critical type of argument, and I lay the foundation for this chapter by considering it, it also carries across into familiar psychotherapeutic arguments, as to whether the frame of psychotherapy is autonomous, and, if it is not, what relation it has, in context, to the rest of the life context of the client(s).

This parallelism between the frames of literature, theatre, artistic performance, religious ritual, and the "rite" of the psychotherapy session (Ekeland, 1997), is part of what has led me to draw the close analogy I am doing between psychotherapy and poetry.

So, then, does the artist create in a pure realm of genius, which takes on itself different values than anything about the actual intentions and personal history of the author or creator? Or is the work of the artist inherently grounded in the life—albeit in no neat or merely auto-biographical fashion? Is there a third position? What is the complex relation between fiction and personal psychology?

All this summons up such literary critical themes as Wimsatt and Beardsley's famous discussion (1951/1967b) of the *intentional fallacy*, DH Lawrence's (1990) maxim, *Never trust the artist, trust the tale*, (though this has a different thrust when taken in its totality), TS Eliot's (1920/1932) very ambiguous discussion of the impersonality of the artist, in *Tradition and the Individual Talent*, and similar themes. I explore one of many variant views of this—that of G Wilson Knight—shortly, in the context of Shakespeare.

In virtue of the fact that, with regard to our greatest genius of all, Shakespeare, his life, *if he was William Shakespeare of Stratford*, affords us *virtually nothing which can be correlated independently with the works*, as opposed to *postulated conjecturally on the basis of them*, we may conjecture that many of the normally extremely pragmatic, realis-tic, empirical and anti-Platonic, Anglo-Saxons have, in their literary critical speculations, been pushed unduly in the former direction, of "the imagined pure realm of genius".

This, then, left an open field for imaginative speculation about the workings of genius, and has intensified a somewhat un-Anglo-Saxon trend towards a form of Platonism, which is certainly a valid polarity—but which downgrades the implication of actuality, and the specific how of the implication of actuality, in an author's work.

We shall shortly come to Wilson Knight's version of this, but it is worth illustrating from a more recent and very significant critical voice (from whose powerful insight I shall draw again later in relation to the character of Edgar in *King Lear*), that of Harold Bloom, who is explicitly anti-Oxfordian. He betrays *his profound need for the author to be non-specific in nature* in such (something for Bloom, that notorious anti-post-modernist, rather post-modern!) passages as the following:

> The best principle in reading Shakespeare is Emerson's: "Shakespeare is the only biographer of Shakespeare, and even he can tell us nothing except to the Shakespeare in us." I myself deviate a touch from Emerson, since I think only Shakespeare has placed the Shakespeare in us. [Bloom, 1998/1999, p. 488]

This is extremely curious, since, if Shakespeare invented, as Bloom says, the human as we know it, then realistic drama (not solely that, but that in major part) which points us towards the real life of living people, is precisely part of what he invented—together with, again and again, the "drama" used explicitly as a metaphor for life! We shall soon see what Hamlet has to say on this!

But, as we shall see, even this points us in the direction of the special role, partially yet acutely grasped by Bloom, within *King Lear*, of Edgar, since Edgar, too, is *non-specific* in a very important way.

*My case is that we cannot present an existentially grounded author*, in the sense of "existence" I am trying to define in this book, *if we go with William Shakespeare of Stratford*. We cannot present a credible genius if we go with him—and we are dealing with one of the most towering geniuses of all time. When we are dealing with major literary creativity, we have two vast existential complexities, which do not have a one-to-one relationship, to be sure, but which do have a relationship, and cannot not have a relationship—the complexity of the life, and the complexity of the work.

But this requirement is fulfilled—in spades! And more and more the deeper we explore!—if we relate the life of Edward de Vere to the plays and the poems. Of course, that is a seductive possibility, which can tempt us to overlook evidence, also. But it is also a hypothesis we can explore.

And so, methodologically, I shall carry forward the exploration with the same freedom to interweave the life and the work as I would with, say. Wagner, Byron, or Gerard Manley Hopkins. This in one sense begs the question, but in another it is the hypothetico-deductive testing of hypothesis (Popper, 2002). It is not possible to do it at all with William Shakespeare of Stratford; there is no basis for it. If, then, we allow it freely with Edward de Vere, how does it look?

So, what is the nature of the presence of an author in relation to their work? (Psychotherapists can compare: what is the relation between the client who is revealed in the creative process of sessional work, and the client outside in their life relations?)

As already mentioned, the temptation, given the impossibility for most critics to contemplate the possibility that the Stratfordian attribution may be false, is to go in the direction exemplified (in the abstract, but not in the concrete, as we shall see) by (as well as Bloom) that supreme Shakespearian, and large and grand Shakespearean mind, G Wilson Knight:

> Reference to the author's "intentions" is usually a sign that the commentator—in so far as he is a commentator and not a biographer—has lost touch with the essential of the poetic work. He is thinking in terms of the time-sequence and causality, instead of allowing his mind to be completely receptive. It will be clear, then, that the following essays say nothing new as to Shakespeare's "intentions"; attempt to shed no light directly on Shakespeare the man; but claim rather to illuminate our own poetic experiences enjoyed whilst reading, or watching, the plays. In this sense, they are concerned only with realities, since they claim to interpret what is generally admitted to exist: the supreme quality of Shakespeare's work. [Wilson Knight, 1949/1960, p. 7]

Despite the saving caveat of that use of "directly", above, the general tendency of such passages is clear.

In some sense, their argument is, the work exists in an ideal realm, which has its own kind of logic, its own internal laws, and to which contingent coincidences of relationship with external events in the author's life, are actually irrelevant and misleading. (Wilson Knight also brings in the contrast between conscious intention and the penumbral potency of unconscious creativity—but this, however, is a red herring, since unconscious intentionality *is still intentionality*.

But that it can so readily be confused with the other issue illustrates the complexity we are dealing with here.)

This is parallel in its logic to a certain kind of purism in psychoanalysis and psychotherapy! The three aspect model I have expounded earlier is intended amongst other things to dissolve the basis for such a narrow purism, as is my multi-discipinary conception of psychotherapy. (These remarks in parallel relate to disputes within psychotherapy, which will in turn seem parochial to literary persons!)

In terms of this three aspect model I have expounded in earlier chapters:

1. the *interactive-dialectical* view, which overturns that preciousness and purism of self-containedness, invokes the *relational field* aspect, the assumption that persons inherently exist in relationship;

2. the whole *interpretative detective enquiry elucidatory* process is in terms of *text and context*, the hermeneutic dimension of meaning, which also gives us that *symbolic* dimension which means that a *literal realist* one-to-one relational understanding (which would be another version of a reductive model, in the lineage of classical psychoanalytic interpretations; Freud's view in *The Three Caskets*, 1913/1990, see below, is another matter) is recognised as not working in a simple form (and this can open the way also to dramatic license, and counterfactual imaginal enactments);

3. but where, now, where is the dimension of the *pre-communicable*, the prior to words? Well when I was first beginning to articulate all this in my psychotherapeutic work, it was Cordelia (and Little Dorrit) whose deep and rich silence was my paradigm to begin with ... But what place does it occupy in this process of enquiry? It is part and parcel of the *negative capability* element (Keats, 1817b/1947), which I am applying to the authorship quest itself, so as to be able to live with its part-certainties; and pre-communicability also comes up in the intuitive-embodied exploration of *character* which undercuts mere interpretation, and enables the exploration to take place on the basis of very deep identifications, identifications, and field processes, which enable deep psychic shifts.

This has enabled me to engage with the profound *embodied* aspect of *King Lear*, which in this chapter released me to access the deep and central, and extraordinary and hidden, meaning of Edgar in the play, almost "the body itself", to which we shall come in due course.

The tri-aspect model can be considered itself as a silent partner, an invitation to translate discussions of this or that character in Shakespeare, or in relation to Shakespeare the author, into the terms of our own identifications—those identifications which drive us (and myself in particular) so profoundly, whether we realise it or not, in these enquiries!

On Wilson Knight's model, it would be argued, then, in knock down either/or fashion, either the work works in its own terms—in which case the external relationship is irrelevant; or it does not—in which case nothing will be salvaged by dragging in these secondary linkages.

The work is a completely self-contained whole, on this model. But then the third possibility of a *relatively* or *contextually* self-contained whole is not entertained, one which would be *dialectical* in its relation to the "outside", in the way the therapeutic frame is dialectical in its relation to the "outside", and to the past (Malan, 1979/1995).

Now, it is noteworthy that Shakespeare himself, in *Hamlet*, both in his practice *as* Hamlet, in the "play within the play", and in Hamlet's ad hoc critical theory, takes the view that the work of art is highly relevant to the actual social world (this is addressed to Polonius, who, as the fictional equivalent of Lord Burghley, is *doubly* the target of the remark!):

> Good my lord, will you see the players well bestowed? Do you hear, let them be well used; for they are the abstract and brief chronicles of the time: after your death you were better have a bad epitaph than their ill report while you live. (Shakespeare, 2005, *Hamlet*, II, ii)

To himself (and of course, by implication, to us as audience, instructing us indirectly, in Pirandello-esque fashion, about the significance of a play called *Hamlet*):

> 'I'll have these players
> Play something like the murder of my father
> Before mine uncle: I'll observe his looks;
> I'll tent him to the quick: if he but blench,
> I know my course. (Shakespeare, 2005, *Hamlet*, II. ii)

Here one might almost say that Hamlet views theatre as analogous to effective *interpretation*, in the psychoanalytic sense. And I, as I embark on the journey through Shakespeare, am I being subjected, in a manner, to a psychoanalysis? Does great literature psychoanalyse us?

*Inversely, is interpretation then a form of fiction or theatre?* (c.f., McDougall, 1986) Is the price of the purism of classical psychoanalytic interpretation and frame in effect that it creates a Platonic fiction, out of touch with existence? A very Derridean deconstructive question, taking us from text into context, and from context into precommunicability, and apprehension of sheer existence. (This is the reverse order from the understanding of ready-to-hand existence, leading on to text and context/meaning, which I mapped in the chapter on Heidegger ... .)

"Inside" and "outside" the text, criticism, and creation, are relative concepts. We shall return to this in the poetry and objectivity chapter.

To the players Hamlet says:

> Be not too tame neither, but let your own discretion be your tutor: suit the action to the word, the word to the action; with this special o'erstep not the modesty of nature: for any thing so overdone is from the purpose of playing, whose end, both at the first and now, was and is, to hold, as "twere, the mirror up to nature; to show virtue her own feature, scorn her own image, and the very age and body of the time his form and pressure. (Shakespeare, 2005, *Hamlet*, III, ii)

The "as 'twere", whose significance the late great Peggy Ashcroft (Ashcroft, unknown date) grasped profoundly, indicates that art is *contextualized*, not merely a biographical reportage, but communicating a multitude of things, a deep complex whole—but yet relevantly to the actual social world. It is part and parcel of the poetic paradigm, combining all three aspects or dimensions, which I am offering, that, *the either/or of mirror versus self-contained Platonic whole dissolves.*

And additionally Hamlet, as we shall see, and as frequently recognised, has a special relationship to the author.

But Shakespeare—but for largely contingent reasons, due to the absurd discrepancy between the life of William Shakespeare of Stratford, and the works—*accidentally and fascinatingly becomes the very archetype of the situation and model in which the work is entirely self-contained.*

When I upheld the Stratfordian view, for over twenty years until I stumbled upon Ogburn's book (Ogburn, 1988, Wilkinson, 2005b), I was fascinated, seduced, and hypnotised, by this unique situation that these huge creations had miraculously emerged from a complete unknownness, magically descending like the Grail, and I overlooked the fact that this creativity, above all, is about the human in its context, and that it was impossible the laws of artistic creation could have been overthrown in this one unique case only! More recent defences of the Stratfordian position now, significantly, endeavour to give him a real identity (e.g., Wood, 2003, Ackroyd, 2005, the film *Shakespeare in Love*, 2003), and the "pure poet" theory (along with the "spontaneous genius" theory) has mostly been tacitly abandoned!

I continue to refer to William Shakespeare of Stratford, when speaking of the orthodoxly assumed proper author of the plays; as I have said, the Oxfordian practice of referring to Shagsper or Shaksper (e.g., Ogburn, 1988) is unworthily tendentious and demeaning, *even if* the names were variable, as they were, and *even if* Shakespeare himself ridiculed the names of the lower classes, as he did, (for instance, with Falstaff the recruiting sergeant, in *Henry IV part 2*). I shall therefore refer to William Shakespeare of Stratford when referring to the putative author and simply to Shakespeare when talking of the author whoever he/she is.

But Wilson Knight's second essay, his second thoughts, on *Hamlet* in *The Wheel of Fire*, entitled *Hamlet Reconsidered* (Wilson Knight, 1949/1960, pp. 298–325), graphically and instinctively, in a masterly and extraordinarily sure essay, deconstructively undermines his own previous position in the passage quoted above. It is an essay which has the kind of certainty and mastery of, and argues a somewhat similar position as, DH Lawrence in the remarkable (though with some standard Lawrentian exaggerations) passage on *Hamlet* in *Twilight in Italy* (Lawrence, 1997).

> What is the reason? Hamlet goes mad in a revulsion of rage and nausea. Yet the women-murderers only represent some ultimate judgement in his own soul. At the bottom of his own soul Hamlet has decided that the Self in its supremacy, Father

and King, must die. It is a suicidal decision for his involuntary soul to have arrived at. Yet it is inevitable. The great religious, philosophic tide, which has been swelling all through the Middle Ages, had brought him there.

The question, to be or not to be, which Hamlet puts himself, does not mean, to live or not to live. It is not the simple human being who puts himself the question, it is the supreme I, King and Father. To be or not to be King, Father, in the Self supreme? And the decision is, not to be.

***

The King, the Emperor is killed in the soul of man, the old order of life is over, the old tree is dead at the root. So said Shakespeare. It was finally enacted in Cromwell. Charles I took up the old position of kingship by divine right. Like Hamlet's father, he was blameless otherwise. But as representative of the old form of life, which mankind now hated with frenzy, he must be cut down, removed. It was a symbolic act.

The world, our world of Europe, had now really turned, swung round to a new goal, a new idea, the Infinite reached through the omission of Self. God is all that which is Not-Me. I am consummate when my Self, the resistant solid, is reduced and diffused into all that which is Not-Me: my neighbour, my enemy, the great Otherness. Then I am perfect. [Lawrence, 1997]

Here there is no thought that the author himself, in his true self-hood, his true intentionality, is not writing within and about his world! And Lawrence, obviously, also makes the connection, which undercuts Wilson Knight's points above about specific intentions, with the *general historical and Zeitgeist situation*, to which any fictional work may be legimately related, quite regardless of such arguments as those earlier about "the intentional fallacy", etc. If so, then we confirm the opening of the door to a middle position, in which there is a real relation between the author and their works, *but a dialectical one, not a literal one-to-one relation which overlooks the creative and fictional context* (and hence, certainly, there is much latitude for detailed argument!), about all this. Wilson Knight also, as we shall see, invokes the general historical situation, in a way which relates likewise to the specific.

In the final lines of the essay Wilson Knight clearly returns to the ambiguous and hesitant Eliot-like position indicated above, in the first quotation, and I quote this too first only to bring out the contrast (once more, there is the parallel but irrelevant implicit appeal to the unconscious):

> That these deeper issues were not planned out by Shakespeare is likely enough; it is probable that he could not have planned them. *The poet, as such, does not think thoughts* [my italics]; he makes them; though it may be for us to think the thoughts that he has made. The meanings here discussed are not insisted on by the poetry; they emerge only to a sensitive and listening enquiry. They are rather suggested than said. But that is no reason why we, with due care, should not proceed to say them; it is our business to say them. [Wilson Knight, 1949/1960, pp. 324–5]

*But we can also apply this ironically here to Wilson Knight himself* (as it may also be applied to me! to the extent that all art is enactment before it is propositional, the thesis of this book), and, in the previous pages of this second essay, Wilson Knight has shown how, in the last Act, Hamlet—hitherto a divided, merely potential, partially realised, Superman, who cannot sustain outwardly his own image of himself at his peak introspective moments—gains, or regains, his identity and panache *as Renaissance courtier and as such becomes whole and integrated*. And in the process Wilson Knight's own writing takes on that kind of confident mastery in which their deepest truth speaks through a writer (responding to this level of truth, is the level of the pre-communicable)—the positive meaning of Lawrence's "Don't trust the Artist, trust the Tale", the deeper impersonality that is a realisation, not a denial, of a writer's identity.

Hamlet becomes, or becomes again, what Ophelia saw in him:

> O, what a noble mind is here o'erthrown!
> The courtier's, soldier's, scholar's, eye, tongue, sword;
> The expectancy and rose of the fair state,
> The glass of fashion and the mould of form,
> The observed of all observers, quite, quite down!
>     (Shakespeare, 2005, *Hamlet*, III, i)

In this essay Wilson Knight oscillates, but—like the skilful sleepwalker he himself thinks Shakespeare the poet is (and as seen from the point of view of the Oxfordian thesis of this chapter)—serendipitously communicates (with a fine honesty and integrity) more than he perhaps intends.

From here on in, I shall develop, in the light of this second essay of Wilson Knight's, the general model of a rich, but not one-to-one, relationship between work and author, specifically in terms of the Oxfordian hypothesis. Then I turn to *King Lear*, supplemented with *Little Dorrit* to explore the subtle relation in more depth.

First, following Keats, for instance, in his view that Hamlet is indeed *"more like Shakespeare himself in his common every day Life than any other of his characters"*, (Keats, 1819b/1947), Wilson Knight lets the cat out of the bag about the special position Hamlet has in the Shakespeare oeuvre, and draws some frank potential implications (I note where it is I, who am italicising such particular significant items and implications, in this and the following):

> The poet, by projecting and mastering mad themes in literature, is able to make certain daring explorations without risking personal insanity. His art is at once an adventure into and a mastery of the demonic, Nietzsche's "Dionysian" world. *Now Hamlet the man has often enough been felt to reflect, in some especial sense, the poet himself, the artistic temperament as such* [my italics]; and if this be so, it is quite natural that he should be shown in a state of variously controlled insanity. Here, as in other matters, the play tries to strike a peculiarly subtle balance. So, like many a poet or dramatist (e.g., Byron, Shaw), Hamlet attacks society by wit and buffoonery, *as well as by actual play production* [I cannot resist italicising this also!], in order to make an all but impossible relation or reference where disparity is clear and the time "out of joint" (I. v. 188). Hamlet suffers for his profundity, for his advance, prematurely hastened by his ghost-converse, beyond normality and mortality. He is on his way to superman status in the Nietzschean sense. [Knight, 1949/1960, pp. 300–1]

In the next piece of the jigsaw he imagines what Hamlet, who is clearly changed by his English adventure, and his encounter (parallel to Oxford's! twice!) with the pirates, might have transmuted into at the ending of the play, on his return from England, had he not been exactly the Hamlet of the play. He explores options relating to outcomes in other Shakespeare plays, then he goes on:

> If he returned with a sense of artistic superiority, washed his hands of the whole nasty business and confined himself to writing a Ph.D thesis at Wittenberg on satiric literature; or, *better still, set himself to compose explosive dramas calculated to terrify all the kings of Europe* [I cannot resist italicising this either!], we, today, should be very pleased with him indeed. [Wilson Knight, pp. 320–1]

But maybe he did! Is the latter necessarily an either/or?

Wilson Knight graphically recognises that something else happens—Hamlet's solution in the fifth act is *that of the Renaissance Courtier*. A long quotation is needed to get the full flavour of this:

> The "time" is no longer "out of joint"; a relation has been established.
>
> What, on Hamlet's side, does this mean? He has attained humility before his society, the world as it is; that is, therefore, before the King as King. Surely the reader has been struck, during our talk of beyond-ethic possibilities and compulsions, by the thought that, failing a kingdom of heaven on earth, morals are an essential? Law and order must be preserved. The second best is needed to avoid disaster. But Hamlet has pushed beyond the second-best; and what is he to do? What are others, such as he, Nietzscheans, to do? Art and reverie are not enough. Is there not a second-best for them to *live* by? There is. It is simple. It is love; love of a very simple and realistic kind; a love which is humility before not God's ideal for the race but God's human race as it is, in ones own time and place. Hamlet has somehow reached it and hence his new courtesy before men and acceptance before God:
>
>> Not a whit, we defy augury; there's a special providence in the fall of a sparrow. If it be now, tis not to come; if it be not to come, it will be now; if it be not now, yet it will come. The readiness is all. Since no man has aught of what he leaves, what is't to leave betimes? Let be. (v. ii. 232)

Hamlet has accepted not only his surroundings, but himself. We may suppose he knows himself now neither saint nor soldier, but a Renaissance gentleman of finely tuned sensibility; and that is saying a lot. He now knows intuitively that he will do the work in front of him; and mark what happens. As soon as he attains this state of being, the contact formerly missing is at once established and *everything falls into line for him*. [Then Wilson Knight discusses the detail of this in the duel—then goes on ...]

\*\*\*

Hamlet has won this success by humility and acceptance. In his own, Renaissance, terms, he has attained to his Kingdom of Heaven and all the rest is at once added: "To be or not to be: that is the question".

\*\*\*

It is true that this conclusion is not one which an age which regards *Henry V* as a pot-boiler and *Henry VIII* as an enigma will most readily appreciate; but I believe that it is good for us to observe it. We must remember that the courtly value of the Renaissance touched the hem, at least, of religion, *as that text-book of contemporary idealism, Castiglione's* Il Cortegiano, *shows* [my emphasis]. Their importance in *Hamlet* as a standard of reference is clear from Ophelia's speech attributing to Hamlet "The courtier's, soldier's, scholar's eye, tongue, sword" (iii. i. 160). In its conclusion, moreover, *Hamlet* only the more clearly shows itself to be, what it is generally supposed, the hub and pivot of Shakespeare's whole work in its massed direction: for both the Duke in *Measure for Measure* and Prospero return finally to take up their ducal responsibilities, *and Shakespeare himself concludes his great sequence of more personal works* [my italics] with the nationalistic and ritualistic *Henry VIII*. (Wilson Knight, 1949/1960, pp. 322–4)

Now if we are to take the implication of all this in some measure *literally*—if partly literally Hamlet the poet and playwright could, in some sense, translate into Shakespeare the poet and playwright— then we must be willing to take the position in its fullness, let the train run right on to the buffers! At the very least, in that case, we cannot arbitrarily rule out the full scope of the parallel.

If, in the light of this, we test out the hypothesis of Hamlet, as he is astutely represented in the Wilson Knight passages I have quoted, as very close to Oxford, even if reshaped into art, what do we get?

Well! the first thing we get is the striking recognition, endorsed independently by Wilson Knight, (no Oxfordian), of the centrality of Castiglione's *The Courtier* in the understanding of the value system of *Hamlet*—and, reflexively, the centrality of literary values (Ophelia's "the scholar") in this affirmation.

When he was 21 years old Edward de Vere wrote the preface, and gave his patronage, to Bartholomew Clerke's translation of *The Courtier*. In that preface was even included the following remarkable and accomplished, as well as youthfully hyperbolic, passage:

> For what more difficult, more noble, or more magnificent task has anyone ever undertaken than our author Castiglione, who has drawn for us the figure and model of a courtier, a work to which nothing can be added, in which there is no redundant word, a portrait which we shall recognize as that of a highest and most perfect type of man. And so, although nature herself has made nothing perfect in every detail, yet the manners of men exceed in dignity that with which nature has endowed them; and he who surpasses others has here surpassed himself and has even out-done nature, which by no one has ever been surpassed. (de Vere, 1571)

If we assume the author was the same writer, then, strikingly, a later, much more ripely mature and subtly paradoxical, version, almost a mature man's commentary on the earlier version of the same thought, is to be found in this, from *A Winter's Tale*, a passage which has always been recognized as peculiarly central to Shakespeare's own vision:

POLIXENES
Wherefore, gentle maiden,
Do you neglect them?

PERDITA
For I have heard it said
There is an art which in their piedness shares
With great creating nature.

POLIXENES
Say there be;
Yet nature is made better by no mean
But nature makes that mean: so, over that art
Which you say adds to nature, is an art
That nature makes. You see, sweet maid, we marry
A gentler scion to the wildest stock,
And make conceive a bark of baser kind
By bud of nobler race: this is an art
Which does mend nature, change it rather, but
The art itself is nature (Shakespeare, 2005, *A Winter's Tale*, IV, iv)

We shall return to the "awesome paradoxes" (Lionel Trilling's, 1965/1967, phrase about Freud's *Beyond the Pleasure Principle*) of our relation to "nature", for Shakespeare, when we come to *King Lear*, where the valuation of "art" is shaken. But, generally, the centrality of art, and the indispensability of nobility and lineage ("degree", c.f., Shakespeare, 2005, *Troilus and Cressida*, I, iii), and the high culture and breeding that goes with it, are emphasised again and again in Shakespeare. And, correspondingly, the recognition that art is essential to Shakespeare's vision, that he was no naïve uneducated genius (generally accepted now by Stratfordians also), is emphasised in vital contemporary documents, of which far the finest and most famous is Ben Jonson's majestic poem in the First Folio (Jonson, 1623/1981): *To the memory of my beloved, The Author Mr William Shakespeare: and what he hath left us.*

Perhaps the key lines concerning this, which are as emphatic as one could wish, both about Shakespeare's art, and his gentlemanly (i.e., noble, aristocratic) lineage, are these:

The merry *Greeke*, tart *Aristophanes*,
Neat *Terence*, witty *Plautus*, now not please;
But antiquated, and deserted lye
As they were not of Natures family.

Yet must I not give Nature all: Thy Art,
My gentle *Shakespeare*, must enjoy a part;
For though the *Poets* matter, Nature be,
His Art doth give the fashion. And, that he,
Who casts to write a living line, must sweat,
(Such as thine are) and strike the second heat
Upon the Muses anvile: turne the same,
(And himselfe with it) that he thinkes to frame;
Or for the lawrell, he may gaine a scorne,
For a good *Poet's* made, as well as borne.
And such wert thou. Looke how the fathers face
Lives in his issue, even so, the race
Of *Shakespeares* minde, and manners brightly shines
In his well turned, and true-filed lines:
In each of which, he seemes to shake a Lance,
As brandish't at the eyes of Ignorance. (Jonson, 1623/1981)

All this is congruent with the supreme role within the author's value system of Castiglione's model for Renaissance Man. And, all the evidence exists for Oxford as both the supreme literary patron, and greatest nobleman poet-patron, the Maecenas, of the age. Professor Steven May, who emphatically does not support the Oxfordian attribution for Shakespeare, and certainly thinks Oxford made a comprehensive and dangerous fiasco of his life, nevertheless writes (in his *Introduction* to Oxford's Poems, 1990):

> Much as Oxford's rash, unpredictable nature minimized his success in the world of practical affairs, he deserves recognition not only as a poet but as a nobleman with extraordinary intellectual interests and commitments.

***

The range of Oxford's patronage is as remarkable as its substance. Beginning about 1580 he was the nominal patron of a variety of dramatic troupes, including a band of tumblers as well as companies of adult and boy actors. Among the thirty-three works dedicated to the Earl, six deal with religion and philosophy, two with music, and three with medicine; but the focus of his patronage was literary, for thirteen of the books presented to

him were original or translated works of literature. Besides
Munday and Lyly, the list includes Underdowne's translation
of *Heliodorus*, Greene's *Gwydonius*, and Spenser's *Faerie Queene*.
Thus forty per-cent of the books offered to the Earl were literary, and even if we subtract all seven dedications by the prolific
Munday, this category would still account for almost one fourth
of the total. By contrast, peers of similar means and with some
reputation for cultivating the arts were rather less sought after
by Elizabethan men of letters.

***

We know, too, that Oxford was in close contact with a number
of writers; he read Watson's *Hekatompathia* while it was still in
manuscript, and personally encouraged Bartholomew Clerke's
translation of Castiglione's *Courtier*, and Bedingfield's translation of *Cardanus*. Besides Lyly and Munday another writer,
Thomas Churchyard, claimed to have been in Oxford's service and twice advertised his plans to dedicate a book to his
patron. Oxford's genuine commitment to learning throughout
his career lends a necessary qualification to Stone's conclusion
that De Vere simply squandered the more than 70,000 pounds
he derived from selling off his patrimony, for with some part of
this amount Oxford acquired a splendid reputation for nurture
of the arts and sciences. [May, 1990]

Of the works dedicated to Oxford, Spenser's *Faerie Queen*, by far the
pre-eminent Elizabethan narrative poem (Spenser, 1589/1924), is the
most significant poem. Spenser's dedicatory poem to Oxford includes
the following unequivocal remarks about Oxford's equally pre-eminent
relation to the Muses (the Heliconian imps—he also asks Oxford to protect him from envy):

And also for the loue, which thou doest beare
To th'*Heliconian* ymps, and they to thee,
They vnto thee, and thou to them most deare:
Deare as thou art unto thy selfe, so loue
That loues & honours thee, as doth behoue.
    (Spenser, 1589/1954)

In turn, "Ignoto" ("the unknown one")—almost certainly Oxford, from the authority with which he writes, and from the date, together with Ben Jonson's allusion quoted below (and another echo of the quoted Preface to Bartholomew's translation of *The Courtier*—"a work to which nothing can be added") below—writes of Spenser (the "envy" theme continues) as follows:

> Thus then to shew my iudgement to be such
> As can discern of colours blacke, and white,
> As alls to free my minde from enuies tuch,
> That neuer giues to any man his right,
> I here pronounce this workmanship is such,
> As that no pen can set it forth too much. (in Spenser, 1589/1954)

Which is clearly ("envy" again!) directly echoed in the opening lines of Ben Jonson's poem to Shakespeare quoted above:

> To draw no envy (*Shakespeare*) on thy name,
> Am I thus ample to thy Booke, and Fame;
> While I confesse thy writings to be such,
> As neither Man, nor Muse, can praise too much.
> 'Tis true, and all men's suffrage. (Jonson, 1623/1981)

This material is some of the most significant on the theme, but it is the merest tip of the evidential iceberg. But so much for Oxford the literary Renaissance man alongside of the man of action.

Secondly, Wilson Knight lightly throws out: or, *better still, set himself to compose explosive dramas calculated to terrify all the kings of Europe* (p. 320). But, if Hamlet is indeed *"more like Shakespeare himself in his common every day Life than any other of his characters"*, as we have noted Keats wrote (1819b/1947), and if Hamlet writes a speech and commandlingly directs the players, as to the manner born, then we must consider too the possibility that the author is indeed a nobleman who writes "explosive dramas", and who directs theatrical productions, and manages a troupe of players, all of which the Earl of Oxford probably was.

Thirdly, if Hamlet returns to acceptance of a role as a *doer* in the world of the court, and if this is confirmed by Fortinbras, who plays a key role, as Wilson Knight argues, as a kind of role model for Hamlet, and whose final words on him are:

> Let four captains
> Bear Hamlet, like a soldier, to the stage;
> For he was likely, had he been put on,
> To have proved most royally: and, for his passage,
> The soldiers' music and the rites of war
> Speak loudly for him.
> Take up the bodies: such a sight as this
> Becomes the field, but here shows much amiss.
> Go, bid the soldiers shoot. (Shakespeare, 2005, *Hamlet*, V, ii)

In other words, Hamlet, as the prototype of the author, is a doer in the royal world. But he goes through a process marked equally by vision, and by huge ineptitude and blundering, and dangerous loss of control, before he reaches equipoise in the fifth act.

Now, it is certainly clear that Oxford's fiery, mercurial, and highly dubious temperament (however parallel it is in many ways to the volatile, and sometimes contextually craven, dramatic characters of Hamlet, Othello, Anthony, Leontes, Richard II, Coriolanus, and many others) did result in his not being given the senior military leadership positions he constantly craved.

There is some evidence that (like Marlowe, for example) he may have held a kind of secret service role (c.f., Hess, 2002).

This is indirectly confirmed by the longest contemporary poem directly *about* Oxford, Gabriel Harvey's *Speculum Tuscanismi* (Harvey, 1580), which (in Harvey's peculiar, yet not inappropriate, language and grammar) drips with both venom, and a richly ambiguous, but very high, admiration. (Inconsistency, and a very high level of ambivalence, was much more the norm in those times, *King Lear*, *Anthony and Cleopatra*, and Falstaff in *Henry IV parts 1 and 2*, being perhaps the most splendid Shakespearean illustrations of this.) It includes the following lines (succeeding a passage of insult)—but these ones in the register of ambivalent admiration (!):

> Every one A per se A, his terms and braveries in print,
> Delicate in speech, quaint in array: conceited in all points,
> In Courtly guiles a passing singular odd man,
> For Gallants a brave Mirror, a Primrose of Honour,
> A Diamond for nonce, a fellow peerless in England.

Not the like discourser for Tongue, and head to be found out,
Not the like resolute man for great and serious affairs,
Not the like Lynx to spy out secrets and privities of States,
Eyed like to Argus, eared like to Midas, nos'd like to Naso,
Wing'd like to Mercury, fittst of a thousand for to be
    employ'd,
This, nay more than this, doth practice of Italy in one year.
None do I name, but some do I know, that a piece of a twelve
    month
Hath so perfited outly and inly both body, both soul,
That none for sense and senses half matchable with them.
A vulture's smelling, Ape's tasting, sight of an eagle,
A spider's touching, Hart's hearing, might of a Lion.
Compounds of wisdom, wit, prowess, bounty, behavior,
All gallant virtues, all qualities of body and soul. (Harvey, 1580)

(Notice Harvey's praise of Oxford's *intense sensibility*—something notorious in Shakespeare.) *Hamlet* of course is through and through and monumentally a play about spying, and counter-spying (and the plays in general are riddled with dramatisations of espionage, counter-espionage, and disguise).

And this is also tied in with Hamlet's (and others in the plays, crucially Edgar's, to whom we shall come, in *King Lear*—and in a sense Oxford's) feigning madness, and with his putting "an antic disposition on" (I, v. 169–171), burlesquing or playing the eccentric, madman, or the fool (something of course hugely frequent in the plays).

What arguably informs us most tellingly that the author of *Hamlet* was directly involved in the world it portrays (the world of the poisoner Leicester/Claudius, and of the conniving, highly capable and resourceful, yet deeply avoidant, statesman Lord Burghley/Polonius, declared blatantly in this drama drawing upon the most notorious scandals of the Elizabethan period, in an age when, for instance, authors', such as John Stubbes', hands were cut off if their writings gave offence) is that—*nothing happened*! that the author escaped scot free!

Unless, indeed, such considerations did indeed necessitate his taking on a pseudonymous identity—which, however, would not apply to a rising commoner, but only to a nobleman who had possibly somehow besmirched his own name, in being implicated in the drama, or in respect of drama of such unexampled frankness (and there is still substantive debate as to the nature and necessity of the cover-up, on an Oxfordian analysis).

But first let us turn back briefly to the "might of a lion" mentioned by Harvey here. Oxford defeated all comers (including Sir Henry Lee, the Queen's champion, and later partner of Oxford's erstwhile mistress, Anne Vavasour!) at the joust in the two major royal tournaments of 1571, and 1584 (and in one other, of which I do not have the date) (Ogburn, 1988). Edward Webbe wrote in his *Travels*:

> Many things I have omitted to speak of which I have seen and noted in the time of my troublesome travel. One thing did greatly comfort me which I saw long since in Sicilia in the city of Palermo, a thing worthy of memory, where the right honourable the Earl of Oxenford, a famous man for chivalry at what time he travelled into foreign countries, being then personally present made there a challenge against all manner of persons whatsoever and at all manner of weapons, as tournaments, barriers with horse and armour, to fight a combat with any whatsoever in the defence of his prince and country, for which he was very highly commended, and yet no man durst be so hardy to encounter with him, so that all Italy over he is acknowledged the only chevalier and nobleman of England. This title they give unto him as worthily deserved. [Webbe, 1590]

Both in *Henry V* and *Hamlet* allusion is made, as it was to Oxford, to an almost magical ability to horse-ride in complete unity with the horse, thus Claudius to Laertes speaks of the Norman Lamond:

> I've seen myself, and served against, the French,
> And they can well on horseback: but this gallant
> Had witchcraft in't; he grew unto his seat;
> And to such wondrous doing brought his horse,
> As he had been incorpsed and demi-natured
> With the brave beast: so far he topp'd my thought,
> That I, in forgery of shapes and tricks,
> Come short of what he did. (Shakespeare, 2005, *Hamlet*, IV, vii)

Such was Oxford's reputation. Oxford's challenge included Don John of Austria—who, like Achilles, (but unlike Edmund in *King Lear*! see below) was not to be drawn. But there is some possible evidence that Oxford was involved in the outmanoeuvring of the threat to Elizabeth's rule, before the Armada of 1588, posed by Don John (Hess, 2002).

Despite the high degree of prestige all this connotes, however, here we are entering the characteristic *area of uncertainty* of the Oxfordian attribution. Evidence here is cumulative, intricate, and *highly* and minutely detailed—but mostly also highly open to rival interpretations.

The paucity of the direct Stratfordian evidence would be completely overwhelming—but for the uncertainties and deep ambiguities, the state of suspense, of much of the evidence and material relative to rival positions, especially that whose congruence between life and drama is most authentic, Oxford's. In case of doubt, (human) "Nature abhors a vacuum", or—perhaps!—"Nothing will come of nothing." (*King Lear*, I, i)

Notoriously, for instance, since Oxford died in 1604, whilst William Shakespeare of Stratford died in 1616, and the standard datings of the plays are developed on the latter assumption, Oxfordians cannot avoid a major dialogue about the dating, and, although this is more and more going their way (in such texts by Stratfordians as, e.g., Chambers, 1930/1989, Honigmann, 1985, Sams, 1995), the accepted dating, especially of *The Tempest*, remains a hard psychological barrier to overcome. And there is a great deal else that is problematic, of a complexity I cannot begin to convey here (c.f., Wilkinson, 2005b).

We do not yet have a truly professional, non-partisan, Life of Oxford—but, mind you, we do not have a truly professional, non-partisan, *Life of Shakespeare* (as William Shakespeare of Stratford)! That is, we have no 'life' of thick immediate non-conjectural dense and idiosyncratically characteristic material, in the way we have of, say, Samuel Johnson, David Hume, or John Donne; how could we have? That precisely is the problem! (Emerson implicitly notes this in the remark quoted by Bloom, op. cit., above.) Since writing the above I have read what is far the nearest to a completely professional and fully integrated life of Oxford as Shakespeare, with only a narrow layer of the speculative in its methodology, namely Mark

Anderson's *"Shakespeare" by another name* (Anderson, 2005). It is good enough to test the hypothesis in biographical mode!

I myself now find it well-nigh psychologically impossible to consider or imagine William Shakespeare of Stratford as author of these works, but, as with my view of Nietzsche's *My Sister and I* (Wilkinson, 2002), my journey to certainty in this is a personal one, whose total grounds could not be conveyed briefly to anyone else. There is no knock out argument here, no smoking gun, which is precisely why circumstantial evidence has become so crucial.

But some things are very emphatic, even if ambiguous.

One of them is a fact we virtually nowadays take for granted, so familiar is it to us—but we certainly should not so take it.

It is the nearly unprecedented fact that the author of these plays has uniquely mapped the world he lives in, and its historical antecedents, with a comprehensiveness comparable to that of Zola or Balzac.

He has, firstly, as Wilson Knight (above) obliquely invokes, written a substantially uninterrupted *sequence of accounts of the English monarchy*, and its accompanying history, from Richard II onwards (leaving out the Edwards mainly!) up to Henry VIII of the Tudors. (This list may indeed be extended if certain plays attributed to Shakespeare are indeed his, such as *Edmund Ironside, Edward III,* and *Woodstock.*)

Secondly, the author has provided a many-sided fictional commentary on a considerable number of the personages and situations in *Elizabethan* life—such as, for instance, in *Twelfth Night*, Sir Philip Sidney, Sir Christopher Hatton, the Duc d'Alencon, Mary Vere, and Queen Elizabeth (c.f., Barrell, 1944)—in the non-historical plays, both comedies and tragedies. In addition, an accurate detailed awareness of many aspects of contemporary French and Italian geography, culture and politics is articulated (Ogburn, 1988)—suggesting an intimate in depth knowledge not capable of having been acquired merely second hand.

Thirdly, the author has articulated *Classical-Renaissance political values* in a most emphatic way through the Roman and Greek plays, which even that master classicist Nietzsche found authentic in their classical qualities, e.g., in *Ecce Homo* 2, iv (Nietzsche, 2005).

And fourthly the author, in the tragedies, addresses and evokes the deepest, most abysmal, political (and more than political) fears, terrors, nightmares, of the epoch—especially such as overthrow of monarch and monarchy—in an unexampled way (DH Lawrence's comments quoted above being *one* emphatic illustration of this).

All this is offered in modes simultaneously of the utmost *realism*, and of *symbolic and dramatic sophistication*; in these works the English Drama virtually moves from its beginnings right to maturity almost single-handedly (contrast the situation of the great Greek drama) in one lifetime and lifework—and against the background of a contempt for the stage, both from puritans, and from aristocratic class values and snobbery, which was at the opposite pole to the Greeks' recognition of theatre as sacred religious festival (Nietzsche, 1872/1999).

Dryden's (1668) comment on it was: *Shakespeare was the Homer, or father of our dramatic poets; Jonson was the Virgil, the pattern of elaborate writing. I admire him, but I love Shakespeare.* But Dryden here is assuming the "artless Shakespeare" model; whereas, in terms of the mastery of language, and of courtly sophistication, *Shakespeare is simultaneously Homer and Virgil.* And it is a Drama which provides both a sustained commentary upon how England had come to be, and how she was endangered, and thereby effectively creates a national consciousness (albeit from a monarchist sustaining the Elizabethan settlement).

If Tyndale's Bible awoke the English language, in Shakespeare it takes on infinitude, in a manner parallel to, though greater than, the way in which Luther's Bible created German consciousness and the German language. Shakespeare occupies the role in the creation of English consciousness which Luther occupies in the creation of German consciousness, and this says something very deep about the different way the two nations and peoples hold their respective "world-views"! One may say, for instance, that Shakespeare made P.G. Wodehouse and Churchill possible; but there is no equivalent of P.G. Wodehouse or Churchill for Germany!

Samuel Johnson (1765/1958) writes:

> Shakespeare's plays are not in the rigorous and critical sense either tragedies or comedies, but compositions of a distinct kind; exhibiting the real state of sublunary nature, which partakes of good and evil, joy and sorrow, mingled with endless variety of proportion and innumerable modes of combination; and expressing the course of the world, in which the loss of one

is the gain of another; in which, at the same time, the reveller is hasting to his wine, and the mourner burying his friend; in which the malignity of one is sometimes defeated by the frolick of another; and many mischiefs and many benefits are done and hindered without design.

Chaucer and Shakespeare—principally the latter—created this "mixed" English consciousness.

We don't need to be Oxfordians to hold these things as true; as staunch a Stratfordian as Harold Bloom goes so far as to believe that Shakespeare *invented the human* as we know it, no less (Bloom, 1998/1999), and we can certainly say that it is unlikely that English would have become the current language of the West (possibly the evolving world language), if there had been no Shakespeare.

If indeed he was the Earl of Oxford, then this falls into place as primarily an achievement of *Elizabeth's* reign, when the foundations of English imperialism, English nationalism, English intellectual and scientific achievement, and English (Anglican) Christian religion, were laid. Something of the poignancy and weight of the achievement of that epoch is intimated in Oxford's letter to Robert Cecil on the death of Elizabeth (de Vere, 27th April 1603)—with its echoes of the Epilogue of *The Tempest* and of *Anthony and Cleopatra* (Shakespeare, 2005)

> I cannot but find a great grief in myself to remember the mistress which we have lost, under whom both you and myself from our greenest years have been in a manner brought up and, although it hath pleased God after an earthly kingdom to take her up into a more permanent and heavenly state wherein I do not doubt but she is crowned with glory, and to give us a prince wise, learned and enriched with all virtues, yet the long time which we spent in her service we cannot look for so much left of our days as to bestow upon another, neither the long acquaintance and kind familiarities wherewith she did use us we are not ever to expect from another prince, as denied by the infirmity of age and common course of reason. In this common shipwreck, mine is above all the rest who, least regarded though often comforted of all her followers, she hath left to try my fortune among

the alterations of time and chance, either without sail whereby
to take the advantage of any prosperous gale or with anchor to
ride till the storm be overpast. There is nothing therefore left to
my comfort but the excellent virtues and deep wisdom where-
with God hath endued our new master and sovereign Lord,
who doth not come amongst us as a stranger but as a natural
prince, succeeding by right of blood and inheritance, not as a
conqueror but as the true shepherd of Christ's flock to cherish
and comfort them (de Vere 27th April 1603)

If we now imagine a man who achieved this titanic, this Promethean,
lifework, yet whose own life, simultaneously, was marked not only
by failure, but by humiliation and loss of wealth and estate on a vast
scale, within a process of concealment, pseudonymity, and denial
to posterity (that posterity, which the Sonnets show he wrote for,
beyond all men—whilst knowing at the same time, that: "My name
be buried where my body is"! *Sonnet 72*) of his authorship, not to
mention moral ambiguity (at the very least!) on a colossal scale, what
kind of works would we expect him to have written? And what can
we infer from the works he has written? And among other things,
are they the works of a creditor or of a debtor, a squanderer or a
hoarder, a waster or an accumulator, an abdicator or an acquisitor?

The contrast is as extreme as possible: William Shakespeare of
Stratford, whatever else he was, is in the record as being a highly,
somewhat unexpectedly, successful minor moneylender, thug, play-
house investor, actor probably, and financial acquisitor, (we have just
*two* authenticated oral remarks of his, both about land enclosures!)
as well as tax evader, and probably recusant Catholic, and is in the
record unambiguously for very little else:

(Ogburn, 1988, pp. 28–35, Price, 2001, and Bacon F, website: http://
home.hiwaay.net/~paul/shakspere/evidence1.html)

The morally dubious aspects are matched quite as starkly in Oxford's
case, but pointing in a different direction.

The historian Hugh Trevor Roper wrote:

One-hundredth part of the labor [expended on Shakespeare's
curriculum vitae] applied to one of his insignificant contempo-
raries would be sufficient to produce a substantial biography.
[Trevor-Roper, 1962, cited in Ogburn, 1988]

Of Edward de Vere, 17th Earl of Oxford, a very great deal indeed is known, much of it certainly highly ambiguous, but what is not in doubt is that he ran through virtually his entire fortune in his lifetime, and was by the 1590s known probably by the nickname Thomas Nashe gave him of "Pierce Pennilesse"! In the process he had also marred his reputation in a multitude of ways, in every possible way, morally and prudentially, some would say (e.g., Nelson, 2003), on several fronts. Financially, to take the obvious case, he fulfils the requirements to be the original of Timon of Athens, who squanders his entire fortune, in Shakespeare's play. He was a debtor on the grand scale.

*Part II*
The Author of Shakespeare and King *Lear*
and *Little Dorrit*

Can we start from the other end, and infer *from the greatest plays themselves* that they are written from within an experience of the author's own life as being a squanderer, and a squanderer on the grand scale, a "spender", not only financially, but psychologically in many ways? This is the attempt I wish to make.

Although a ready case can be made by referring directly not only to *Timon of Athens*, but also to Falstaff, and the fortunes of Anthony, Coriolanus, Antonio, Richard II, and other lesser squanderers, I set out to ascertain this by taking the greatest of the tragedies, *King Lear*, as a test. When I began I had no idea of the scale, but also the subtlety—the "open secrecy"—of the confirmation the play would provide. And I found the view further corroborated by the fact that Dickens's great novel about debt, affluence, and speculation—and reality and illusion—*Little Dorrit*, turns out to be substantially a commentary on *King Lear* (reasons of space limit me to only touching on this at the end of the chapter).

I found myself seeing for the first time the kinds of thing which, once seen, are inescapable and obvious, so blatant one does not notice them.

I must first note that, so unbelievably great is *King Lear*, that *any* actual real live man proposed as the author must still seem utterly inadequate to it. And to respond to the play means a kind of submission to it (a submission modelled *within* it particularly in the roles of Cordelia and Edgar) which in my terms puts our relation to it in the dimension of pre-communicability!

With those provisos I continue my hermeneutic detective work!

To begin with, the first thing that hit me right away, on re-reading the very first lines of *King Lear*, is that, between Lear and Gloucester (who are uncannily linked as ego and alter ego, as their "incognito encounter"[1] near Dover suggests), Edward de Vere's entire family situation is duplicated, in terms of number, gender, and legitimacy status:

**KENT**
Is not this your son, my lord?

**GLOUCESTER**

His breeding, sir, hath been at my charge: I have
so often blushed to acknowledge him, that now I am
brazed to it.

**KENT**

I cannot conceive you.

**GLOUCESTER**

Sir, this young fellow's mother could: whereupon
she grew round-wombed, and had, indeed, sir, a son
for her cradle ere she had a husband for her bed.
Do you smell a fault?

**KENT**

I cannot wish the fault undone, the issue of it
being so proper.

**GLOUCESTER**

But I have, sir, a son by order of law, some year
elder than this, who yet is no dearer in my account:
though this knave came something saucily into the
world before he was sent for, yet was his mother
fair; there was good sport at his making, and the
whoreson must be acknowledged.

*** 

**KING LEAR**

Meantime we shall express our darker purpose.
Give me the map there. Know that we have divided
In three our kingdom: and 'tis our fast intent
To shake all cares and business from our age;
Conferring them on younger strengths, while we
Unburthen'd crawl toward death. Our son of Cornwall,
And you, our no less loving son of Albany,
We have this hour a constant will to publish
Our daughters' several dowers, that future strife
May be prevented now. The princes, France and Burgundy,

> Great rivals in our youngest daughter's love,
> Long in our court have made their amorous sojourn,
> And here are to be answer'd. Tell me, my daughters—
> Since now we will divest us both of rule,
> Interest of territory, cares of state—
> Which of you shall we say doth love us most?
> That we our largest bounty may extend
> Where nature doth with merit challenge. Goneril,
> Our eldest-born, speak first.
>     (*King Lear*, I, i, Shakespeare, 2005)

The family situation of Edward de Vere in the 1590s was: three surviving daughters from his first marriage to Anne Cecil, Lord Burghley's daughter (Elizabeth, b. 1575, Bridget, b. late 1570s, Susan, b. 1587) and two surviving sons—one legitimate from his second marriage to Elizabeth Trentham (Henry, b. 1593) and one illegitimate (Edward, b. 1581, from his liaison with Anne Vavasour—who, *possibly* (there is also an Oxfordian case for Rowse's Emilia Bassano, Prechter, 2005, Rowse, 1973), corresponds in character and appearance to the embittering "dark lady" of *The Sonnets*, and who may still be seen in her portrait (Sir Henry Lee nearby!) at the Armourers' Hall in Moorgate, London, (Armourer's Hall, online).

We know of the situation of his son Edward in depth from the researches of Charles Wisner Barrell, a brilliant and profound Oxfordian, published in the 1940s (Barrell, 1941–2), who includes in his account the conjecture that the "paternal" sonnets in Shakespeare's sonnet sequence are in fact written to Edward, something which may (though the enigmas of the Sonnets have as many lives as ninety nine cats! here, below, for instance, "entitled" in line 7 might lead enquiry in another direction, to the Earl of Southampton, for instance) account for certain anomalies otherwise unaccounted for, in such sonnets as No. 37:

> As a decrepit father takes delight
> To see his active child do deeds of youth,
> So I, made lame by fortune's dearest spite,
> Take all my comfort of thy worth and truth.
> For whether beauty, birth, or wealth, or wit,
> Or any of these all, or all, or more,

> Entitled in thy parts do crowned sit,
> I make my love engrafted to this store:
> So then I am not lame, poor, nor despised,
> Whilst that this shadow doth such substance give
> That I in thy abundance am sufficed
> And by a part of all thy glory live.
> Look, what is best, that best I wish in thee:
> This wish I have; then ten times happy me!
>     (*Sonnet* 37, Shakespeare, 2005)

Other highly relevant sonnets are Sonnets 36, 39, 71, and 72.

The whole situation of being a bastard son is explored in *King Lear*, as previously in *King John*. (Let us also remember that Elizabeth 1st herself's legitimacy was permanently in question, and that Mary Tudor never accepted her as her blood sister—hence the long agony of Mary Queen of Scots!—as the blood daughter of Henry VIII. Why are the three "great" tragedies, *Hamlet*, *King Lear*, *Macbeth*, all about usurpation or abdication?)

Oxford, when in early puberty, faced a legal challenge to his legitimacy, which, as a youthful poem on "Loss of good name", Looney, 1921, indicates, highly sensitised him to such matters. His illegitimate son Edward, who went to University abroad in Leyden, Holland, and who was eventually knighted by King James 1st, established himself as a comrade in arms of Oxford's cousins Francis and Horace/Horatio (Bowen, 1966), as one of the "fighting Veres", who are then celebrated in Marvell's "Upon Appleton House" and then in turn in Hermann Melville's *Billy Budd*, who significantly names his Napoleonic War Captain Edward Fairfax Vere (Oxford's emblem was the star). This all suggests—with much other evidence—that Edward was not denied and neglected by his father. The relevant and significant passage in Melville (was there something Melville knew?) is:

> In the navy he was popularly known by the appellation—Starry Vere. How such a designation happened to fall upon one who, whatever his sterling qualities, was without any brilliant ones was in this wise: A favorite kinsman, Lord Denton, a free-hearted fellow, had been the first to meet and congratulate him upon his

return to England from his West Indian cruise; and but the day
previous turning over a copy of Andrew Marvell's poems, had
lighted, not for the first time however, upon the lines entitled
Appleton House, the name of one of the seats of their common
ancestor, a hero in the German wars of the seventeenth century,
in which poem occur the lines,

"This 'tis to have been from the first
In a domestic heaven nursed,
Under the discipline severe
Of Fairfax and the starry Vere." [Melville, 1986, Ch. 6]

Both in *King Lear*, and in the relevant Sonnets, shame, "burning shame",
is the central emotion we begin from (we may add, in *Little Dorrit*
also, c.f., Welsh, 2003), and whose nature and roots we are to explore.
Gloucester's opening remarks both indicate his own shame, and are
themselves shaming, in their "nod and wink" masculine freemasonry;
Edmund deals with his shame by a "brazing" (in Gloucester's word)
it out into, converting it into, a deeper, and nihilistic, character.

Without turning Shakespeare into a developmental psychologist
(though the grasp of such issues is totally there! in Cordelia and
her sisters, for instance!—goodness knows how much we do, retrospectively, take for granted!—when it suits his dramatic purpose),
we note that, despite Edmund's nearly complete and utter villainy
(countermanded genuinely but ineffectually for a moment when
he is dying), which results directly in his father's blinding, and his
brother's banishment and intended death, and much else of evil,
there are many tokens in the text which reveal that the author by
no means has the same contempt and disgust towards him which
he clearly bears towards Iago, in *Othello*, whose villainy is comparable. His brother Edgar, despite Edmund's utter treachery to him
and his father, treats him with forgiveness after their fight, when he
is dying.

Shakespeare clearly also regards him as significantly embodying *one
view* of nature (roughly that which was later articulated by Hobbes in
*Leviathan*, in contemporary terms perhaps that of Machiavelli) which
is not simply false in the final analysis, though it is grossly incomplete. John Danby articulates Shakespeare's three main views, though
they oscillate and interchange wildly, of Nature in *King Lear* in Danby,

1949—as cosmic order (Gloucester's view); as raw power and force (Edmund's view); and as healing reconciliation/restoration/trans-formation based in restored equilibrium (Cordelia's view). All three leave little room for the positive dialectic with culture earlier touched upon. Here is Edmund:

> **EDMUND**
> Thou, nature, art my goddess; to thy law
> My services are bound. Wherefore should I
> Stand in the plague of custom, and permit
> The curiosity of nations to deprive me,
> For that I am some twelve or fourteen moon-shines
> Lag of a brother? Why bastard? wherefore base?
> When my dimensions are as well compact,
> My mind as generous, and my shape as true,
> As honest madam's issue? Why brand they us
> With base? with baseness? bastardy? base, base?
> Who, in the lusty stealth of nature, take
> More composition and fierce quality
> Than doth, within a dull, stale, tired bed,
> Go to the creating a whole tribe of fops,
> Got 'tween asleep and wake? Well, then,
> Legitimate Edgar, I must have your land:
> Our father's love is to the bastard Edmund
> As to the legitimate: fine word—legitimate!
> Well, my legitimate, if this letter speed,
> And my invention thrive, Edmund the base
> Shall top the legitimate. I grow; I prosper:
> Now, gods, stand up for bastards!
>   (Shakespeare, 2005, *King Lear*, I, ii)

Now, there is virtually no direct exploration of monetary issues in *King Lear*; the word "debt" occurs once, and "usury" and "usurer" are as infrequent. If there is a presentation of squandering it is *purely symbolic*, in the form of the direct and absolute—and deliberately unanalysed—abdication of the monarchy, the datum, the premise, from which the play starts (far starker, and more abruptly started, than in the possibly earlier *The True Chronicle History of King Leir and His Three Daughters*, (Anonymous, 1605).

In a manner Shakespeare excludes the monetary equation entirely from the *peripiteia* (dramatic reversal), so that the theme of squandering could be traced to its source in dereliction/abdication of duty, without distractions.

What is included in *King Lear* is an exploration, connected with the "nature" theme, of the most extreme kind, of *the stripping off of garments, of coverings, falsifications, both real and symbolic, and reduction of "culture" to "nature" and "truth" in every sense.* (Yet it is also, by the same token, in an uncanny doubling, which is the heart of the paradox and the "equation" of the play, about the necessity of disguise, to which we shall return.) This theme provides a profound link with those of *Little Dorrit*, which draws deeply upon Thomas Carlyle's (1838) Philosophy of Clothes in *Sartor Resartus* (Carlyle, 1838/1999) and which defines Society through and through in terms of clothes and surfaces and analogous phenomena, and we can indeed wonder what connection this has with squandering (in a very Freudian reversal of Freud, "civilisation" itself is a squandering, in *King Lear*), and how the themes connect? Lear struggles to articulate this when Goneril and Regan are about to deny him his unruly followers:

> **GONERIL**
> Hear me, my lord;
> What need you five and twenty, ten, or five,
> To follow in a house where twice so many
> Have a command to tend you?
>
> **REGAN**
> What need one?
>
> **KING LEAR**
> O, reason not the need: our basest beggars
> Are in the poorest thing superfluous:
> Allow not nature more than nature needs,
> Man's life's as cheap as beast's: thou art a lady;
> If only to go warm were gorgeous,
> Why, nature needs not what thou gorgeous wear'st,
> Which scarcely keeps thee warm. But, for true need—
> You heavens, give me that patience, patience I need!
>     (Shakespeare, 2005, King Lear, II, iv)

Now, *King Lear* in actuality has more interwoven themes than any other Shakespeare play.

So let us briefly pause and consider the central themes of *King Lear*, before proceeding to see whether we can identify a fundamental pathway through this hugely overdetermined, multi-faced, mass and clustering of issues. Several profound themes are almost cosmically intermingled in this extraordinary play; in a way they are all included in this over-theme of civilisation as squandering, civilisation as excess, civilisation as superfluity, superflux. They include those of: shame and nature, (already touched upon); kingship and authority; power and powerlessness; poverty and riches, and wretchedness; that of "legitimacy", both in legal and symbolic senses; justice and corruption, and punishment and mercy; there is the theme, with which the play is riven (and whose connection with "legitimacy" and authority is partly obvious, but to be explored), of the nature of women, and of sexuality, themes we are very familiar with from Shakespeare's own autobiographical writing in *The Sonnets*; filial duty and ingratitude; the theme of nakedness already noted, in all its implications concerning culture and nature; the clash of pagan, sceptical, and implicitly Christian values; madness and sanity, and the (profoundly modern) understanding of psychological collapse; despair and acceptance; goodness and evil; and, last but not least, the whole question, wrestled with in Lear's ragings in the storm on the heath, of *the roots and limits of morality in nature*, which is what, in effect, the whole play is struggling with.

These are some of the major ones, a hugely rich tapestry.

*King Lear*, like Wagner's *Ring Cycle*, combines, along with grotesque melodrama, extreme concentrated intricate suggestiveness and reach, with an extraordinary clarity, like that of *Othello* or *Coriolanus*. And we, transposingly, can draw as freely from Wagner's own life in understanding *The Ring*, as we do here from Oxford's, in understanding *King Lear*.

The play plummets downwards from its first moments of Lear's abdication, to the abyss of the ejection of Lear on to the heath in the storm, and the blinding of Gloucester, with a cataclysmic ferocity which reminds us of the terrible discordant, yet also utterly orgasmic and ecstatic, climaxes of the first movements of Beethoven's Third and Ninth Symphonies, and of Mahler's Ninth and Tenth. *King Lear* of all the Shakespeare plays carries most powerfully the resonance of Nietsche's concept of *The Birth of Tragedy out of the Spirit of Music* (Nietzsche, 1872/1999). It is not an accident that, at the key moments of Lear's restoration, and Edgar's (last-trump like) challenge to Edmund, music is involved. *King Lear* combines the terrible concentration of drama and action of *Macbeth* and *Othello*, with the vastness carried within the sprawling spaciousness of *Hamlet*, and it has a cosmic reach and interconnectedness which is unique in literature, despite, and because of—in a complex unity—the sheer *ineptitude*, though not merely ineptitude, as one may call it, of Lear and Gloucester.

The musical dimension of *King Lear* is commensurate with, in my terms, the pre-communicable dimension, and goes with the general sense of cosmic "beyondness", neither purely Christian, nor purely pagan, nor purely naturalistic, but utterly, enormously, *numinous*, of the play, of what Wilson Knight calls "the *Lear* universe" (Wilson Knight, 1949/1960, p. 177ff).

My sense of the utter ineptitude (but the paradoxical *masterly ineptitude*) of the great Shakespeare heroes once led me to feel that Nietzsche and Heidegger were right in denying the fullest accolade of tragedy to Shakespeare; but, as will be seen below, *King Lear* points us towards another way of understanding this—one which, in Hegelian mode, *positively incorporates the ineptitude* right into the heart of the tragedy as such.

Significantly, there is a very great deal of ineptitude in Oxford's own life, which anti-Oxfordians like Rowse and Nelson are not slow to point out. *But it operates in favour of the case for his authorship, not the reverse.* (And the miserly characteristics of William Shakespeare of Stratford do not count against him because he is *bad*, as Ogburn, 1988, for instance, is drawn constantly into implying, but simply because these characteristics *do not fit* the author of the plays. As in psychotherapy process, moralistic valuations, or at any rate narrowly moralistic valuations, on either side, nearly always get in the way, in this enquiry.)

Let us take up the last issue I named, and consider *the roots and limits of morality in nature*. Is God dead? Are the gods dead? Do they torture us for their pleasure? Is there any basis in nature for our "natural" or human desire for providential justice? Why does someone as totally good-hearted as Cordelia die?

These Nietzschean questions, three centuries before their time, are right at the heart of *King Lear*, nor is it likely that the play offers any final answers; *negative capability* (Keats, 1817b/1947), and multiple perspective, reigns. But it certainly underlines the questions.

The seventeenth and eighteenth centuries—the centuries of Leibniz's optimistic *Theodicy*, and Voltaire's and Dr Johnson's response to it (*Candide* and *Rasselas*), and the questioning provoked by the Lisbon earthquake of 1751—found it simply impossible to cope with the death of Cordelia following upon her reconciliation with the King. Even Dr Johnson (hardly a natural optimist about the state of things in this life!) wrote:

> In the present case the publick has decided. Cordelia, from the time of Tate, has always retired with victory and felicity. And, if my sensations could add any thing to the general suffrage, I might relate, that I was many years ago so shocked by Cordelia's death, that I know not whether I ever endured to read again the last scenes of the play till I undertook to revise them as an editor. [Johnson, 1765/1958]

That this is not an isolated reaction, confined to its own time, is indicated by a representative remark, from two centuries later, of FR Leavis's from around 1958 (quoted in MacKillop and Storer, 1995):

> "King Lear", certainly there the disturbing radical attitude to life. The desperate Shakespeare is definitely there. The last turn of the screw, really disturbing. Not prepared to talk glibly about it. No one is. Not prepared to say anything about it.

Bloom (1998/1999, p. 485) says simply:

Every attempt to mitigate the darkness of this work is an involuntary critical lie.

This is the same fundamental reaction, in more sophisticated modern dress—and it is shared by many more critics. Wilson Knight also struggles with it, despite his insistence that he is clear about the significance of Cordelia's death.

It is extremely difficult for us to imagine that the universe has not got a moral response to us. Even the Nietzschean position oscillates between cosmic neutralism, and a doctrine akin to Edmund's, in which "Nature" is taken to support values such as power, strength and beauty. Darwinism exhibits the same oscillation in its history. And so it is hard not to interpret *King Lear* in the light of this. At some level we can take Shakespeare to be wrestling with such a view, even though it constantly deconstructs it through the impingement of the presence of a stark absolute realism which is indifferent (or, alternatively, hostile) to man. But this deconstructing is dialectical, not abstract; it interacts with other frameworks. Alongside of this, we have, at the same time, to assume the creative process of *King Lear*, which has the "cosmic" dimension touched upon, and assumes an animated universe, is charged with symbolic-alchemical, as well as talionic ("measure for measure"), significance, not a mere affirmation of indifference.

If we start with this, then why does Cordelia die?

In Cordelia we have the greatest, the most overwhelmingly moving, heart-rending portrayal of devoted filial love since Antigone in Sophocles, and it is only matched by the poignancy of the character who is undoubtedly based upon her in some way (as her father William Dorrit is based upon Lear in some way), Amy Dorrit in Dickens' *Little Dorrit*. (We should also mention Wotan and Brunnhilde in *The Ring*—also created in the image of Greek Tragedy and Shakespeare!) The scene where Lear is restored to sane consciousness, surrendered to his extreme *contrition* towards Cordelia, but overcoming his shame through her total acceptance and love (his "do not laugh at me" is exceptionally poignant and telling, in relation to the expression of shame), in her presence is beyond all description in its sublime simplicity and nobility:


**CORDELIA**
How does my royal lord? How fares your majesty?

**KING LEAR**
You do me wrong to take me out o' the grave:
Thou art a soul in bliss; but I am bound
Upon a wheel of fire, that mine own tears
Do scald like moulten lead.

**CORDELIA**
Sir, do you know me?

**KING LEAR**
You are a spirit, I know: when did you die?

**CORDELIA**
Still, still, far wide!

**DOCTOR**
He's scarce awake: let him alone awhile.

**KING LEAR**
Where have I been? Where am I? Fair daylight?
I am mightily abused. I should e'en die with pity,
To see another thus. I know not what to say.
I will not swear these are my hands: let's see;
I feel this pin prick. Would I were assured
Of my condition!

**CORDELIA**
O, look upon me, sir,
And hold your hands in benediction o'er me:
No, sir, you must not kneel.

**KING LEAR**
Pray, do not mock me:
I am a very foolish fond old man,
Fourscore and upward, not an hour more nor less;
And, to deal plainly,
I fear i am not in my perfect mind
Methinks I should know you, and know this man;
Yet I am doubtful for I am mainly ignorant
What place this is; and all the skill I have
Remembers not these garments; nor I know not
Where I did lodge last night. Do not laugh at me;
For, as I am a man, I think this lady
To be my child Cordelia.

**CORDELIA**
And so I am, I am.

**KING LEAR**
Be your tears wet? yes, 'faith. I pray, weep not:
If you have poison for me, I will drink it.
I know you do not love me; for your sisters
Have, as I do remember, done me wrong:
You have some cause, they have not.

**CORDELIA**
No cause, no cause. (Shakespeare, 2005, *King Lear*, IV, vii)

Now, in life, Oxford's youngest daughter was Susan Vere, who later married Philip Herbert, Earl of Montgomery, one of the "incomparable paire of brethren" (William Herbert, Earl of Pembroke, and at that time Lord Chamberlain, with power to control what was and was not printed, a post he had fought for tenaciously, was the other) to whom the First Folio of Shakespeare's plays was dedicated, and who shared with his brother, Ben Jonson, and Heminge and Condell, the cunning plan of achieving the mysterious publication of this enigmatic and extraordinary volume (together, probably, with the erection of the Stratford-Upon-Avon monument to Shakespeare) in 1623. In 1602 a student at the Middle Temple, something of a gossip, who kept a diary for a year (Manningham, ed. Sorlien, 1976), to whom we owe a fortunate knowledge of several vital things, recorded an epigram couplet of John Davies addressed to Susan Vere:

**LA[DY] SUSAN VERE**
Nothing's your lott, that's more then can be told
For nothing is more precious then gold.

This relates to the early dialogue between Lear and Cordelia:
Now, our joy,

Although the last, not least; to whose young love
The vines of France and milk of Burgundy
Strive to be interess'd; what can you say to draw
A third more opulent than your sisters? Speak.

**CORDELIA**
Nothing, my lord.

**KING LEAR**
Nothing!

**CORDELIA**
Nothing.

**KING LEAR**
Nothing will come of nothing: speak again.

**CORDELIA**
Unhappy that I am, I cannot heave
My heart into my mouth: I love your majesty
According to my bond; nor more nor less.

**KING LEAR**
How, how, Cordelia! mend your speech a little,
Lest it may mar your fortunes.

**CORDELIA**
Good my lord,
You have begot me, bred me, loved me:
I return those duties back as are right fit,
Obey you, love you, and most honour you.
Why have my sisters husbands, if they say
They love you all? Haply, when I shall wed,
That lord whose hand must take my plight shall carry
Half my love with him, half my care and duty:
Sure, I shall never marry like my sisters,
To love my father all.

**KING LEAR**
But goes thy heart with this?

**CORDELIA**
Ay, good my lord.

**KING LEAR**
So young, and so untender?

**CORDELIA**
So young, my lord, and true.

**KING LEAR**
Let it be so; thy truth, then, be thy dower:
　　(Shakespeare, 2005, *King Lear*, I, i)

The pun on Vere/Ver ("verity", "verily", "verie", "very") as Truth is one Oxford made lifelong. Nathaniel Baxter had traveled to Italy with Oxford in their youth, and writes a fairly frank poem about him to Susan in 1606 (he died in 1604), whose first letters form the words:

VERA NIHIL VERIUS SUSANNA NIHIL CASTIUS,

that is,

Nothing truer than truth, nothing chaster than Susan.

Alan Nelson (Nelson, undated) interprets Davies' 1602 couplet as a mocking allusion to Oxford as a "deadbeat dad", who had handed the care of his daughters over to Lord Burghley when he had lost all his estates and become virtually destitute. But as Warren Hope (quoted by Ligon, 2006) argues, this overlooks the connection with Cordelia's dialogue with Lear in this passage, which brings home that the "nothing" which is more precious than gold, is *truth*. As the King of France says of her:

Fairest Cordelia, that art most rich, being poor;
Most choice, forsaken; and most loved, despised!
Thee and thy virtues here I seize upon:
Be it lawful I take up what's cast away.
Gods, gods! 'tis strange that from their cold'st neglect
My love should kindle to inflamed respect.
Thy dowerless daughter, king, thrown to my chance,
Is queen of us, of ours, and our fair France:
Not all the dukes of waterish Burgundy

> Can buy this unprized precious maid of me.
> Bid them farewell, Cordelia, though unkind:
> Thou losest here, a better where to find.
> (Shakespeare, 2005, *King Lear*, I, i)

In many ways Cordelia aletheiaically enacts truth as "nothingness"; the spectres of Heidegger and the Buddha hover here; and she was always mysteriously and poignantly for me the paradigm and the prototype of what I have latterly come to identify under the rubric of *pre-communicability* in this book (and which helped me immensely to value creative silence in my work and in my clients). Yet Cordelia is murdered—and murdered following her most poignant moments of reconciliation and transfigured love with her father.

What does this symbolise? Does truth condemn her to death? The possibility is by-passed of such a miraculous ending as those of *The Tempest* or *A Winter's Tale*, which show, by contrast, there is no inevitability about this, and therefore that it is intentional, that it is clearly deliberately passed over by Shakespeare, who indeed produces, by the medium of Edgar's story telling of his and Kent's sagas, such a degree of delay as guarantees Edmund's belated repentance, of his murderous orders against Lear and Cordelia, will be too late. At some level we know and understand—yet cannot readily fully articulate into reason—that Cordelia's death is inevitable, that Nahum Tate's "happy ending" is a kind of travesty.

In fact, four of the five children die: Edmund, bastard son of Gloucester, and the three daughters of King Lear, all die, within minutes of one another; only Edgar, Gloucester's legitimate son, is left alive at the end—and left to rule the kingdom.

Now let us pause from the situation of Cordelia to consider the implication of the role of Edgar in the play.

What marks Edgar is that *he is apparently without relationships*, except of loving service, by contrast with all four of the others (three of whom, further, are engaged in lustful and passionate advances between themselves, as reflected in Edmund's wry and witty remark at the death of Regan and Goneril:

> I was contracted to them both: all three
> Now marry in an instant.)

Edgar has no ordinary human position in the play (and his peculiar combination of melodramatic sententiousness, with imposed roles, has been often noted, e.g., negatively, by Mason, 1967); his position is one of *filling a role*—whether as the stooge his brother sets up at the start of the play; as Poor (mad) Tom; as Gloucester's "most poor man" guide after his suicide attempt; as the fake peasant who kills Oswald in protecting Gloucester; or as Edmund's mysterious, and Knight of the Round Table like, challenger (to which we shall return)—in each case a role which is crucial at the time, but which in a sense melodramatically denies him personhood. (They are also roles into which the extremes of the suffering of others are poured, within the field conditions of the play.)

He is, in a way, the most *depersonalised* individual in the whole drama. One cannot but see him as *celibate*, which none of Cordelia, Goneril, Regan, and Edmund are (France's signs of passion in the passage just quoted are clear, and he is accepted by Cordelia).

Bloom, who *does* recognise his central importance in the play, albeit on a naturalistic model which I think ultimately prevents him seeing its significance, says:

> There is something so profoundly disproportionate in Edgar's self-abnegation throughout the play that we have to presume in him a recalcitrance akin to Cordelia's, but far in excess of hers. Whether as bedlamite or as poor peasant, Edgar *refuses his own identity* [my italics] for more than practical purposes. (op. cit., p. 480)

Now, there is a link with Shakespeare, who portrays himself several times as lame in the Sonnets (for instance, Sonnet 37, quoted above, almost the very phrase: "So I, made lame by fortune's dearest spite,"), when in the Quarto version of *King Lear* of 1608 Edgar describes himself to Gloucester as:

**EDGAR**
A most poor man, made lame by fortune's blows;
Who, by the art of known and feeling sorrows,
Am pregnant to good pity. Give me your hand,
I'll lead you to some biding. (Shakespeare, 2005, p. 935)

In the Folio of 1623 this becomes:

A most poor man, made tame to fortune's blows;
(Shakespeare, 2005, p. 1178)

Frank Harris (who, despite or because of his own profligacy, has a keen intuition of the exceptionally autobiographical character of the Shakespeare writings—though he never remotely deals with William Shakespeare of Stratford's usurious aspects; for instance, in his remarks on "a most poor man" below), in The Man Shakespeare writes

> In "Lear" Edgar is peculiarly Shakespeare's mouthpiece, and
>    to Edgar
> Shakespeare gives some of the finest words he ever coined:
> "The gods are just, and of our pleasant vices
> Make instruments to plague us."
>
> Here, too, in what Edgar says of himself, is the moral of all
>    passion:
> it is manifestly Shakespeare's view of himself:
> "A most poor man, made tame to Fortune's blows,
> Who by the art of knowing and feeling sorrows
> Am pregnant to good pity."
>
> Then we find the supreme phrase—perhaps the finest ever
>    written:
> "Men must endure
> Their going hence even as their coming hither.
> Ripeness is all." [Harris, 2004]

But, what, then, do we make of the fact that, as Poor Tom, but as acting a part (and how does this literal-minded man manage that, considered naturalistically?), *Edgar takes on the lustful persona of both his father, and of Edmund (and Goneril and Regan)*? (Notice how this is also linked with the squandering motif—c.f., below, "thy pen from lenders' books"; it is one of my theses about this play that they are profoundly linked):

**KING LEAR**
What hast thou been?

**EDGAR**
A serving-man, proud in heart and mind; that curled
my hair; wore gloves in my cap; served the lust of

my mistress' heart, and did the act of darkness with
her; swore as many oaths as I spake words, and
broke them in the sweet face of heaven: one that
slept in the contriving of lust, and waked to do it:
wine loved I deeply, dice dearly: and in woman
out-paramoured the Turk: false of heart, light of
ear, bloody of hand; hog in sloth, fox in stealth,
wolf in greediness, dog in madness, lion in prey.
Let not the creaking of shoes nor the rustling of
silks betray thy poor heart to woman: keep thy foot
out of brothels, thy hand out of plackets, thy pen
from lenders' books, and defy the foul fiend.
Still through the hawthorn blows the cold wind:
Says suum, mun, ha, no, nonny.
Dolphin my boy, my boy, sessa! let him trot by.
      (Shakespeare, 2005, III, iv)

Where has the author got this all from? Well, first I cannot help
but note the affinity of this to Harvey's "animal" list in *Speculum
Tuscanismi*:

A vulture's smelling, Ape's tasting, sight of an eagle,
A spider's touching, Hart's hearing, might of a Lion. (op. cit., 1580)

and find myself initially asking whether Oxford is putting *himself*
into this also—that Edgar's simulated madness is an expression of
Oxford's own real near-madness—but also, in his role-playing, what
is closely allied to that near-madness, *Oxford's huge self-concealment
and psychological carrying of the predicament of his time*. Lear's mockery
of Edgar's (lack of) dress even possibly replicates all this in the context of *clothing*; in a part of his poem I could not quote Harvey mocks
Oxford's Italianate penchant for archaically elegant clothing; and here
Lear comments (ironically to us, but "seriously" for Lear):

**KING LEAR**
*To EDGAR*

You, sir, I entertain for one of my hundred; only I do not like the
fashion of your garments: you will say they are Persian attire:
but let them be changed. (Shakespeare, 2005, *King Lear*, III, vi)

When Edgar has mortally wounded Edmund in their duel (which Edmund, in the same strange non-naturalistic way, accepts, though having no obligation to do so under the rules of chivalry, as Goneril comments after Edmund falls) he reveals himself to him exchanging forgiveness, in a way which conveys the same strange affinity between them, and they comment in somewhat Karmic fashion:

> Let's exchange charity.
> I am no less in blood than thou art, Edmund;
> If more, the more thou hast wrong'd me.
> My name is Edgar, and thy father's son.
> The gods are just, and of our pleasant vices
> Make instruments to plague us:
> The dark and vicious place where thee he got
> Cost him his eyes.
>
> **EDMUND**
> Thou hast spoken right, 'tis true;
> The wheel is come full circle: I am here.
>     (Shakespeare, 2005, V, iii)

The Karmic or perhaps Zodiacal connection between them also points to this strange affinity, between darkness and light, perhaps— which also reminds me of the earlier incognito encounter (*this one too is* also an incognito encounter) already mentioned, between Lear and Gloucester, which it perhaps parallels and mirrors.

And in becoming Poor Tom, also, Edgar takes on his "other" imaginatively, both sexually and psychically. (And, conversely, in becoming Edgar, perhaps the author "takes on *his* other"! We return to this, with its resonances of the Freudian "Uber-Ich"—Over-I, or Super-Ego!) Generally he, in his own persona, is the most sane and stoical of individuals, albeit excessively sententiously virtuous, but who, in the famous remark, "Ripeness is all", utters this play's equivalent of Hamlet's beautiful speech:

> **HAMLET**
> Not a whit, we defy augury; there's a special providence in the fall of a sparrow. If it be now, "tis not to come", if it be not to come, it will be now; if it be not now, yet it will come: the readiness is all. Since no man knows aught of what he leaves, what is't to leave betimes? Let be. (Shakespeare, 2005, *Hamlet*, V, ii)

But, also like Hamlet, *he feigns madness*. There is a clue in this, to which we shall return. The Fool, however wonderfully Joycean in his witticisms and linkages, remains very much his own person; *but Edgar is, uniquely, through and through Other-determined throughout the play.*

It seems that, in a way, he seems like a kind of dream (or entry into the darkness, "the dark and vicious place") of his father and brother, through whom they enact their mutual hatred, and their shared hatred of women.

For we must now come to the oft noted central hatred of women (or, not to be simplistic, *however we describe what this is*) which is at the heart of this play.

This connects with Freud's profound interpretation of this play (Freud, 1913/1990), in conjunction with the theme of the three caskets in *The Merchant of Venice*, by relation to which he interprets *King Lear* as *also* representing a love-contest. Along with the interpretation of Cordelia's death as the expression of the indifference of nature, and as punishment (e.g., for Lear's continued infantile self-absorption) there is now the Freudian interpretation of Cordelia as death, as the third of the Fates, the Parcae, Atropos the inexorable, Death. Truth as Death, Death as Truth, Woman as Death, Death as Woman (Freud here is foreshadowing *Beyond the Pleasure Principle*, 1920/1984, and the relation of Truth and Death is, as we have already seen, highly germane to De Vere and Shakespeare). Freud's is an interpretation that does justice to our sense that a happy ending, such as Nahum Tate's (c.f., Johnson, op. cit.), is utterly impossible here.

Clearly, in the general overdetermination, this is not incompatible with the first two interpretations. Nor is it incompatible with a view of Cordelia tacitly functioning as scapegoat-sacrifice for the depravity and cruelty of "woman" in general, and as innocent scapegoat-sacrifice for the irresistibility of sex, which in *King Lear* is very much, though not entirely, projected on to women.

Once again, this is very far from absent from the Sonnets, in particular and notoriously (though directed more against "sex" than "women" as such—and note the link with "expense", "expenditure", "spending", etc) 129 ("shame" again!):

> The expense of spirit in a waste of shame
> Is lust in action; and till action, lust

Is perjured, murderous, bloody, full of blame,
Savage, extreme, rude, cruel, not to trust,
Enjoy'd no sooner but despised straight,
Past reason hunted, and no sooner had
Past reason hated, as a swallow'd bait
On purpose laid to make the taker mad;
Mad in pursuit and in possession so;
Had, having, and in quest to have, extreme;
A bliss in proof, and proved, a very woe;
Before, a joy proposed; behind, a dream.
All this the world well knows; yet none knows well
To shun the heaven that leads men to this hell.
    (Shakespeare, Sonnet 129, 2005)

In *King Lear* it comes out in representative form during the period of Lear's madness:

**GLOUCESTER**
The trick of that voice I do well remember:
Is 't not the king?

**KING LEAR**
Ay, every inch a king:
When I do stare, see how the subject quakes.
I pardon that man's life. What was thy cause? Adultery?
Thou shalt not die: die for adultery! No:
The wren goes to 't, and the small gilded fly
Does lecher in my sight.
Let copulation thrive; for Gloucester's bastard son
Was kinder to his father than my daughters
Got 'tween the lawful sheets.
To 't, luxury, pell-mell! for I lack soldiers.
Behold yond simpering dame,
Whose face between her forks presages snow;
That minces virtue, and does shake the head
To hear of pleasure's name;
The fitchew, nor the soiled horse, goes to 't
With a more riotous appetite.
Down from the waist they are Centaurs,

> Though women all above:
> But to the girdle do the gods inherit,
> Beneath is all the fiends';
> There's hell, there's darkness, there's the
> sulphurous pit,
> Burning, scalding, stench, consumption; fie,
> fie, fie! pah, pah! Give me an ounce of civet,
> good apothecary, to sweeten my imagination:
> there's money for thee.
>     (Shakespeare, 2005, IV, v)

(How, on a naturalistic basis, is Lear supposed to have come to all this, when there is next to no reference whatsoever, unlike Gloucester, to any woman he has been sexually associated with? and on what basis would he have figured the degree of lust of his elder daughters?—there is a significant gap here, which again may point to something in the author as such.) In all of this "hatred of women" there are a mass of themes which we need only note in passing, without succumbing to reductive temptations, which invoke both the psychoanalytic dimension and other related dimensions: castration anxiety (which is also expressed in Gloucester's blinding, if we follow Freud on such matters); "procreation envy", as one might call it; fear of the "terrible mother" (Jung); birth anxiety; sexual guilt; and so on and on.

At the root of it, arguably, is *sexual shame*, together with other forms of shame; shame is what, at this point, is keeping Lear away from Cordelia (as it originally prevented Cordelia from speaking of her love for him), as emerges clearly in the "wheel of fire" passage already quoted (and is his "wheel of fire", like Schopenhauer's "wheel of Ixion", a sexual wheel?)

Like Yeats (and Schopenhauer, and Beckett), Lear believes (though without Yeats' releasing addition!):

> How could passion run so deep
> Had I never thought
> That the crime of being born
> Blackens all our lot?
> But where the crime's committed
> The crime can be forgot. (Yeats, *Consolation*,
>     in Yeats, 1983, p. 272)

We thus get a strange and, as yet, enigmatic, inference; in a manner, *only in relation to Edgar is the play free of shame.*

But Edgar *takes on the whole shame of others.*

Immediately following the passage quoted above where Edgar as Poor Tom explains what he is to Lear, we have the following, relating to the "clothing" issue touched upon above:

> **KING LEAR**
> Why, thou wert better in thy grave than to answer with thy uncovered body this extremity of the skies. Is man no more than this? Consider him well. Thou owest the worm no silk, the beast no hide, the sheep no wool, the cat no perfume. Ha! here's three on's are sophisticated! Thou art the thing itself: unaccommodated man is no more but such a poor bare, forked animal as thou art. Off, off, you lendings! come unbutton here.
> *Tearing off his clothes* (Shakespeare, 2005, *King Lear*, III, iv)

And this "animal" theme connects with the whole clothes and nature and "society" issue, with which it runs right on even into Lear's final speech:

> **KING LEAR**
> And my poor fool is hang'd! No, no, no life!
> Why should a dog, a horse, a rat, have life,
> And thou no breath at all? Thou'lt come no more,
> Never, never, never, never, never!
> Pray you, undo this button: thank you, sir.
> Do you see this? Look on her, look, her lips,
> Look there, look there!
> *Dies* (Shakespeare, 2005, *King Lear*, V, iii)

We are, then, dealing with something like a conception of the Fall of Man, in which, in some way, it is connected with the whole theme of sexuality. In parallel with the reduction to nature and animality element, in short order, we might first say that the reason Cordelia has to die, is the same as the reason why Christ has to die, (and perhaps also *why Edgar has to live*), the utterly innocent facing the utmost abyss of despair, abandonment, and retribution, and all of Wilson

Knight's intuitions regarding the Christian dimension of the plays come into their own.

> And about the ninth hour Jesus cried with a loud voice, saying, Eli, Eli, lama sabachthani? that is to say, My God, my God, why hast thou forsaken me? (Mt., 27:46)

**KING LEAR**
Howl, howl, howl, howl! O, you are men of stones:
Had I your tongues and eyes, I'ld use them so
That heaven's vault should crack. She's gone for ever!
I know when one is dead, and when one lives;
She's dead as earth. Lend me a looking-glass;
If that her breath will mist or stain the stone,
Why, then she lives.

**KENT**
Is this the promised end

**EDGAR**
Or image of that horror?

**ALBANY**
Fall, and cease! (Shakespeare, 2005, V, iii)

The intimate connection between Cordelia and Lear's Fool, which has even led some (Marks, 1995) to conclude that Cordelia *is*, disguised, the Fool, which is expressed in this reminiscence at the point of Lear's death, is reflected in the Fool's profound "truth-telling", which is aletheiaic (that is, based upon veiling/unveiling, *as is Cordelia herself*—and that is also the point in John Davies' couplet whose significance Alan Nelson, loc. cit., misses), and sacrificial.

Here also (and this leads on to *Little Dorrit*) is a Pauline understanding (*First Letter to the Corinthians*), a *Kenotic* understanding[2], of tragedy, which Shakespeare somehow (defying, in anticipation, Nietzsche and Heidegger on the nature of tragedy!) combines with a capacity to evoke the tragic equal, if not superior, to that of the great Greeks:

> 27 But God hath chosen the foolish things of the world to confound the wise, and God hath chosen the weak things of the world, to confound the mighty things, 28 And vile things of the

world, and things which are despised, hath God chosen, and
things which are not, to bring to nought things that are, 29 That
no flesh should rejoice in his presence. [1 Cor. 1. vv. 27–9]

That this Cordelian motif of "nothing" can be combined with an
erotic evisceration is illustrated by Donne in *A Nocturnall Upon St
Lucies Eve* (where the Pauline echo is equally clear):

> Study me then, you who shall lovers bee
> At the next world, that is, at the next Spring:
> For I am every dead thing,
> In whom love wrought new Alchimie.
> For his art did expresse
> A quintessence even from nothingnesse,
> From dull privations, and leane emptinesse:
> He ruin'd mee, and I am re-begot
> Of absence, darknesse, death; things which are not.
>     (in Donne, 1941, p. 32)

But Christ's way of life, too, in the Gospels is portrayed as celibate,
annulling of sexuality, as Paul was celibate, and there is the famous
passage in Matthew:

> For there are some eunuchs, which were so born of their
> mother's belly; and there be some eunuchs, which be gelded
> by men; and there be some eunuchs, which have gelded them-
> selves for the kingdom of heaven. He that is able to receive this,
> let him receive it. (Mt., 19., v.12)

We shall return to the connection of this appeal to nothingness with
the "animal" dimension.

How far can the epiphanies of Christian forgiveness encompass
sexual affirmation as opposed to sexual denial?

It can be! Sexual affirmation is integrated within the Christian forgiveness enacted in the great Mozart operas, (apart from
*Don Giovanni*, where sexuality is punished in similar fashion as
in these relevant parts of Shakespeare), and it is also integrated
within Shakespeare's own *Anthony and Cleopatra*, *A Winter's Tale*
and *The Tempest*. Indeed we may say that in *Anthony and Cleopatra*

Shakespeare has transformed the very same feminine traits, which evoke his hatred and ambivalence in the *Sonnets* and *King Lear*, into something glorious and incandescent; he apotheoses (if Oxford is the author, and among other sources, including probably the Queen) Anne Vavasour, or later replacements, with all her/their faults and all! *King Lear* was perhaps, indeed, the route through which he released himself from his own fear and hatred of women.

However, I think *King Lear* (with much else of Shakespeare) falls within the group of those works, in which human sexuality is either repudiated (Wagner's *Parsifal*, Schopenhauer's philosophy), treated as a profound disturbance (Kierkegaard, Henry James, Thomas Mann, Beckett), or anatomised and belittled (Swift, Flaubert, Eliot, Proust).

> **Vladimir:** Astride of a grave and a difficult birth. Down in the hole, lingeringly, the grave digger puts on the forceps. We have time to grow old. The air is full of our cries. [Beckett, 1953]

But this happens, as with Wagner's *Parsifal*, in the context of what is otherwise a profound life-affirmation (for *King Lear*, though a work in many ways savage in the extreme, never loses its sense of meaning and of the cosmos, is never merely cynical—and Edgar, to whom we shall return in a moment, is central to the accomplishment of this)—through the Christian resonances in particular.

What is going on?

It seems to me, reflecting upon the play in the light of the hypothesis of the autobiographical elements, however transformed they are in it, that this play, like *Measure for Measure* especially, *is one of those Shakespeare plays in which he splits himself*, between on the one hand dramatisations of aspects of himself of which he is profoundly ashamed, and about which he feels profound contrition, and on the other a non-naturalistically conceived *deus ex machina* Super-Ego self (or Ego-Ideal), which is in some way exempted from, or lifted above, the ordinary course of procreative mortality, and through which he is enabled to "redeem" the base self or selves, as in *Measure for Measure*:

> ANGELO
> O my dread lord,
> I should be guiltier than my guiltiness,

> To think I can be undiscernible,
> When I perceive your grace, like power divine,
> Hath look'd upon my passes. (Shakespeare, 2005, *Measure for*
>      *Measure*, V, i)

And the figures which embody *that* position, like Edgar, *do* have the "indeterminate" "No-Self" status ("As to the poetical Character itself ... it is not itself—it has no self—it is every thing and nothing—It has no character"—Keats, 1818/1947) which Emerson and Bloom attribute to William Shakespeare of Stratford, but which belonged in another way to Oxford—*the humiliated abyss of his ultimate non-personality, his un-personing, as creator of literature,* which made the Stratford man so paradoxically fascinating to me as the ultimate mystery non-person whose creativity came from the beyond, in my youth.

*This is perhaps the element of truth which is transposed into the Strat-fordian orthodoxy!*

Lear's three children are, all three of them, utterly real and convincing characters. Of Gloucester's children, Edmund, whilst there is a "morality play villain" touch about him, is nevertheless consistently presented, has enormous charm, and a human touch of vanity, and need for love, and a quixotically chivalric style, which comes out both in relation to Goneril, and at the end, and enables him humanly to respond "despite of mine own nature", and which also makes him respond, as he had no need to, to Edgar's anonymous challenge (perhaps there is a touch of Don John *manqué* about Edmund!)

Neither brother is entirely naturalistically convincing (it may be not irrelevant that Oxford had no brothers). But Edgar's character is on the face of it *a thoroughgoing non-naturalistic* anomaly, which has to be accounted for (for instance, Bloom talks about his self-humiliation, for which he gives no adequate reason). As already indicated, he has no overt character of his own (he is on the run from the very start of the play) *but only a series of functions,* dictated by the needs of others (even his Tom a' Bedlam disguise mirrors or emerges from a remark of his brother's:

> And pat he comes like the catastrophe of the old comedy: my
> cue is villanous melancholy, with a sigh like Tom o' Bedlam.

O, these eclipses do portend these divisions! fa, sol, la, mi).
(Shakespeare, 2005, I, ii)

At the end he emerges as a true challenger, only appearing on the
third sound of the trumpet, like a Knight of the Holy Grail.

In between he acts like a psychopomp (an underworld guide,
like Dante's Virgil in *L'Inferno*) leading Lear into the madness he,
Lear, seeks, partly as relief (unlike Gloucester, for whom madness is
not available, Act 4, sc. vi) from his "huge sorrows"—but also as the
license to release Lear to utter, in madness, the wisdom in madness
which has not been available to him whilst he is still sane, and whilst
he still seeks to retain the needs which vanity and esteem, as the
antithesis to shame, appear to require. (See above: "O reason not the
need …".) And then, next, Edgar acts as the psychopomp who, conversely, leads Gloucester back to life affirmation. He is in many ways
the "touchstone" for all in the play (see below).

The world which opens up for Lear is the world, the antithesis
to royalty, royalty which Lear has forfeited, but which, in forfeiting,
opens to him a world of which he had no comprehension before,
the world of poverty, of the recognition of "wretches" (the key word
Gerard Manley Hopkins picked up from these passages, as we have
seen in an earlier chapter):

**KING LEAR**
Prithee, go in thyself: seek thine own ease:
This tempest will not give me leave to ponder
On things would hurt me more. But I'll go in.

*To the Fool*

In, boy; go first. You houseless poverty,—
Nay, get thee in. I'll pray, and then I'll sleep.

*Fool goes in*

Poor naked wretches, whereso'er you are,
That bide the pelting of this pitiless storm,
How shall your houseless heads and unfed sides,
Your loop'd and window'd raggedness, defend you
From seasons such as these? O, I have ta'en

Too little care of this! Take physic, pomp;
Expose thyself to feel what wretches feel,
That thou mayst shake the superflux to them,
And show the heavens more just.


**EDGAR**
[Within] Fathom and half, fathom and half! Poor Tom!
*The Fool runs out from the hovel*
    (Shakespeare, 2005, *King Lear*, III, iv)

It is clear, incidentally, in connection with this moment of realisation of Lear's, that Oxford was fantastically generous to his beneficiaries, on a Timon-like scale, whereas William Shakespeare of Stratford was a sharp litigator for small debts, and a participant in enclosures of the common land.

Now, Edgar's Grail-quest-like "entering into his opposite" is prefigured in an allusion which invokes something equivalent:

**EDGAR**
Child Rowland to the dark tower came,
His word was still—Fie, foh, and fum,
I smell the blood of a British man.
    (Shakespeare, 2005, *King Lear*, III, iv)

The Student's Encyclopaedia Britannia notes:

> Childe Roland (sometimes spelled Rowland) is a character in an old Scottish ballad. A son of the legendary King Arthur, he is the youngest brother of Burd Ellen, who has been carried off by the fairies to the castle of the king of Elfland. Guided by the enchanter Merlin, Childe Roland undertakes a quest to Elfland and rescues her. Shakespeare alludes to the ballad ...

Edward de Vere's ancestor, who came over with the Conqueror (Gardner, 1999), was Alberic de Vere—Albry, Aubrey, Auberon, Oberon (the fairy king in *A Midsummer's Night's Dream*)—Albe Righ (= the Elf King;—as also the anti-hero, the Nibelung dwarf, King of the Underworld, of Wagner's *Ring* Cycle, who shows himself here fully conversant with the lore, as we must assume Shakespeare to have been, is likewise Alberich; and arguably Cordelia is related to Persephone, visitant to Hades, a connection which is explicit in Perdita in *A Winter's Tale*:

> O Proserpina,
> From the flowers now that, frighted, thou let'st fall
> From Dis's waggon!—daffodils,
> That come before the swallow dares, and take
> The winds of March with beauty; violets, dim
> But sweeter than the lids of Juno's eyes
> Or Cytherea's breath; pale primroses ...) (Shakespeare, 2005,
>     *A Winter's Tale*, IV, iv)

Edgar, like Parsifal in Wagner's final opera, is making a journey into his non-respectable "other", his "alter", his "dark tower", his opposite, sexuality, madness, poverty, nakedness, degradation, victimisation, illegitimacy, sacrifice ("No worst, there is none.", in Hopkins' epitomisation); and then he describes "himself", his previous self, to Gloucester, after he has engineered Gloucester's faked suicide by throwing himself over the cliff which did not exist:

> **EDGAR**
> As I stood here below, methought his eyes
> Were two full moons; he had a thousand noses,
> Horns whelk'd and waved like the enridged sea:
> It was some fiend; therefore, thou happy father,
> Think that the clearest gods, who make them honours
> Of men's impossibilities, have preserved thee. (Shakespeare,
>     2005, IV, v)

This is a fine evocation (which Wilson Knight, op. cit., p172, thinks simply "a fantastic picture of a ridiculously grotesque devil") precisely of the Elf King, or the Celtic Horned god Cernunnous (Mystica Encyclopaedia, no date), or the phallic Green Knight of *Sir Gawain and the Green Knight*. This is the kind of territory we are in here.

Similarly, the names of the fiends which torment poor Tom, through which he is able to simulate hallucinatory behaviours extremely graphically, are derived ostensibly from a book by

Samuel Harsnett, about exorcisms performed by Roman Catholic priests, published in 1603 (Bowen, 1965). But Bowen shows that this in turn relates back to an earlier book of "Miracles", from around 1585–6, and this, however contemporary its form, was the title given to the Mediaeval Mystery Cycle Plays (Chambers, 1945); so this derivation not only enables us to place *King Lear* much earlier than the standard dating of 1605/6, but also takes us right back to the world of the Mediaeval Drama and the origins of drama, as one would expect from the author whose childhood memories included such as these:

**HAMLET**
Let me see.

*Takes the skull*

Alas, poor Yorick! I knew him, Horatio: a fellow
of infinite jest, of most excellent fancy: he hath
borne me on his back a thousand times; and now, how
abhorred in my imagination it is! my gorge rims at
it. Here hung those lips that I have kissed I know
not how oft. Where be your gibes now? your
gambols? your songs? your flashes of merriment,
that were wont to set the table on a roar? Not one
now, to mock your own grinning? quite chap-fallen?
Now get you to my lady's chamber, and tell her, let
her paint an inch thick, to this favour she must
come; make her laugh at that. (Shakespeare, 2005, *Hamlet*, V, i)

So, taking all this, together with his Parsifal-like challenge, clad in armour, to Edmund at the end, it is possible to fairly plausibly confirm that Edgar is *one of those disguised presences of the author in the play* as magician or psychopomp (guide to the "other-world"—Oxford, like Francis Bacon, knew well John Dee, the greatest necromancer of the Elizabethan world) familiar in Shakespeare, which we find as Prospero in *The Tempest*, the Duke in *Measure for Measure*, and also there is an element of this in Touchstone the Clown in *As You Like It* (where Touchstone's affinity and connection with the Hamlet-esque figure of Jacques is significant).

Edgar is *unique in the scale* of his purgatorial descent into the darkness, which in psychotherapeutic terms has Jungian alchemical connotations, and which for me has been the central nucleus or eye of the vortex of this journey of discovery. But the appearances of such figures in Shakespeare always signify *attempts at exorcism of wrongs*, and cleansings of the body politic, along the lines of Jacques' own comment in *As You Like It*:

> He that a fool doth very wisely hit
> Doth very foolishly, although he smart,
> Not to seem senseless of the bob: if not,
> The wise man's folly is anatomized
> Even by the squandering glances of the fool.
> Invest me in my motley; give me leave
> To speak my mind, and I will through and through
> Cleanse the foul body of the infected world,
> If they will patiently receive my medicine. (Shakespeare, 2005,
>     *As You Like It*, II, vii)

On which the Duke Senior comments significantly:

> Most mischievous foul sin, in chiding sin:
> For thou thyself hast been a libertine,
> As sensual as the brutish sting itself;
> And all the embossed sores and headed evils,
> That thou with licence of free foot hast caught,
> Wouldst thou disgorge into the general world.

When Shakespeare is in this mode, it is a fair preliminary inference that, among others, it is always also *himself* he is condemning—it is a Super-Ego indictment—and whose aspects are brought forward in contrition. And so, in this aspect, when Cordelia dies the ultimate judgement on Lear's dereliction is enacted.

Now Touchstone, with whom as Fool in his Motley Jacques is identifying, as Edgar is associated with the Fool in the Storm scenes in *King Lear*, is the significant utterer of one of those moments in the plays and sonnets where an absolute identity claim, an absolute authority claim, is implied. They invoke either "the thing itself" or the I AM THAT I AM of Moses' vision of Jahweh in Exodus (Ch. 3, v. 14). In the case of Touchstone the moment comes significantly in rebuking, contemptuously, the country character, significantly called "William", but also implying that the water of identity has been poured into the wrong receptacle (though this is swiftly sidestepped again as soon as it has appeared):

TOUCHSTONE
You do love this maid?
WILLIAM
I do, sir.
TOUCHSTONE
Give me your hand. Art thou learned?
WILLIAM
No, sir.
TOUCHSTONE
Then learn this of me: to have, is to have; for it
is a figure in rhetoric that drink, being poured out
of a cup into a glass, by filling the one doth empty
the other; for all your writers do consent that ipse
is he: now, you are not ipse, for I am he.
WILLIAM
Which he, sir?
TOUCHSTONE
He, sir, that must marry this woman. (Shakespeare, 2005, *As You Like It*, V, i)

We see the affinity with Lear's evocation of Edgar *as animal*:

Ha! here's three on's are sophisticated! *Thou art the thing itself* [my italics]: unaccommodated man is no more but such a poor bare, forked animal as thou art. (Shakespeare, 2005, *King Lear*, III, iv)

A letter of Oxford's to Burghley (c.f., for what follows, Barrell, 1941–2, also de Vere, 30 October, 1584) challenging his spying on him (this is in parallel, of course, with *Hamlet*), which also mirrors Lear's famous "I know not what they shall be but they shall be The terrors of the earth" threat to Goneril and Regan, 4. sc. ii, at the end of the "reason not the need" speech already quoted, contains an analogue comment:

My Lord, this other day your man Stainer told me that you sent for Amys, my man and, if he were absent, that Lyly should come unto you. I sent Amys, for he was in the way. And I think very strange that your Lordship should enter into that course toward me whereby I must learn that I knew not before, both of your opinion and goodwill towards me. But I pray, my Lord, leave that course, for I mean not to be your ward nor your child. I serve her Majesty, *and I am that I am* [my italics], and by alliance near to your Lordship, but free, and scorn to be offered that injury to think I am so weak of government as to be ruled by servants, or not able to govern myself. If your Lordship take and follow this course, you deceive yourself and make me take another course that yet I have not thought of. Wherefore these shall be to desire your Lordship, if that I may make account of your friendship, that you will leave that course, as hurtful to us both.

This, again, is paralleled in Sonnet 121, we can almost feel it being dashed off to relieve his feeling (!):

"Tis better to be vile than vile esteem'd,
When not to be receives reproach of being,
And the just pleasure lost which is so deem'd
Not by our feeling but by others" seeing:
For why should others false adulterate eyes
Give salutation to my sportive blood?
Or on my frailties why are frailer spies,
Which in their wills count bad what I think good?
No, *I am that I am* [my italics], and they that level
At my abuses reckon up their own:
I may be straight, though they themselves be bevel;
By their rank thoughts my deeds must not be shown;
Unless this general evil they maintain,
All men are bad, and in their badness reign. (Shakespeare,
    2005, *Sonnet* 121)

Which in turn reminds us of (significantly, in its arrogance, just before the "no worst" moment when Edgar's hubris is deflated, when he encounters his father, blinded):

**EDGAR**
Yet better thus, and known to be contemn'd,
Than still contemn'd and flatter'd. To be worst,
The lowest and most dejected thing of fortune,
Stands still in esperance, lives not in fear:
The lamentable change is from the best;
The worst returns to laughter. Welcome, then,
Thou unsubstantial air that I embrace!
The wretch that thou hast blown unto the worst
Owes nothing to thy blasts. But who comes
    here? (Shakespeare, 2005, *King Lear*, IV, i)

There are also similarities between Edgar's flight, and Oxford's attempt at flight, as reported by Sir Francis Walsingham, when Oxford's pregnant mistress Anne Vavasour was taken to the Tower of London to give birth (to Edward):

On Tuesday at night Anne Vavasor was brought to bed of a son in the maidens' chamber. The E. of Oxeford is avowed to be the father who hath withdrawn himself with intent as it is thought to pass the seas. The ports are laid for him and therefore if he have any such determination it is not likely that he will escape. [Walsingham, 1581, in Bowen, 1966]

**EDGAR**
I heard myself proclaim'd;
And by the happy hollow of a tree
Escaped the hunt. No port is free; no place,
That guard, and most unusual vigilance,
Does not attend my taking. (Shakespeare, 2005,
    *King Lear*, II, iii)

Likewise, as we have noted, Edgar duplicates Hamlet in *mimicking madness*. Hamlet, in a catastrophic kind of way, and unable to master his relation to the whole situation until the very end of the play, as we have seen, nevertheless, in a Prospero-like fashion, *stage manages* the whole denouement of the process of the play, as the authentic representative of the author, and as heaven's "scourge and minister" (as well as Catholic notes, *Hamlet* simultaneously strikes a very Calvinistic predestinarian note).

Edgar facilitates Lear's descent into madness (truth-in-madness) which enables him to return, though partly in a second childhood way, to Cordelia (and Lear only returns to "truth" in the loss of her; Lear is unable, whilst she is living, to see her as a person in her own right, as opposed to a derivative of himself, even in the exchange when they are led off to prison, and maybe this is his ultimate egotism which can only be surpassed towards the other, by her loss through death), and he equally facilitates, in a psychopomp way, which, in the characteristic style of behaviour of psychopomps, seems ruthless and inhumane (as noted in Mason, 1967) Gloucester's return to truth, and his refusal of both madness and suicide.

Both Lear and Gloucester incur, in a non-moral unfolding, the consequences of their derelictions, and egotisms, and it is Edgar who, in a way, ruthlessly stage-manages and orchestrates that unfolding, and likewise the subsidiary one of the melodrama of Edmund, Goneril, and Regan. Edgar, like Prospero, and the Duke in *Measure for Measure*, is left, sole, to rule the kingdom at Lear's death, when Kent declines the task. Accordingly, it seems to me that we must reconsider the famous moment, which we have already touched upon, of Lear's realisation of the nature of man:

**KING LEAR**
Why, thou wert better in thy grave than to answer with thy uncovered body this extremity of the skies. Is man no more than this? Consider him well. Thou owest the worm no silk, the beast no hide, the sheep no wool, the cat no perfume. Ha! here's three on's are sophisticated! Thou art the thing itself: unaccommodated man is no more but such a poor bare, forked animal as thou art. Off, off, you lendings! come unbutton here.

*Tearing off his clothes* (Shakespeare, 2005, *King Lear*, III, iv)

If we are to consider only the author in his projection of himself into the play, then *this becomes the most extreme of all the self-identity formulations in the plays and poems*, one in which, in shame, and destitution, and reduction to animality, shame-less nothingness, paradoxically (as the being who is *only* role in the play; the denial of personal identity—representing both tenacious and unconquerable social order, and its sheer annulment, the twin poles of the play) absolutely deprived of role, "unaccommodated", he is penitentially *reduced entirely to his animal and elemental cosmic being solely*:

> … unaccommodated man is no more but such a poor
> bare, forked animal as thou art. (Shakespeare, 2005,
> *King Lear*, III, iv)

This, as we have seen, is poignantly echoed in Lear's final speech. In the loss of Cordelia he himself has become Other, become "wretch", become "unaccommodated man". Edgar's Grail Journey in search of identity, and of his sister (Burd Ellen, who, perhaps like Cordelia, "ran the reverse way round the church") to the abode of the Elf-King has led him to this. And Lear attributes it to his "daughters":

> Death, traitor! nothing could have subdued nature
> To such a lowness but his unkind daughters. (Shakespeare,
> 2005, *King Lear*, III, iv)

It seems to me that, symbolically, Lear and Gloucester are *conducted by Edgar into the loss of everything*, as they approach death. Edgar is the emblem and instrument ("scourge and minister") of their reluctant renunciation. In a way, in terms of Freud's (1913/1990) model, therefore, *Edgar also* is Death. The final loss is the sacrificial death of Cordelia, which Edgar inadvertently, by delay, brings about, symbolising, in an overdetermined way, the many things touched on in this chapter.

By enacting *the loss of everything* the author symbolically commands something which was in reality beyond his control, but in the expiatory total reduction to "thou art the thing itself", which is enacted in the total trajectory of the play, he surrenders it again—except in the form of the act of renunciation which he enacts through the "null character" Edgar, "the thing itself". (Freud makes similar comment about the reversal of the reversal in which Lear carries Death—as Cordelia/Atropos—dead in his arms, in Freud, 1913.)

This is what I meant by Oxford as the author in a manner neutralizing himself penitentially, more than in any other play, in Edgar—who nevertheless, parallel to Prospero, takes over the Kingdom at the end, and, *in a disguised way*, is in a way more potent than anyone else in the play.

Indeed, one might go further and say that, in Edgar, Shakespeare has *dramatised disguising itself*, in an uncanny double take.

In which case *King Lear* is also dramatising the agony and shame of the authorial concealment as such—which is so often expressed in the *Sonnets*:

LXXII.
O, lest the world should task you to recite
What merit lived in me, that you should love
After my death, dear love, forget me quite,
For you in me can nothing worthy prove;
Unless you would devise some virtuous lie,
To do more for me than mine own desert,
And hang more praise upon deceased I
Than niggard truth would willingly impart:
O, lest your true love may seem false in this,
That you for love speak well of me untrue,
*My name be buried where my body is*, [my italics]
And live no more to shame nor me nor you.
For I am shamed by that which I bring forth,
And so should you, to love things nothing worth.
(Shakespeare, 2005, *Sonnet* 72)

I cannot see this as anything less (though it is also more) than comprehensive penitence and alchemical descent; and therefore I cannot conceive of the author as doing anything other than enact his comprehensive losses, and abdications, for which he feels responsible to an abyssal extent, in this profound symbolic expiation.

This only partially matches the life of Oxford in a literal way, in the way much of *Hamlet* does, but it is profoundly *symbolically* congruent with what we know of it (in much the same way as, for instance, Wotan's relation to Fricka in *The Ring* is congruent with Wagner's own relation to Minna). And indeed the symbolic aspect of it is expressed monumentally in the *disguise* motif which Edger embodies—*as the iconic enactment of the author who, if the hypothesis is true, is the greatest disguised genius in history*!

I cannot see that there is anything remotely comparable in what we know of the life of William Shakespeare of Stratford, nothing which could *come to life specifically*, as congruent, in the way Oxford's life does, or Wagner's in the parallel case (or that of Dickens' own father's time in *Little Dorrit's* Marshalsea Prison, c.f., Dickens, 1857/2003); the only serious possible exception to this argument, it seems to me, is the Catholic Recusant dimension of the Shakespeares of Stratford. But this creates a mass of puzzles of its own in relation to the Authorship, though I shall have to leave it unresolved here.

In so doing Oxford/Shakespeare creates one of the greatest of all dramas—in which his own "he hath ever but slenderly known himself" is conducted into the profoundest self-knowledge through the impersonal cypher character Edgar.

Edgar is a kind of "reserve" of the aletheiaic hidden thoughts—or unthoughts—of the play. By creating the character of Edgar as this "reserve", he is able to submit his own conduct to the most comprehensive and appalling total examination, "without reserve". The abyss of Edgar's descent, accompanying companion to that of Gloucester and Lear, symbolizes the depth of the author's self-imposed penitence—yet apotheosis of that penitence—for his "abdication". There is nothing manifest in the life of William Shakespeare of Stratford which corresponds to this (with the possible exception mentioned).

*Edgar never meets Cordelia alive during the play.* But Nahum Tate's modification in which Cordelia lives and marries Edgar—paradoxically, the two "death" figures of the play—nevertheless does, therefore, symbolically and mysteriously correspond to something fitting, which is enacted in Dickens' *Little Dorrit*. I turn briefly to *Little Dorrit* to evoke this connection and parallel.

Dickens' *Little Dorrit*, though a redemptive work and not a tragedy, offers in many ways both a contextual updating of *King Lear*, and an emotional and psychological elucidation. The issues have been reduced more nearly all to money, both in the concrete and as metaphor, in a mercantile age. *Little Dorrit*, in its turn, forms the base for an intriguing "line" of character influences in the English novel; Henry Gowan in *Little Dorrit* is the prototype for Grandcourt in George Eliot's *Daniel Deronda*, who in turn (as Leavis points out in *The Great Tradition*, 1983) forms the prototype for Osmond in Henry James' *The Portrait of Lady*. (If we bring in Gowan's diabolical friend Rigaud/Blandois, they all indeed go back to Edgar's:

> The prince of darkness is a gentleman
> Modo he's called, and Mahu. (Shakespeare, 2005,
>     *King Lear*, III, iv)

I am invoking such transmission of influence in relating the main characters and psychological assumption to those of *King Lear* (Welsh, 2003, op. cit.)

In Dickens's *Little Dorrit* the character of Arthur Clennam (the name Arthur is significant for *his* Grail Search) corresponds to that of Edgar in *King Lear*, and Lear and Cordelia correspond to William Dorrit and Amy Dorrit—"Little Dorrit" (Welsh, 2003, op. cit.). And Clennam and Amy eventually marry, after many long detours which include Clennam's "descent into Hell" sojourn in the debtors' prison in which Amy was born, without which he cannot be stripped of his pride which prevents him accepting the grace of her love.

In this prison William Dorrit, arrested as a debtor early in his life, has lived most of his adult life. He holds the honorific nickname/title, "Father of the Marshalsea"—while Flora Casby's—Clennam's first love—father, who is eventually shorn of his hair in a "castration" gesture by his rent "grubber" Mr Pancks, is nicknamed "The Patriarch", and in a bizarre and perverse manner fills the role position of Gloucester. Inept fathers again hold the stage. In the prison Amy learns to love by looking after her father as his "Little Mother" (the name the brain-damaged Maggie gives her), a love he both leans on, and repudiates as humiliating (which is the fate Mason, 1967, suggests Lear most fears at the start of the play—dependence as a child on Cordelia).

Dickens' implicit "commentary" is fairly straightforward, at the point we have now reached. Dickens reverses Shakespeare's sequence, by showing the family as moving from poverty and suddenly made rich (through the agency of Mr Pancks, who, like the Ferryman in Hades, takes on the activity, in compensation for his extortionist rent-grubbing day job, of finding out lost inheritances for people for whom he cares, such as Clennam and Little Dorrit). But riches in no way negate the hidden shame, as the passage, in which William Dorrit directly most reminds us of Lear, (a Lear whose self-deception never attains even partial insight), illustrates, where his hypersensitivity to the assumed slight on the part of the hotelier is dictated by hidden paranoia about the shame of the Marshalsea past:

"Is it possible, sir," said Mr Dorrit, reddening excessively, "that you have—ha—had the audacity to place one of my rooms at the disposition of any other person?"

Thousands of pardons! It was the host's profound misfortune to have been overcome by that too genteel lady. He besought Monseigneur not to enrage himself. He threw himself on Monseigneur for clemency. If Monseigneur would have the distinguished goodness to occupy the other salon especially reserved for him, for but five minutes, all would go well.

"No, sir," said Mr Dorrit. "I will not occupy any salon. I will leave your house without eating or drinking, or setting foot in it.

How do you dare to act like this? Who am I that you—ha—separate me from other gentlemen?"

Alas! The host called all the universe to witness that Monseigneur was the most amiable of the whole body of nobility, the most important, the most estimable, the most honoured. If he separated Monseigneur from others, it was only because he was more distinguished, more cherished, more generous, more renowned.

"Don't tell me so, sir," returned Mr Dorrit, in a mighty heat.

"You have affronted me. You have heaped insults upon me. How dare you? Explain yourself."

Ah, just Heaven, then, how could the host explain himself when he had nothing more to explain; when he had only to apologise, and confide himself to the so well-known magnanimity of Monseigneur!

"I tell you, sir," said Mr Dorrit, panting with anger, "that you separate me—ha—from other gentlemen; that you make distinctions between me and other gentlemen of fortune and station. I demand of you, why? I wish to know on—ha—what authority, on whose authority. Reply sir. Explain. Answer why."

Permit the landlord humbly to submit to Monsieur the Courier then, that Monseigneur, ordinarily so gracious, enraged himself without cause. There was no why. Monsieur the Courier would represent to Monseigneur, that he deceived himself in suspecting that there was any why, but the why his devoted servant had already had the honour to present to him. The very genteel lady—

"Silence!" cried Mr Dorrit. "Hold your tongue! I will hear no more of the very genteel lady; I will hear no more of you. Look at this family—my family—a family more genteel than any lady. You have treated this family with disrespect; you have been insolent to this family. I'll ruin you. Ha—send for the horses, pack the carriages, I'll not set foot in this man's house again!" [Dickens, 1857/2003, Part II, Ch. 3]

Beneath this social veneer (manifest in both parts of the book, and incarnate in the aptly named Mrs General, and in the speculating Mr Merdle's Chief Butler) the connection between Amy and her father remains, in which, like Lear, he takes her for granted, but also manages to keep some semblance of connection with emotional reality and congruence going, despite his huge self-deception. In the following passage he has just been cravenly hinting, she remaining silent, that she might marry the son of the turnkey, John Chivery, who is in love with her—but she cannot, she is, unrevealed, in love with Clennam—which would of course have led to William's being treated much better still than hitherto, with considerable privileges:

His voice died away, as if she could not bear the pain of hearing him, and her hand had gradually crept to his lips. For a little while there was a dead silence and stillness; and he remained shrunk in his chair, and she remained with her arm round his neck and her head bowed down upon his shoulder.

His supper was cooking in a saucepan on the fire, and, when she moved, it was to make it ready for him on the table. He took his usual seat, she took hers, and he began his meal. They did not, as yet, look at one another. By little and little he began; laying down his knife and fork with a noise, taking things up sharply, biting at his bread as if he were offended with it, and in other similar ways showing that he was out of sorts. At length he pushed his plate from him, and spoke aloud; with the strangest inconsistency.

"What does it matter whether I eat or starve? What does it matter whether such a blighted life as mine comes to an end, now, next week, or next year? What am I worth to anyone?

A poor prisoner, fed on alms and broken victuals; a squalid, disgraced wretch!"

"Father, father!" As he rose she went on her knees to him, and held up her hands to him.

"Amy," he went on in a suppressed voice, trembling violently, and looking at her as wildly as if he had gone mad. "I tell you, if you could see me as your mother saw me, you wouldn't believe it to be the creature you have only looked at through the bars of this cage. I was young, I was accomplished, I was good-looking, I was independent—by God I was, child!—and people sought me out, and envied me. Envied me!"

"Dear father!" She tried to take down the shaking arm that he flourished in the air, but he resisted, and put her hand away.

"If I had but a picture of myself in those days, though it was ever so ill done, you would be proud of it, you would be proud of it. But I have no such thing. Now, let me be a warning! Let no man," he cried, looking haggardly about, "fail to preserve at least that little of the times of his prosperity and respect. Let his children have that clue to what he was. Unless my face, when I am dead, subsides into the long departed look—they say such things happen, I don't know—my children will have never seen me."

"Father, father!"

"O despise me, despise me! Look away from me, don't listen to me, stop me, blush for me, cry for me—even you, Amy! Do it, do it! I do it to myself! I am hardened now, I have sunk too low to care long even for that."

"Dear father, loved father, darling of my heart!" She was clinging to him with her arms, and she got him to drop into his chair again, and caught at the raised arm, and tried to put it round her neck.

"Let it lie there, father. Look at me, father, kiss me, father! Only think of me, father, for one little moment!"

Still he went on in the same wild way, though it was gradually breaking down into a miserable whining.

***

Thus, now boasting, now despairing, in either fit a captive with the jail-rot upon him, and the impurity of his prison worn into the grain of his soul, he revealed his degenerate state to his affectionate child. No one else ever beheld him in the details of his humiliation. Little recked the Collegians who were laughing in their rooms over his late address in the Lodge, what a serious picture they had in their obscure gallery of the Marshalsea that Sunday night. [Dickens, 1857/2003, Part I, Ch. 19]

In such ways Dickens fills out how the relation between Cordelia and her self-deceiving father might perhaps have been.

In the phase of "riches", on the point of marrying Mrs General on his return from London to Rome, he eventually only reconnects with Amy when he suffers a stroke at a large dinner, and psychologically "returns" to the Marchalsea, and dependence on Amy, for the last days of his life. Like Lear he is saner when "mad", but his "sanity" is explicit dependence on her.

As with the character of *King Lear*'s Cordelia (and Susan Vere), the riches which eventually Amy and Arthur Clennam share are not financial but emotional—they have, eventually, Cordelia-like, "nothing", financially:

"Yes! And it's [Fanny, her sister's, fortune, in Merdle's bankruptcy] all gone.—How much do you think my own great fortune is?"

As Arthur looked at her inquiringly, with a new apprehension on him, she withdrew her hand, and laid her face down on the spot where it had rested.

"I have nothing in the world. I am as poor as when I lived here. When papa came over to England, he confided everything he had to the same hands, and it is all swept away. O my dearest and best, are you quite sure you will not share my fortune with me now?"

Locked in his arms, held to his heart, with his manly tears upon her own cheek, she drew the slight hand round his neck, and clasped it in its fellow-hand.

"Never to part, my dearest Arthur; never any more, until the last!

I never was rich before, I never was proud before, I never was happy before, I am rich in being taken by you, I am proud in having been resigned by you, I am happy in being with you in this prison, as I should be happy in coming back to it with you, if it should be the will of God, and comforting and serving you with all my love and truth. I am yours anywhere, everywhere! I love you dearly! I would rather pass my life here with you, and go out daily, working for our bread, than I would have the greatest fortune that ever was told, and be the greatest lady that ever was honoured. O, if poor papa may only know how blest at last my heart is, in this room where he suffered for so many years!" [Dickens, 1857/2003, Part II, Ch. 34]

I have not space to explore the full interconnections between the two works. Enough has been presented to indicate the central element—which is the dialectic of riches and poverty in the literal and the metaphoric-symbolic senses. Like *King Lear* (indirectly, symbolically), and directly *Timon of Athens*, and *The Merchant of Venice*, the thrust of *Little Dorrit* is against the ancient practice of what used to be known as usury, moneylending, and the psychological background is one in which, at the very core, the main characters, William Dorrit especially, are caught and involved in loss, squandering, and speculation. (This has been disputed regarding Shakespeare and *The Merchant of Venice*, Hunt, 2003, and personal communication, 2007.) But William Shakespeare of Stratford was a successful moneylender and usurer.

The values with which Dickens, like Shakespeare the author of the plays, responds to this are life values, not finance values; in the terms of Christ's parable—which is our first introduction to projection!—of the speck of dust and the beam of wood (Mt ch. 7, v.3) Amy Dorrit rejects the imposition of commercial price on everything (Clennam, caught himself in the commercial trap, fails to grasp her insight, but it is decisive, Leavis and Leavis, 1970):

"Mr Clennam, will he pay all his debts before he leaves here?"
   "No doubt. All."
   "All the debts for which he had been imprisoned here, all my life and longer?"
   "No doubt."
   There was something of uncertainty and remonstrance in her look; something that was not all satisfaction. He wondered to detect it, and said:

"You are glad that he should do so?"

"Are you?' asked Little Dorrit, wistfully.

"Am I? Most heartily glad!"

"Then I know I ought to be."

"And are you not?"

"It seems to me hard," said Little Dorrit, "that he should have lost so many years and suffered so much, and at last pay all the debts as well. It seems to me hard that he should pay in life and money both."

"My dear child—" Clennam was beginning.

"Yes, I know I am wrong," she pleaded timidly, "don't think any worse of me; it has grown up with me here."

The prison, which could spoil so many things, had tainted Little Dorrit's mind no more than this. Engendered as the confusion was, in compassion for the poor prisoner, her father, it was the first speck Clennam had ever seen, it was the last speck Clennam ever saw, of the prison atmosphere upon her.

He thought this, and forbore to say another word. With the thought, her purity and goodness came before him in their brightest light. The little spot made them the more beautiful.

Worn out with her own emotions, and yielding to the silence of the room, her hand slowly slackened and failed in its fanning movement, and her head dropped down on the pillow at her father's side. Clennam rose softly, opened and closed the door without a sound, and passed from the prison, carrying the quiet with him into the turbulent streets. [Dickens, 1857/2003, Part I, Ch. 35]

Leavis comments (op. cit., p. 223–4): "The speck, of course, is on Clennam."

Amy and Clennam achieve the purgatorial purification their alchemical descent from money values into the abyss of the nothing makes possible. The moments of redemption Wilson Knight points to in *King Lear* are swallowed up by the background of an even deeper descent into darkness than Dickens contemplates, and which is embodied in the survival and role of Edgar, but as glimpses they are there, and they are only compatible with an understanding based upon experience of catastrophic loss and personal abdication.

Having myself here made this Keatsian journey of descent into the darkness, the old oak forest, of *King Lear*, once again, and having been privileged to discern the extraordinary role of Edgar which I never saw previously, with Ogburn (1988) I find myself asking: what must have been the depths of the personal descent of the author of a work of such darkness, a work yet imbued, nevertheless, with the sustained and starkest determination to realise the true (ver verius)?! The Oxfordian hypothesis alone gives us an author into whom our fullest intuitions about the plays can expand. This does not as such make it true, of course, but if congruence be part of truth it contributes to it.

Thus our spiritual detective journey into the creative psyche of the authorship points to the character of Oxford as profoundly compatible with the authorship, and William Shakespeare of Stratford (with the mentioned reservation) not at all. And thus this quasi-psychotherapeutic, quasi-literary, methodology, can contribute, in a modest way, to the return of this historically repressed heritage, and so to the longer-term righting of a deep and centuries-long-sustained historical wrong.

It also very graphically supports what I wrote earlier: "Inside" and "outside" the text, criticism, and creation, are relative concepts. The enactment we have been drawn into in exploring this whole issue is one which straddles life and work, and in which a creative totality is at work which transcends both separately. I shall now turn to this, and to the concept of poetic as enactment which makes sense of it all, in the poetry and objectivity chapter.

## Notes

1 The "incognito encounter" is my label for a phenomenon found at peak moments of the greatest literature: the reunion of Joseph and his brethren in *Genesis*, the encounter between Jesus and his disciples on the Road to Emmaus, in Luke's Gospel, Wotan's encounter with Siegfried in *Siegfried in The Nibelung's Ring*, the encounter of Oedipus and Laius on the crossroads outside Thebes, Pip and Magwitch on Magwitch's return in *Great Expectations*, Nostromo with Dr Monygham in *Nostromo*, and so on. It always indicates an hidden relationship—either familial, or by conjoint participation in some fundamental enterprise.

2 From Wikipedia, the free encyclopedia

*Kenosis* is a Greek word for emptiness, which is used as a theological term. The ancient Greek word κένωσις *kénōsis* means an "emptying", from κενός *kenós* "empty". The word is mainly used, however, in a Christian theological context, for example Philippians 2:7, "Jesus made himself nothing (κένωσε *ekénōse*) ..." (NIV) or "... he emptied himself ..." (NRSV), using the verb form κενόω *kenóō* "to empty".

# CHAPTER FIVE

# Poetic Enactment and Propositional Truth: Poetry and Objectivity

*Part I*
*Poetic as enactment*

[Note: *I have also used, in modified form, parts of the analysis of Daniel Stern's narrative and analysis of the skaters, in this chapter, in my contribution of a chapter on Derrida in* Beyond Postmodernism: Extending the Reach of Psychoanalysis, *edited by Roger Frie and Donna Orange,* Routledge, in press.]

Following on from the profound sweep of the large scale communicative dramatic, as I may refer to it, we have been exploring in relation to Shakespeare, this chapter will now seek to:

Clarify what defining poetic communication as *textual enactment* means, and illustrate it through Daniel Stern's work;

Characterise poetic enactment ontologically by linking it to the concept of imaginative synthesis (imagination) as characterised by Kant (Kant, 1781/1964), and give the historical-cultural background for the emergence of this concept;

161

Relate the emerging character of imaginative synthesis to a *modal-social (existential) conception of the self*, which is defined in terms of the tri-structure of temporality;

Show that, in this modal-social way, the character of textual enactment is essentially connected to *the irreducible personhood in which language participates*, but by which it is also defined;

Relate the modal-social concept of self in the later Freudian metapsychology, and its extensive offshoots and derivatives in terms of influence, in terms of the modal understanding of the Trinity in Christian theology as expounded by Karl Barth (Barth, 1932/1936);

Link in this way poetic enactment on through to what I argue is the fundamental reciprocal-social character (Leibniz, 1714/1998, Whitehead, 1929/1979) of being itself;

And, in passing through all this, the rejection of what I call the objecthood model of existence in favour of a reciprocal-social one.

In the chapter on philosophy of existence we got in the end a glimpse of the equi-primordiality of poetry (including psychotherapy, on my argument), and philosophy of existence, and suggested that philosophy of existence could not be separated from the analysis which places poetry and poetic in a fundamental role.

So, next we must see and spell out fully what this centrality of poetic means, when, for instance, Daniel Stern (Stern, 2004, p. 173) writes:

We need another language that does not exist (outside poetry)—
a language that is steeped in temporal dynamics.

We are concerned in this book with poetic process. I shall use the words "poetry", "poetic" (as a generic noun, like "dialogic"), and "poesis", and "poetic process" and variants in a mutually supplementary, contextually appropriate (I hope), way, because it is not simply poetry in the formal sense we are concerned with.

Having given a very full and wide-ranging exemplification of the literary-critical methodology in the chapter on the Shakespeare question, I shall mainly be concentrating on the fundamental concepts required to elucidate the thesis, not putting it to work in detailed poetic analysis. I shall include some exemplification, partly from a Blake poem, partly from an example (not psychotherapeutic, as such, but highly pertinent to psychotherapy) of Daniel Stern's (2004). Then it moves through considering Kant himself on imagination, and then finally uses Freud, Andrew Marvell, Heidegger, and Karl Barth to outline the implications for revisions of developmental psychology in its light (which also takes us into some theological territory). It is more than hermeneutic of poetry; it is the conceptual elaboration corresponding to the developed exemplification in earlier chapters.

The chapter, however abstract, gives the indispensable background for the poetic methodology and way of thinking about psychotherapy to be placed on secure foundations. Again, however abstract, it is nevertheless itself an example of the kind of enquiry which, in more concrete form, opens unexpected doors in psychotherapy itself. This wide-ranging chapter is, indeed, itself a graphic illustration that the mixed psychotherapeutic-literary-philosophical methodology of this book can yield powerful results over a surprising range of material.

Poetic process is often used as the watchword for the indescribable; "the poets" are appealed to as having communicated things otherwise incommunicable. We shall come to the quoted comment by Daniel Stern for other purposes later but for now I take it as an example of what people very often say about poets, that they have a kind of hot-line to the ineffable (yet, as we shall see, underrating his own poetic ability, Stern himself "goes into poetry" to make his argument):

> We need another language *that does not exist* (outside poetry)—a language that is steeped in temporal dynamics. [Stern, 2004, p. 173, my italics]

But poetic process is not in the least conceptually indescribable, as Stern seems possibly to imply. It is not a mere irrational counterpart to propositional and positive truth, as it is often thought. Not that *this* is what Stern is saying, but I think he *is* in some way saying poetry has a fast track to the otherwise ineffable.

The relationship between propositional assertion and poetic/ poesic is much more subtle. In this chapter I am going to try to characterise the essential elements of that relationship.

However, there is a *sense* in which description fails, and must fail, in evoking poetry and poetic. But this way can *itself* be described and explained, and there is *also* a sense in which it is perfectly precise, and therefore describable.

Our task is to explicate this combination of inherent indescribability, in conjunction with precise describability, in what follows, to make this apparent paradox clear, obvious, and non-contradictory. It is quite banal, in a way, the distinction we need to make, but it all-too-easily slips through our hands!

The core of the way that description fails, is that poetry, poetic, is in a way a form of *action*, but in a special way, the way of *enactment, of textual enactment*, this form of action as enactment being also a form of partial deferral, postponement, by entry into the realm of quasi-permanence of the verbally iconic (Wimsatt and Beardsley, 1951/1967a), or "universal", in the Platonic sense—with apologies for the jargon.

So, what *all description* fails in, is in *evoking* what poetic process in fact does, the way it enacts a total situation (a form of action, or participation in action, which is—*in a sense*—repeatable, iterable).

And the reason for this is *simply* that, if it did capture it, it could not do so *without itself being* that enactment, which is what poetry and poetic process are, without repeating precisely that element which participates in its quasi-permanence (to be illustrated shortly).

Poetry, poetic, then, uses language in a special way to achieve *textual enactment*, and it is this we shall seek to elucidate.

Clarity about this distinction, as we shall see progressively, begins to release us from a great many of the confusions over post-modernist positions, in particular, and the mostly misunderstanding-based oppositions to them, or at any rate to the core formulations of them, not the extremer versions.

In the upshot we shall be partly elucidating the philosophical *a priori*, which is essential to this in ways which will become clearer, and again in a way which takes it into some spaces not commonly associated with it, for instance that there is no clear demarcation from the empirical, and that there is an *a priori* of time as such, of temporality, and events, (something which would still be ridiculed in many Anglo-American philosophical contexts).

The peculiarity of poetic enactment, and of all speech which derives from it, is that it carries the indescribability of *action* as action—or rather of action's *not being description* or propositional—*into the quasi-permanence of speech and writing itself.*

Precisely what I am saying is not easy to explain without some familiarity with literary critical concepts. The indescribability of action qua action is existential; I participate my actions, I *am* them, in the way an item of equipment, the ready-to hand, for Heidegger, has its being *in* its employment, (as discussed in Chapter 3 above, c.f., Heidegger, 1927/1967). In that sense, also, I participate, and am, my engagement in poetic and in art. A poem, like a book (like, as we saw before, the book, *Being and Time* itself) *is ready-to-hand in its own way.*

The large realm of "speech acts" promising and marrying, which JL Austin (1962a) identified and classified, are clearly fully-fledged *actions*, in verbal form, as such. They are therefore only the thin end of the wedge of this. It is indeed also true, as Derrida pointed out in *Limited Inc.* (1988), that as verbal actions, they too participate in quasi-permanent forms, repeatability, iterability, and so there is an element of enactment, they are not "pure actions"—if there could be such a thing! (for this is a recognition of a type that clearly begins to "spread wider", to more and more relevant types of communication and action!)

*Poetry, poetic, as a whole communication process is a complex enactment.* I have given substantial exemplification of poetry as enactment in another chapter, but now we have to characterise it.

A poem like William Blake's *Ah Sunflower* (Blake, 1977) can be held to enact a grammatical movement like an Escher painting (it does not matter too much if this interpretation is incorrect, it only needs to be a *possible* interpretation):

That is, we find by the end of the poem that the "goal" (the "sweet golden clime") turns out after all, once again, *da capo*, to be the starting point (the youth and the virgin, after their resurrection, still "aspire", though there is a, possibly deliberately ambiguous, hint of a secondary meaning of "breathing again"), so that we recognise that all that desire enacts—is still just endless *desire*:

> Ah, Sunflower! weary of time,
> Who countest the steps of the sun,
> Seeking after that sweet golden clime
> Where the traveller's journey is done;
>
> Where the youth pined away with desire
> And the pale virgin shrouded in snow
> Arise from their graves, and aspire
> Where my Sunflower wishes to go.

But this is not just stated by the poem, it is enacted by it. It is also, when we think about it, a profound enactment of what desire is, so that the enactment also *expresses* (we participate in) a deep truth of life, like, but in another key from, Oscar Wilde's impish paradox (Wilde, 1891/2004):

> A cigarette is the perfect type of a perfect pleasure. It is exquisite, and it leaves one unsatisfied. What more can one want?

It is an enactment because, as with the Escher painting, we hold in our mind the visual or the grammatical rules, which then lead us on to a "repositioning", based on a second, unexpected, but still congruent, use of the same visual or grammatical rules. And this, then, flips us back and leads us round in the endless circle, realising the quasi-permanence, of re-enactment as we return to the beginning again! Every time we read the poem!

This, in either case, takes the presentation in the direction of an enactment which exploits the rules unexpectedly, as opposed to a straightforward propositional or visual "representation" of a *possible actual* state of affairs—whether that is of a staircase, or a consistent description of a straightforward realisation of desire.

What, then, Escher does, and what Blake does, on this interpretation, is take us though a textual enactment, *unrealisable in physical actuality but only through the quasi-permanence of imagination*, the full description, or evocation, of which cannot abstain from, or fall short of, *the very process and imaginative means of the enactment*.

That is, in grasping this, we ourselves *participate* in the enactment, nothing short of that will achieve understanding here. (And the literary method itself, of course, consists of *brief epitomising selected and selective enactments*, i.e., quotations, but *enactive* quotations, a process therefore which raises the issue, always, how far criticism is itself creative!)

Other examples (among many many others, c.f., Leavis, 1969, and 1975) which would yield a similar result, if anyone wishes to explore, include TS Eliot's *Ash Wednesday*, Macbeth's speech beginning Act I, Sc 7, of Shakespeare's *Macbeth*—and Marvell's *To His Coy Mistress*, to which we return below (Marvell, 1681/1984).

It is an enactment which, unlike, as mentioned, Austin's quasi-propositional "words as deeds" (his "performative utterances", Austin, 1962a), which in a sense, in Quine's phrase, (because of reflexivity), do "*make themselves true*" (Quine, 1969), cannot be consistently realised in the spatio-temporal realm of straightforward events, unless we include imagination, or virtual and holographic imagery, in that.

Austin's performatives are *in that sense* propositional. But when Derrida *begins* a book with the sentence,

This (therefore) will not have been a book. (Derrida, 1972/1983) this is an enactment. Derrida's stylistic innovations are almost invariably aimed at being enactments, and he is always interested in the seamlessness involved in our understanding of enactments. He is implying that the *totality of awareness of being* as a whole *has to be an enactment*, and cannot be non-circularly evoked, and so nothing in it escapes our participatory enactments, they are inherent in the totality which is realised. This is a central element of the meaning of the much misunderstood slogan of deconstruction, "there is nothing outside of the text" (Derrida, 1967/1976, p. 158), which, it ought to be understood, also means, "there is nothing which is *not* text", which I have tried to illustrate in the larger perspective on Shakespeare, in the last chapter. (In a crude and clumsy shorthand, this would mean that Derrida is *not* a relativist, as often thought, he is indeed nearer to being an *objective idealist*, in Hegel's sense. But perhaps—tell it not in

Gath, tell it not to the Philistines!—nearly all of the major modern philosophers, on both sides of the Channel, and on both sides of the Atlantic, with the exception of the commonsense philosophers, if any, actually are thus![1])

I would wish to add that it is possible to make true statements about all of this at a meta-level, even though *they too* are subject to the rule, including the statement I have just made, and that this is indeed not contradictory or relativistic, and that, only if this is true, is it possible for Derrida to claim, as he does in *Limited Inc* (1988), that his position is not a relativism.

We in fact begin to glimpse a false dichotomy here.

This total state of affairs can, then, be *described*, in the sense of pointed to and explicated, elucidated (it is not alien to language, it is not ineffable), except in respect of the limitation I have indicated, and recognising, as has already become pretty apparent, that this description is *an infinite, incompleteable process* (the full meaning of context is not localisable).

Now, once we have recognised the element of enactment in these paradoxical expressions which seem paradigms of it, we can then go on further to grasp that the element of enactment in poetic communication can never be reduced to description, *even when it takes the form of description*. Even then, it is doing something else.

We find this, for instance, in the Wordsworth poem I quoted at the end of the Heidegger chapter:

> No motion has she now, no force;
> She neither hears nor sees;
> Rolled round in earth's diurnal course
> With rocks, and stones, and trees. (Wordsworth, 1799/2004)

This is in the form of statement, but the tacit suggestion, the images evoked for imagination, the choice of words, things like the odd juxtaposition of "rocks" and "stones", and so on, all take us into the realm of enactment. Why "stones", in addition to "rocks"? To ascertain what the last example, what *that* apparently redundant near-repetition is doing, how, in its strange textual doubling, it anchors the elemental worldly whole, which is being evoked, whilst embedding "the human" in it, would take us very far in understanding enactment in poetry, which I must leave here with these hints[2]!

We should not assume this was initially intended or planned by the poet. Poets *discover* these juxtapositions; it is language which enacts them! In a way, the whole of what I am saying is in this remark (and I myself have retraced several of those discoverings as discoveries myself in the course of writing this book). This is also a theme developed at large in Lacan's writings, and taken even further in Derrida's. We don't write, we are written!

Gradually it will becomes clearer that *all* language is enactment, as well as, sometimes but not always, description. And therefore we have to make the distinction in terms of *function*, not just simply of *linguistic means*. Those "means" do however, lead us into, and enable us to introduce, the issue. This is rather in the way that Austin's (Austin, 1962a) performatives, opposed to constatives, eventually lead him into, or on to, distinguishing levels of force *within* communications rather than *between* types of communication, (which are then articulated, rather, within a spectrum).

In accounting for poetic process, as a whole, then, we now need to make *a functional distinction* between a *conceptual analysis or description* of the central elements of such process, and an *enactive evocation* of it.

The latter, an enactive evocation, as we shall see shortly, *is itself an enactment*. It evokes by enacting. I shall give examples shortly. The former cannot do the latter, but it *can* point to its features. But most, if not all, of both poetry and philosophy is an inextricable combination of both aspects.

And this conceptual pointing must also *participate* in the enactive evocation; it probably cannot avoid fundamental metaphors, or very general terms used in such a way that they break out of their circumscriptions, and are themselves implicated in the indefinite cross-connections of meaning, even if they are purely analytic-descriptive. The characterisation of poetic, circularly, cannot itself avoid an irreducible element of poetry. As we shall see in the cases of Kant and Hume, and more recent thinkers, such as Daniel Stern, the "third possibility", which is the "indeterminate" dimension of poesis, cannot be kept out, and keeps flipping the neat distinctions upside down.

This is the basis of the "flipping upside down" of deconstruction, at least as Derrida practices it—which always heads for the fault-lines where the hidden, "supplementary", recognition is inscribed. Deconstruction, in this, is simply an *exaggeration* of something which is inherent in literary exegesis and hermeneutics. Deconstruction is the elucidation of poesis. Literary criticism has always had the power to do this[3]. I invoke it in discussing Wilson Knight, for instance, in the Shakespeare chapter, whose belying his own thesis is a characteristic *concrete* piece of deconstruction (apparently empirical, but actually corresponding to a fundamental principle, that of the contextual external relevance of art, of which Knight has a profound implicit grasp, counter to his overt official position, which he is only ambivalently committed to, as I argue). And later I consider some of Stern's analyses, as well as Kant's, in a deconstructive light, in this way.

However, whilst doing philosophy, it so frequently happens, as Wittgenstein noted, that we must, embarrassed, again and again return to the recognition of the obvious—yet though, or because, obvious, easily overlooked.

> The aspects of things that are most important for us are hidden because of their simplicity and familiarity. (One is unable to notice something—just because it is always before ones eyes.) The real foundations of his enquiry do not strike a man at all. Unless that fact has at some time struck him. And this means: we fail to be struck by what, once seen, is most striking and most powerful. [Wittgenstein, 1967, § 129]

And the obvious right in front of my nose here, which we already just noticed, but which can as easily be overlooked, and which I had to drag myself clumsily back to, is that, even though poetic process i.e., enactment, will in some way be *involved* in the characterisation, it can still be *functioning as* characterisation, rather than primarily as enactment. And likewise something which is pure description *can evoke and enact by what it brings before the mind*.

We shall shortly see this illustrated in relevant passages from Daniel Stern (2004), but this overlapping and leap-frogging makes it very difficult to disentangle the aspects.

Indeed, this distinction, conceptually, is beginning to wear a little thin by now, methinks! But it is important to hold on to it, at least provisionally, in the functional sense.

Similarly, philosophical insight can be part of such a poem as *Four Quartets* by TS Eliot, or *Duino Elegies* by Rainer Maria Rilke, but in the way of a poem and a poem's enactments. Yet it is certainly disconcerting—as Austin (Austin, 1962a) also found—how readily characterisation can pass over into enactment, and vice versa, constative into performative and mutatis mutandis! (Thus Austin, op. cit., realised that "to state" is also perfomative, whilst Quine, as already noted, op. cit., reminded us that performatives are still propositionally true or false, in one dimension.) It's as if each side of the antithesis is already reaching towards the other or towards some third thing!

These are, in a way, very elementary and simple distinctions and clarifications. Yet they puzzle the mind to which they are unfamiliar, like the Escher painting. We endlessly attempt to make a watertight demarcation, and then we find some third possibility invades it. *And that constant shifting, that refusal of neat demarcations, that refusal to stabilise, is itself the nature of poetry, poetic process or poesis, and is an indicator of the fundamentally poetic or poesic character of human communication.* And, *mutatis mutandis*, it is an indicator of the creative shifts of psychotherapy also (we shall discuss Stern's "ordinary life", but through goingly relational, example of such a shift, shortly).

It is the representational-propositional ("objecthood") paradigm that prevents us grasping what is involved here and hypnotises us, for it is not that any of this is intellectually extremely complicated. Rather, the ideas violate what feels to be our deepest commonsense. But this "deepest commonsense" in fact turns out to be our being hypnotised by the objecthood paradigm, which lies behind the representational-propositional model. I shall return to this issue of the paradigms involved progressively as we go on.

Daniel Stern (2004, p. 173), who wrestles with all of this as I am wrestling with it, in his chapter, on *The Process of Moving Along*, which includes the excellent and highly relevant discussion of the *sloppy* in psychotherapy, indicates the distinction between enactment and description, in rather elusive fashion, when he, all too casually, but therefore in a sense the more significantly, throws out, presumably about this kind of enactment, the passage I have already cited:

> We need another language that does not exist (outside poetry)—
> a language that is steeped in temporal dynamics.

So then, in the terms we have just defined, the language that "does not exist outside poetry" is simply *poetic enactment*, whilst the "language that is steeped in temporal dynamics" is the *descriptive conceptualisation* of those temporal dynamics, but in a way which does inescapably participate in, or implicitly invoke, poetry, and its paradoxes, and trades on poetry in its descriptive task.

It begins to look as if, in the end, this participation in poetic and enactment may apply to all language, and that *this is essentially connected to the irreducible personhood in which language participates, but by which it is also defined*. There is an ostensible conflict between relationally based and textually based models or analyses; I am going to try to show they are essentially correlative. We shall work our way round to this, especially via a consideration of Kant, and it is also the emergence of a different conception of the *a priori* which is the culmination of our enquiry.

To pursue and illustrate this further, in relation to the point we have now reached, I now indeed turn to Stern, who makes the quoted throw-away remark, (which might indeed be taken as a motto for this book), in a passage of *The Present Moment* (2004, P. 172–3). I shall need to quote at some length the whole passage where the *en passant* remark takes on its full weight in context. Regarding the necessary conceptual distinctions we are concerned with, there are here a number of confusions, helpful confusions to be sure, whose sorting out helps us clarify what is involved here, in this passage. I shall make observations as seems needful as we go along.

This is an ordinary human situation he is describing, but the description can be applied *mutatis mutandis* to psychotherapy process, as Stern does in other passages in his book. It is just a very vivid, and indeed excellently chosen and portrayed, example, for reasons which will become clear, and which will—of course, on my view, inevitably!—take the form of poetic, in the way Stern evokes it.

Stern is writing about *experienced*—and hence *enacted*, lived, not merely *narrated*—and *shared* feeling processes, (which he designates "shared feeling voyages"). He wrestles to elucidate this—as I am doing here—in a complex, many-faceted, awkward—partly deft and poetic, and partly cliché, and partly tautological—linguistic process.

It is apparent that he himself, not accidentally if I am correct in the above, is riding on a wave of metaphor, some of it cliché, some of it quite vivid, metaphor much of it akin to the cliché one I have also (!) just used. For instance, is the doubling of metaphor between wave and mountain, in what I am about to quote, here, creative metaphorisation, a Shakespearean merging of metaphors, or just confused and mixed metaphor? It is hard to tell (but we shall see later, that out of the "ocean" aspect of this metaphor eventually nevertheless emerges a genuinely "Shakespearian" metaphoric enactment):

> During a shared feeling voyage (which is the moment of meet-
> ing) two people traverse together a feeling-landscape as it
> unfolds in real time. Recall that the present moment can be a
> rich, emotional lived story. During this several-second journey,
> the participants ride the crest of the present instant as it crosses
> the span of the present moment, from its horizon of the past to
> its horizon of the future. As they move, they pass through an
> emotional narrative landscape with its hills and valleys of vital-
> ity effects, along its river of intentionality (which runs through-
> out), and over its peak of dramatic crisis. It is a voyage taken as
> the present unfolds. A passing subjective landscape is created
> and makes up a world in a grain of sand.

[Comment: it is clear that any metaphoric physical evocation of temporal dynamics presumes the temporality it seeks to clarify, and that
therefore, if it is indeed to elucidate it, it at least has to be metaphor
*used in a certain way*, as (Heidegger, 1927/1967) for instance, does it
(1962). Here also "real time" is a questionable concept. That does not
mean *no* clarification is attained, but it does not seem itself to bump
explicitly up against the inherent *trans-physicality or trans-factuality
of the temporal*, with which Augustine, Kant, Husserl, and Heidegger
all wrestled so tenaciously!]

> Because this voyage is participated in with someone, during an
> act of affective intersubjectivity, the two people have taken the
> voyage together. Although this shared voyage lasts only for the
> seconds of a moment of meeting, that is enough. It has been
> lived-through-together. The participants have created a shared
> private world. And having entered that world, they find that

when they leave it, their relationship is changed. There has been a discontinuous leap. The border between order and chaos has been redrawn. Coherence and complexity have been enlarged. They have created an expanded intersubjective field that opens up new possibilities of being-with-one-another. They are changed and they are linked differently for having changed one another.

[Comment: Stern resorts to the language of chaos and catastrophic change, in my view, partly because he is embarrassed by the risk of accounting for intersubjectivity in purely personal, phenomenological, non-physical, terms, which would take the matter out of the realm of neurological investigation, and into the realm of the temporal intersubjective *a priori*. This I think would be too metaphysical, mystical, and anti-postivist, in its full-fledged form, for him. I think he would definitely be wary of the full Husserlian transcendental idealist reduction to which Nissim-Sabat, 2005, invites him! Hence the appeal of physical, and turbulently concrete, metaphors for him. However, I think he is also moving towards an analytic-description characterisation of time process. But see below.]

Why is a shared feeling voyage so different from just listening to a friend or patient narrate episodes of their life story? There, too, one gets immersed in the other's experience through empathic understanding. The difference is this. In a shared feeling voyage, the experience is shared as it originally unfolds. There is no remove in time. It is direct—not transmitted and reformulated by words. It is cocreated by both partners and lived originally by both.

Shared feeling voyages are so simple and natural yet very hard to explain or even talk about. *We need another language that does not exist (outside poetry)—a language that is steeped in temporal dynamics.* [my italics] This is paradoxical because because these experiences provide the nodal moments in our life. Shared feeling voyages are one of life's most startling yet normal events, capable of altering our world step by step or in one leap. [Stern, 2004, p. 172–3]

Stern is writing about what I am calling enactment here. As anyone who reads his remarkable book may know, he moves his dialectic forward by way of generating antitheses, antitheses which, however, like Freud's own use of them, continually dissolve and themselves reshape (c.f., Wilkinson, 2003a; for an opposed view, Nissim-Sabat, 2005). Here he is playing with the antitheses of the *implicit* and the *explicit*, and the *non-verbal* and the *verbal*, the latter as foils to the former. These readily ally themselves with his concern for the neuroscientific level!

He is playing these against the conception of cocreation, intersubjective moments of meeting, but he finds a very strong pull (and this is a very classical pull and temptation[4] to contrast element in that which are *absolutely immediate*, with ones which are secondary, verbal, and "after the event". But this pull towards a *concrete* (non-reflexive) characterisation of enactment is what now leads him into the conceptual trap of momentarily equating *the enacted* with *the non-verbal*:

> In a shared feeling voyage, the experience is shared as it originally unfolds. There is no remove in time. It is direct—not transmitted and reformulated by words. It is cocreated by both partners and lived originally by both.

Here is manifest the temptation of the objecthood paradigm, of course by no means confined to Stern, here in the form of having to resort to characterisations involving the conception of the direct, or of presence, or of the immediate, or of "pure expression", or parallel such conceptions. "It is direct—not transmitted and reformulated by words." He later (see below) attacks what to me seems a pretty straw man "purely verbalist" psychoanalytic position, which would buttress the apparent compatibility of this immediacy of experience with the neurological dimension.

But, as we have now seen by way of the distinctions I have drawn, *the enacted can be as verbal, reflexively invoking quasi-permanence of language and writing, as one pleases,* and yet still be an enactment!

And what—illustrating this point right on cue!—does *he himself* do next? He *narrates and evokes* an enactment! In other words, to make sense of what this is about, *he himself resorts to poetic process*—and also in so doing enacts the distinction I have drawn!

Here, in parallel with what has been said already, we must pause to more sharply distinguish two further aspects of the characterisation process.

*First*, there is a dimension of the evocation of a poetic process which consists in an epitomisation, *and at the same time a reproduction of it*.

(Literal, total reproduction is, for an immense number of reasons, a logically contradictory conception, but yet the reproduction participates in that deferral, that quasi-permanencing aspect, of the poetic process of events which makes them *universals*, in the Platonic sense. It epitomises in varying measure, essentially.)

I shall awkwardly label this *enactive-reproductive epitomisation*. This mode of evocation *is itself an enactment*. Drama and dramatic narrative—whether fictional or historical—are paradigms (the dramatic parts or scenes of Boswell's (1791/1998) *Life of Johnson*, and his *Journals*, are an archetype of the tension I am evoking here, between fiction, and reporting, which is why, despite Boswell's not possessing inventive gifts, they express a creativity, *based in re-creation*, of which Frederick Pottle can rightly say:

> Boswell was a great imaginative artist—the peer in imagination
> of Scott and Dickens. [Pottle, 1950, c.f., Wilkinson, 2005a]

*Secondly*, the relevant aspect is the *descriptive* task which involves *process-characterising* conceptualisations, which may well also involve poetic coinage. This would include both *evocative characterisation*, which this passage mainly illustrates (this, however, is not redundant, and may also be an essential first step), and *technical characterisation*.

All these are illustrated, positively or negatively, in the graphic transition Stern now makes; another long quotation is necessary. It's significant that here Stern, in however sober academic terminology, is actually describing a *seduction*, with all the viscerally physical intersubjective potency a seduction involves, and, despite his academic mask, he actually manages to characterise it quite evocatively, in other words, he is also functioning as a poet in evoking one of the great subjects of poetry (!).

But a seduction is also peculiarly central to his purpose because of the profound level of intersubjectivity achieved in deep erotic encounter. In his academic evocation, with a quotation from the writing of a peer ("Kendon"), of the process of "intention movements", leading up to the "moment of meeting" of holding hands, it may occur to us that, erotically, *he is also paralleling and cross-referencing the process of foreplay in sexual intercourse*, the consummation which is overtly omitted from the account, but surely implied!

How dare I suggest such a thing!? Well, to the extent that it is valid (and actually, once more, it only has to be *possible*, irrespective of Stern's own intentionality), it illustrates the inherent "textuality", the multiplicitous metaphoricality, and so the musical quasi-permanence and "non-presence" of the evoked "field" of mnemic resonance and instinct, the poetic, of the sexual, as he is invoking it, and thus poetically enacting it! (And, as we shall see, in a special way, the whole account very graphically "reaches a climax"!) Once again, it is not essential that this was, consciously or unconsciously, in his intentionality as he wrote; it is enough that it is a significant possibility in the language used.

All the time, Stern's analysis is bedevilled by the power of the objecthood or objectivity paradigm; his instinct is to feel that an event must have occurred in the spation-temporal physical realm or an analogue of it *really to have happened*.

(By contrast, an enactment, in our sense, never *simply* happens; that is its peculiarity; though that does not mean it does *not* happen either! It is inherent in it that it is repeatable, iterable. And I am claiming Stern evokes an enactment in the iterable sense.)

Hence he strongly desires to emphasise the non-verbal and the implicit, and the neurological. Yet he cannot—of course—help invoking an element of irreducible intersubjectivity! I shall quote the whole long passage, once again, with occasional comment, and then discuss it:

> One major difficulty in grasping the concept is that explicit content must be momentarily put aside and out of mind. Another is to stay focused on the temporal unfolding of feelings. Finally, it is difficult to think of two people cocreating their joint experience in an intersubjective matrix. Another nonclinical example that picks up pieces from previous chapters may be useful here.

[Comment: but the exclusion of "explicit content" does not mean the exclusion of *implicit metaphoric meaning and cross-referencing*, as we have seen. And it is only "difficult to think of two people cocreating their joint experience in an intersubjective matrix" because *it cannot be done* within the framework of the objecthood paradigm, for which there is no intrinsic connection between what happens in me and what happens in you!—or at any rate not non-metaphorically!]

> A young man and woman go out together for the first time one winter evening. They barely know each other. They happen to pass a lighted ice-skating rink. On the spur of the moment they decide to go ice-skating. Neither of them is very good at it. They rent skates and stumble onto the ice. They trace a clumsy dance. She almost falls backwards. He reaches out and steadies her. He looses his balance and tilts to the right. She throws out a hand and he grabs it. (Note that each is also participating neu-rologically and experientially in the bodily feeling centred in the other. And each of them knows, at moments, that the other knows what it feels like to be him or her.) For stretches they manage to move forward together, holding hands with a vari-ety of sudden muscular contractions sent from one hand and arm to the other's to keep them together, steady, and moving. There is much laughing and gasping and falling. There is no space in which to really talk.

[Comment: the significance of Stern's parenthesis—"(Note that each is also participating neurologically and experientially in the bodily feeling centred in the other. And each of them knows, at moments, that the other knows what it feels like to be him or her.)"—is the blurring of the differentiation between the *physical body* and the *experienced phenomenological body* (c.f., Wilkinson, 2000a), which opens the way to either a neurological reduction or thorough going psychophysical parallelism, without heading further towards mysticism than that. But the neurological reference in this example is *an inference for us* here, however direct it may be "in itself". So, on the account of intersubjectivity in, for instance, any of Buber, or Husserl, or Heidegger, we have to take the experienced phenomenological body a great deal more seriously than that! This is a characteristic instance of how Stern elides this difference, and does not tackle the dualistic issue.]

At the end of half an hour, tired, they stop and have a hot drink at the side of the rink. But now their relationship is in a different place. They have directly experienced something of the other's experience. They have vicariously been inside the other's body and mind, through a series of shared feeling voyages. They have created an implicit intersubjective field that endures as part of their short history together. When they now have the physical ease and freedom to look at each other across the table, what will happen? There may be an initial social disorientation between them. They do not yet know each other officially, explicitly. But they have started to implicitly. They are in a no-man's land. And what will they see? Different people with a different past, and different potential futures than before they skated. One could attempt to explain the altered relationship on the grounds of the symbolic and associative meanings attached to their touching and acting on each other. I find this explanation weak and round about even though it could add additional meaning.

[Comment: now Stern heads boldly towards a "mystical" or "telepathic" strand when he says, unequivocally, "They have directly experienced something of the other's experience. They have vicariously been inside the other's body and mind, through a series of shared feeling voyages. They have created an implicit intersubjective field that endures as part of their short history together." This, if taken at all literally, seems a far cry from *The Motherhood Constellation*, Stern, 1995, with its blunt repudiation, (p. 42) of the mystical and telepathic elements in projective identification, not to mention from the neurological references of the previous paragraph.

What seems to me Stern's over-emphasis on the *non-semantic dimension* of the implicit, which enables hims to relegate, what he thinks of as the *verbal unconscious* dimension, to the realm of the repressed, the Freudian unconscious (c.f., Wilkinson, 2003a), this over-emphasis enables him to retain the posit that this will all eventually be assimilated by the neurological accounts of it all. Hence, I believe, as I say, as he struggles with his own inversion of psychoanalysis, the attack on the psychoanalytic straw man in the last sentence! This must here remain simply an opinion of mine, short of analysing the whole book!]

What will our skaters say? They will talk across the table and share meanings. And while they talk, the explicit domain of their relationship will start to expand. Whatever is said will be against the background of the implicit relationship that was expanded before, through the shared feeling voyages they had on the ice. Once they start talking, they will also act along with the words— small movements of face, hands, head, posture. The explicit then becomes the background for the implicit, momentarily. The expansion of the implicit and explicit domains play leapfrog with each other, building a shared history—a relationship.

If their implicit and explicit shared intersubjective field has altered enough that they mutually feel that they like one another, enough to want to go further in exploring the relationship, what might happen? They will engage in a sequence of intention movements. Kendon (1990) described intention movements exchanged between people to test the waters of their motivations towards each other. They con- sist of split-second, incomplete, very partial fullness of dis- play, abbreviated movements that belong to the behavioural sequence leading to the communication of an intention or motivation. (They are the physical-behavioral analogs of intersubjective orienting.)

Our skaters will now engage in a series of intention move- ments. Short head movements forward, stopped after several centimetres, slight mouth openings, looks at the other's lips and then their eyes, back and forth, leaning forward, and so on, will take place. This choreography of intention move- ments passes outside of consciousness but is clearly captured as "vibes". These vibes are short-circuited shared feeling voy- ages and deliver a sense of what is happening. An evolving patterns develops as the sequence of intensity, proximity, and fullness of display, of their intention movements progresses. These relational moves are enacted out of consciousness, leading up to the moment of meeting—their hands move to meet.

Here, too, a notion of readiness is needed, because suddenly the full act is executed in a leap. The present moment surfaces quickly like a whale breaching the water's surface. There is not an incessant, agonizing progression up to the final act.

The above account can only make limited sense if we remain
blind to temporal dynamics and fail to see them as the tissue of
lived experience. [pp. 173–6]

Here, now, is the promised very striking exemplification of a poetic
shift in the emergence of a metaphor (from the earlier "ocean" of the
waves of temporal dynamic), namely in the movement from:

Here, too, a notion of readiness is needed, because suddenly
the full act is executed in a leap.

Of course, here there is a hint of the "leaps" which the skaters have
just been involved in. But in a Shakespearean shift, a piece of genuine poetry, not cliché, the characterisation suddenly emerges from
its dormancy within the image of "leap"—literally, as it were!—in a
fully developed and very graphic metaphor.

The present moment surfaces quickly like a whale breaching
the water's surface.

Now, the event of the hand-contact is also *the present moment*, in Stern's
terms. So there is a sudden shift—like one of Andrew Marvell's

But at my back I always hear
Times winged chariot hurrying near (Marvell, 1681/1984)

*—into the metaphysical or the conceptual.*

The resonance of penetration which I earlier invoked is not at all
gainsaid by this, and the summoning up of an enactment at this
moment is corroborative; the resort to metaphor, in this instance,
is sudden and graphic and has the startling quality of true metaphor ["pity, like a naked newborn babe, striding the blast."[5]] and
as such, *and precisely in its startlingness, enacts the enactment and the
conceptuality it is evoking.*

*In this evocative character of double metaphoric enactment, Stern comes
as near as is possible for him, whilever he does not move into full conceptual
description, to evoking the temporality of enactment.*

Thus he himself *enacts*, as vividly as he can without saying it, the
character of an enactment—for of course the essence of a "present
moment" in Stern's terms has to be an enactment—and it is an

epitome of the task at issue, that he should himself have "leapt" into enactment in this way, in evoking "temporal dynamics", that is, enactment (the whale breaching, with its sheer mass of erotic, animal, metaphoric, mythic—Melville's *Moby Dick*!—and epiphanic resonances). He thus realises his own precept in the most vivid possible way (2004, p. 173):

> We need another language that does not exist (outside poetry)—
> a language that is steeped in temporal dynamics.

In the combination of the conceptual-metaphysical with the concrete in this particular enactment, we also have the element of *literal impossibility* we spoke of earlier (and therefore the impossibility of any "direct" expression of it).

In my terms, Stern has carried out the element of *evocative characterisation*, from the second aspect of the development of a language for temporal dynamics.

[Viz., my earlier remarks:

*Secondly*, the relevant aspect is the *descriptive* task which involves *process-characterising* conceptualisations, which may well also involve *poetic coinage*. This would include both *evocative characterisation*, which this passage mainly illustrates (this, however, is not redundant, and may also be an essential first step), and *technical characterisation*.]

And he has carried it out, though an enactment of his own, *so graphically as to establish the character of what he is talking about*, by default as it were.

I shall now move on to think about what the *technical characterisation* involves, which Stern has only carried so far as a mapping, really, here. Stern, though, has come far, very far, *far enough to have brought into view, in several ways, but especially by the enactment he employs in evoking the temporal dynamics, the phenomena Stepped to characterise*.

But that is not enough, in itself, to establish conclusively that poetic, and the poetic paradigm, is incompatible with any objecthood based paradigm, and the danger remains, apparent also in Stern's work, in my view, of sliding back into covert dependence upon precisely the paradigm from which he sought to emancipate us!

For the most important step in the *technical characterisation* of the nature of poetic, I believe we have to offer it in terms of the concept of *imagination* and analogues of that. Now, these concepts, which I have thus blithely introduced, are, in a sense, only placeholders, until we have seen how they are used; they are the bridging concepts, the Koans, which reach beyond themselves, however difficult to articulate, implicit in the poetic enactment model. To go beyond the objecthood paradigm, we can make progress on this by going to the historical fountainhead himself, fountainhead in the sense that he, who more than anyone else, *set the terms* for the modern science/ extra-science settlement (he *lit the fuse* for the Death of God, in Nietzsche's, 1882/2001, terms), Immanuel Kant, was someone who equally took an extraordinary and revolutionary forward-looking step with the concept of imagination.

The endeavour of overcoming the objecthood paradigm, for instance in the work of Kant, Hegel, Heidegger, Whitehead and Wittgenstein, is so immense, the obstacles opposing it so powerful, tenacious, and so insidious, that the difficulty extends to even the task of accounting for precisely *what* this huge obstacle itself is. No fully consensual account has been achieved, though all of them offer much more than hints, as to why the objecthood paradigm remains so all pervasive, nor is there full consensus as to what the alternative to it is, though there are telling points of overlap. The labour involved in the work of anyone attempting to map a new paradigm, is so intractable, that obscurity seems to descend like the Holy Grail in a mystical cloud upon anyone attempting it, not to mention the liability, in Kant and his successors, for instance (c.f., Heidegger, 1990a), of our backing away from our own deepest insights!

I can only endeavour a glancing tangential "pass" at all this here, for reasons above all of space. What I shall try to establish is:

Firstly, that the technical characterising account of poetic and the poetic paradigm, is *possible*, and can be brought into view,

Secondly, that it takes us into the realm of a new kind of *a priori*, which, as I have said, is compatible with temporality and the event-hood of events, *and which connects the textuality of text with the logic of personhood*.

Thirdly, that it opens the way to gathering together our insights so far gleaned about poetic and psychotherapy process, into formulating a synthesis of the "dimensionality" (past, present, and future) of "temporal dynamics", and Fourthly, that it makes possible a development, in modal-social and temporality-based terms, of the later Freudian metapsychology, which *en passant* draws upon the heritage of the Christian doctrine of the Trinity.

To work our way towards Kant's stunning insights, I begin, then, from one key word and concept central to this whole issue, namely that of *imagination*. TS Eliot, in his pivotal and crucial essay on *The Metaphysical Poets* (1921/1932), gives the following synopsis of the division of the Western mind in the 17th Century (where he, typically cautious, uses the phrase "mechanism of sensibility" instead of the notoriously well-worn one of "imagination", but it is, the word that is not named here, nevertheless his theme!):

> We may express the difference by the following theory: The poets of the seventeenth century, the successors of the dramatists of the sixteenth, possessed a mechanism of sensibility which could devour any kind of experience. They are simple, artificial, difficult, or fantastic, as their predecessors were … In the seventeenth century a *dissociation of sensibility* set in, from which we have never recovered; and this dissociation, as is natural, was aggravated by the influence of the two most powerful poets of the century, Milton and Dryden. Each of these men performed certain poetic functions so magnificently well that the magnitude of the effect concealed the absence of others.

This poetic-historical development was connected with the breakdown of the confidence in the divine right of Kings, the rise of Puritanism and Protestantism, the democratic advance in the 17th Century, the rise of science and technology (the Royal Society was founded in 1660. the year of the Restoration of a—much diminished and rationalised!—monarchy in Britain), and the general surge towards Enlightenment Rationalism. In the context of this emergence—despite Newton's, shared with Leibniz's, own alchemical preoccupations (John Maynard Keynes, 1946, described him as follows:

> Newton was not the first of the age of reason. He was the last of the magicians, the last of the Babylonians and Sumerians, the

last great mind which looked out on the visible and intellectual world with the same eyes as those who began to build our intellectual inheritance rather less than 10,000 years ago. Isaac Newton, a posthumous child born with no father on Christmas Day, 1642, was the last wonderchild to whom the Magi could do sincere and appropriate homage.)

—the world was denuded of its divinity, God was reduced to a rational principle, and the Cartesian separation between rational consciousness and the physical world was carried to a length where the physical, conceived as objecthood, became the criterion of reality.

And so the objecthood paradigm (often, as in Descartes and Spinoza, in the form of the conception, inherited with distortions from Aristotle, of *substance*) gradually assumed a massive dominance, and its dominance was *equated* with the overcoming of religious superstition and enthusiasm. A profound bifurcation took place between conservative-theistic strands in Western culture, and rationalistic-deist or atheistic ones (c.f., Stewart, 2007). Hume's *Essay on Miracles* (in Hume, 1748/2007) rules out testimony for miracles on the basis of a completely circular assumption (an assumption rendered problematic indeed by his own sceptical analysis of causation, and indeed perception, see below, and Hume, 1739–40/1978, Wilkinson, 1999c) of a naturalistic uniformity of nature and evidence (but there is more to this than the circular assumption, as we shall see).

And imagination, accordingly, became identified with excess and irrationalism. Shakespeare, voicing through the dry irony of Theseus, had had a profounder view of imagination, moving from the rationalistic view to something deeper, a classic epitome of poetic creation as *incarnating form from indeterminacy*, the italicised section below, despite himself (Shakespeare, 2005, *A Midsummers Nights Dream V, i.*):

> More strange than true: I never may believe
> These antique fables, nor these fairy toys.
> Lovers and madmen have such seething brains,
> Such shaping fantasies, that apprehend
> More than cool reason ever comprehends.
> The lunatic, the lover and the poet

Are of imagination all compact:
One sees more devils than vast hell can hold,
That is, the madman: the lover, all as frantic,
Sees Helen's beauty in a brow of Egypt:
The poet's eye, in fine frenzy rolling,
Doth glance from heaven to earth, from earth to heaven;
*And as imagination bodies forth*
*The forms of things unknown, the poet's pen*
*Turns them to shapes and gives to airy nothing*
*A local habitation and a name.*
Such tricks hath strong imagination,
That if it would but apprehend some joy,
It comprehends some bringer of that joy;
Or in the night, imagining some fear,
How easy is a bush supposed a bear!

Thus, even Samuel Johnson, despite his own deep Christian alle-
giances, which led him into fierce opposition to Hume (Boswell,
1791/1998), gave an account of rationality and madness in *Rasselas*
(1759/2007), which, brilliantly formulated as it is, and looking for-
wards to Freud (who is indeed very Enlightenment in one of his
myriad identities!), is equally classically Eighteenth Century, and
illustrates Eliot's analysis of the split perfectly. In this example, and
the following one from Hume, I have italicised the manifestation of
the absolutely "imagination"/"reason" dualism in both Johnson and
Hume clear-cut:

> Disorders of intellect, answered Imlac, happen much more
> often than superficial observers will easily believe. Perhaps,
> if we speak with rigorous exactness, no human mind is in its
> right state. *There is no man whose imagination does not sometimes*
> *predominate over his reason* [my italics], who can regulate his
> attention wholly by his will, and whose ideas will come and
> go at his command. No man will be found in whose mind airy
> notions do not sometimes tyrannise, and force him to hope or
> fear beyond the limits of sober probability. All power of fancy
> over reason is a degree of insanity; but while this power is such
> as we can controll and repress, it is not visible to others, nor

considered as any depravation of the mental faculties: it is not pronounced madness but when it comes ungovernable, and apparently influences speech or action.

Philosophically, despite their profound differences of belief, Hume's (1739–40/1978) account of perception gives much the same analytic-functional role to imagination as Johnson's, though in Hume (as indeed elsewhere in Johnson) there are hints of a more positive and purposeful role:

> I believe an intelligent reader will find less difficulty to assent to this system, than to comprehend it fully and distinctly, and will allow, after a little reflection, that every part carries its own proof along with it. 'Tis indeed evident, that as the vulgar suppose their perceptions to be their only objects, and at the same time believe the continu'd existence of matter, we must account for the origin of the belief upon that supposition. Now upon that supposition, 'tis a false opinion that any of our objects, or perceptions, are identically the same after an interruption; *and consequently the opinion of their identity can never arise from reason, but must arise from the imagination* [my italics]. The imagination is seduc'd into such an opinion only by means of the resemblance of certain perceptions; since we find they are only our resembling perceptions, which we have a propension to suppose the same. This propension to bestow an identity on our resembling perceptions, produces the fiction of a continu'd existence; since that fiction, as well as the identity, is really false, as is acknowledged by all philosophers, and has no other effect than to remedy the interruption of our perceptions, which is the only circumstance that is contrary to their identity. In the last place this propension causes belief by means of the present impressions of the memory; since without the remembrance of former sensations, 'tis plain we never shou'd have any belief of the continu'd existence of body. Thus in examining all these parts, we find that each of them is supported by the strongest proofs: and that all of them together form a consistent system, which is perfectly convincing. A strong propensity or inclination alone, without any present

impression, will sometimes cause a belief or opinion. How much more when aided by that circumstance?

But tho' we are led after this manner, by the natural propensity of the imagination, to ascribe a continu'd existence to those sensible objects or perceptions, which we find to resemble each other in their interrupted appearance; yet a very little reflection and philosophy is sufficient to make us perceive the fallacy of that opinion.

Here in Hume is the beginning of the hint of the positive account of the imagination, *as synthesiser of the coherence of our perceptual life*, which then takes on more life in Kant. It then emerges even more emphatically in Hamann, Blake, Coleridge, and Keats, though with loss of Kant's philosophic depth, and then philosophically it comes into its own in Husserl, Whitehead, and Heidegger. To grasp where Kant is on all of this, and how he is wonderfully poised on the cusp between Enlightenment Reasonableness and Romantic Imagination, we need to understand how central providing an account of *science* was to him.

## Part II
### Kant's pioneering evocation of imagination and the social-modal nature of the self

It is Kant who, for the first time, clearly grasps something so radical, in connection with the relation of imagination and science, that we are still struggling with it. For him—*within the citadel itself of that very certainty of the empirical physical world*, which, split off into object-hood, affords the criterion of an objective world apart from the self, and upon which self-certainty of the self is based—there is at the same time a certainty set in place, coming from the other side of the objective–subjective divide, *by means of, and emerging out of, a fundamental requirement of that self.*

This requirement is the thoroughgoing unity of the self's experience, through which alone it can re-identify itself over time, and in time.

*Kant grasps that the requirement of the unity of the self simultaneously makes possible both the objectivity of the physical world, as we experience it, and the continuity of experience and temporality as we know them.* This was a quite extraordinary discovery (the best account of it, and the most gripping, for my money, is Strawson's, in his superb *The Bounds of Sense*, 1966, pp. 97–117). So the physical world, and the objecthood criterion, now cannot be the basis of a split from the experiencing self, but are in some way unified with them. And this unification *turns out to rest upon imagination, which is the index of the overcoming of the split*, and the beginnings of a development into a social concept of the self.

Following Stern, as well as most modern philosophers, we can go on to add that intersubjectivity would nowadays be equally primordially included in that synthesis. Kant accords to imagination, for the first time, a primary *positive* role in this unification of experience (and, in effect, as we shall see, gives an "intersubjective" account of the *internal* relations of the self). When Stern writes (2004), as we have already read:

> They have vicariously been inside the other's body and mind, through a series of shared feeling voyages. They have created an implicit intersubjective field that endures as part of their short history together.

that "vicarious" process is imagination (which incorporates also *mimesis*, c.f., Girard, 1987, and Wilkinson, 2003b, which is, broadly, in psychoanalytic terms, *projective identification*, though these terms are closely related rather than interchangeable). So—allowing for the later steps in philosophy and psychology—we can read Kant with very modern eyes as integrating enactment and propositional truth, science and subjectivity ...

What Kant grasps is the dilemma which, in a way, Hume also grasped, but Kant in a much profounder way: on the one hand, he grasps that science gives us a new means of determining truth which is unheard of previously, namely the experimental method. And, on the other hand, he grasps that this is *accountable at the bar of consciousness*. These twin aspects are grasped simultaneously by Kant. (Whereas for Hume, the connection between them remains unaccounted for.) The experimental method is non-speculative, even though it is hypothetico-deductive.

Kant grasps the nature of the hypothetico-deductive method with a clarity that made Sir Karl Popper recognise him as a clear predecessor, (Popper, 1935/2002):

> When Galileo caused balls, the weights of which he had himself previously determined, to roll down an inclined plane; when Torricelli made the air carry a weight which he had calculated beforehand to be equal to that of a definite column of water; or in more recent times, when Stahl changed metal into lime, and lime back into metal, by withdrawing something and then restoring it, a light broke upon all students of nature. They learned that reason has insight only into that which it produces after a plan of its own, and that it must not allow itself to be kept, as it were, in nature's leading-strings, but must itself show the way with principles of judgment based upon fixed laws, constraining nature to give answer to questions of reason's own determining. Accidental observations, made in obedience to no previously thought-out plan, can never be made to yield a necessary law, which alone reason is concerned to discover. [Kant, 1781/1964]

What underlies the confidence with which Galileo and his successors "put questions to nature"? What had they discovered? However far we are willing, on occasion, to carry philosophical scepticism (c.f., e.g., Hume, 1739–40/1978, Book I, Pt IV, Section vii), we nevertheless cannot help but recognise a difference between those bedrock physical expectations, which carry us forward in our lives and are the bases of our scientific investigations, and speculative *a priori* reasoning, i.e., those which are not in some way correlated with bedrock physical data as the evidential base for enquiry. And by Kant's time, the certainty that the physical world would provide evidence had been gathered in many enquiries. Even then, the steam engine was being developed, and was on the point of being harnessed into a system of transport which would bring to birth the modern world.

The evidential bases for enquiry can be profoundly diverse, and highly recondite; there is nothing to prevent that; and, clearly, in the further reaches of physics and astronomy, and some of the branches of biology, they are indeed so. And they can also be subject to the elusiveness in relation to their evidential base which makes the evolution of science a very open-ended process (c.f., Koestler, 1959, Kuhn, 1962, Pirsig, 1974). And, of course, it is not a matter of its being that there is *not* fundamental and foundational dispute about positions and their analysis in physical science, which fringes over into metaphysics!

Nevertheless, though it is difficult to put into concepts other than the most banal and circular and obvious, we do have a certainty *about the physical evidential basis of science* which we do not have about *any belief generated through the examination of consciousness and experience*. We simply do not have societies and churches founded upon the articles of belief in the sun rising, and the law of gravity! If someone looks as if they are going to jump off a bridge, whatever we may do about it, we don't consider the possibility that perhaps they may not fall down. The neo-Darwinian biologists and the believers in Intelligent Design (ID) are simply arguing past one another, since the latter are not engaging, from the point of view of the former, in serious scientific argument, based on the sort of systematic appeal to specific evidence that science engages in. Much of the discussion is metaphysical-theological argument about origins, much of it a "begging of the question" (for example the ID assumption that where there are indications of "systematic intelligence" in our biological make-up, as there is in respect of genetic structures, and genetic operators and programming systems, in the functioning of organisms, these *have* to be accounted for by conscious design, in parity with, for instance, detective investigations, when it was clearly precisely Darwin's purpose to offer an alternative model of such apparent evidences of design, whether or not the argument succeeds).

Once again, there will be disputes, and Kuhnian issues, in science even about what counts as the evidential base (for example, even in relation to the issues of the paranormal, and also in relation to foundational issues in most of the sciences), but this will still be related to evidential issues in an utterly systematic way.

We indeed think colloquially and jestingly of the Flat Earth Society as the paradigm of holders of a belief system which defies evidence; the Intelligent Design proponents are serious and scientific by comparison. At time of writing (UK Prime Minister's website, 2007) has a disclaimer regarding the teaching of Intelligent Design as science, which is rejected http://www.number-10.gov.uk/output/Page12021.asp and at the same time it is made clear that pupils' questions on this must and will be taken seriously and answered.

We cannot imagine this happening *at all* in relation to the Flat Earth Society!

Not to take this for granted (!), I conscientiously checked, for the record, via Google, websites associated with the Flat Earth belief system. There are indeed several, and to enter them is to enter a mad world (like very much else on the Internet, to be sure) where it is very difficult to tell whether they are serious or spoofs. I realised that I found myself experiencing a sense of madness and destabilisation, as I tried imaginatively to entertain the "Flat Earth" belief system, and at the same time I found myself arguing in my head abjectly and compulsively against the possibility, or the possibility that I might identify with this belief! I also found myself wondering superstitiously and obsessively how many viruses and Trojans had got into my computer as a result of this check, and I found myself feeling ashamed and embarrassed that I had looked at the websites, as if I had been caught looking at pornography!

The Flat Earth Society is a kind of intellectual eclipse of the sun. And I suddenly realised I had thought of that metaphor before I realised its relevant (double-meaning) applicability in this context!

All this illustrates that when it actually comes to *questions of how we hold belief as such*—however rationally unassailable beliefs based upon evidence in the physical realm may be—it is a different matter. That I could find myself being so disconcerted by the impact of mad or eccentric belief systems can only arise because I hold my beliefs, *as beliefs*, in a different way from my "belief", or rather my visceral embodied basic assumption, that I will be hurt if I crash the car into a wall, or that makes me put my hands up reflexly as a cricket ball whizzes towards me. Beliefs are "constructed" in a certain way, in relation to our sense of identity, and this was what Kant was reaching towards.

And when we encounter something that is apparently at odds with our "visceral assumptions", *as they are translated into beliefs*, we find it deeply uncanny or impressive indeed; turning to the example of an actual eclipse (the appositeness of eclipses being reflected in their still-continuing use as metaphor, as above!), the silence of the birds, and the darkening-enshadowing of the land, during a total solar eclipse, are examples which have always haunted the imagination of humankind, and still do, even in the age of science (people do actually cheer, and I with them, total solar eclipses! As if the sun were our friend, as much as it was for an Aztec[6]!)

So *the imaginative organisation of experience*, as articulated into "belief", is the "vulnerable spot" where the certainty of science (something only recently consolidated, in Kant's time, but also deeply founded on far more ancient awarenesses) collides with the disconcerting liability to doubt, and exposure of the uncanny, and to violent anxiety, of consciousness and its underpinnings.

In the light of all this, *Kant implicitly grasped that our human will, in the form of imaginative synthesis, is at the heart of even our most stable and most evidentially based, belief positions or visceral assumptions, and that it must have **already grafted into itself** the basis for such a stability as to enable it to be an identity.*

This became even more fully explicit in Schopenhauer and his successors, but the Enlightenment dilemma comes out in that there is also a greater split, now between "representation" and "will", in Schopenhauer, which Kant integrates by means of the imagination. Kant (1788/1997) had also grasped the specialness of *practical reason*, which connects with his understanding of imagination, and which is implicit in our account of *enactment*.

So Kant connects it fundamentally with identity; in effect, he said that *the stability of my world is the basis of the stability of my identity.* The stability of my world (in early childhood, at the very least, and, in more exceptional circumstances, later) stops me going mad (both Theseus and Samuel Johnson connect imagination fundamentally with the basis of madness). The disconcerting momentary destabilising effect the Flat Earthers had upon me illustrates the point; such an "impossible" belief became uncanny.

*So it was not so "impossible" after all; belief destabilisation is an ever-present possibility. That is why we clutch on to it so anxiously and dogmatically.*

In effect, then, Kant is defining the basis of sanity, and giving us a hidden indication of why it is so precarious—and his account of "imagination" becomes central in this.

Why, then, is Kant himself so certain? Well, *is* Kant so certain? What is he so certain of? Is he so sure, despite that peculiar *magisterial abstractness* of his, his knowledge of the significance of his incomparable synthesis, his grandiose circularity Strawson grasps so well, his "brilliant dryness", as Schopenhauer calls it; I shall quote now a passage, which illustrates this, whilst introducing his use of "imagination" (Kant, 1781/1964):

> *We are conscious a priori of the complete identity of the self in respect of all representations which can even belong to our knowledge, as being a necessary condition of the possibility of all representations.*[italics mine] For in me they can represent something only in so far as they belong with all others to one consciousness, and therefore must be at least capable of being so connected. This principle holds *a priori*, and may be called the transcendental principle of the *unity* of all that is manifold in our representations, and consequently also in intuition. Since this unity of the manifold in one subject is synthetic, pure apperception supplies a principle of the synthetic unity of the manifold in all possible intuition. *This synthetic unity presupposes or includes a synthesis, and if the former is to be a priori necessary, the synthesis must also be a priori. The transcendental unity of apperception thus relates to the pure synthesis of imagination* [italics, mine], as an *a priori* condition of the possibility of all combination of the manifold in one knowledge.

Here the implicit reference to temporality, in "the synthetic unity of the manifold", is apparent, and it turns out, indeed, central to what Kant is doing.

Kant was setting himself the epoch-making task of *reconciling the unassailable certainty of the scientific evidential base, with the highly assailable precariousness and temporality of consciousness*, and there are many signs that he himself *was* exposed to the extreme vulnerability of this process, despite the fact that, on the face of it, *he construes consciousness as the vehicle of certainty*.

The paradox, then, is that he felt he had securely founded, in transcendental analysis (roughly what Strawson, 1959, calls "descriptive metaphysics"), the scientific base, which he rightly saw needed foundations at another level than simply its pragmatic certainty for us, or at least to account for that certainty, precisely in what to us now is rather the quicksand, the quicksand of consciousness!

This is not primarily a personal matter concerning Immanual Kant but a deep indicator of a universal predicament.

First, the introduction of "imagination", illustrated in the quotation above, and to which we shall return, presented as a medium between "intuition" (sense-experience) and "understanding" (the logical conceptualising functions), is radically downgraded between the first and second editions' versions of the *Transcendental Deduction of the Categories*, as if he shrinks back from it.

Secondly, he shows signs of a near-impossible wrestling, with regard to the Transcendental Deduction:

> I know no enquiries which are more important for exploring the faculty which we entitle understanding, and for determining the rules and limits of its employment, than those which I have instituted in the second chapter of the Transcendental Analytic under the title *Deduction of the Pure Concepts of Understanding*. They are also those which have cost me the greatest labour— labour, as I hope, not unrewarded. [Kant, 1781/1964]

(on which Strawson (1966) remarks:

> This thesis, or standard-setting definition [of "experience"] serves as the premise of the Transcendental Deduction of the Categories, that section of the *Critique* which cost Kant, and costs his readers, the greatest labour, being one of the most abstruse passages of argument, as well as the most impressive and exciting, in the whole of philosophy.)

He struggled with the *Critique of Pure Reason* for eleven years, without publishing, after his inaugural dissertation at the University of Konigsberg, of 1770, from the age of forty-six to that of fifty-seven.

Thirdly, there is a huge tension between his aspiration to absolute certainty, and the massively unresolved confusion of the structure he has left us (Strawson, 1966, Bennett, 1966).

Fourthly, he has a great ambivalence about faith and all that goes with it. He mocks the enthusiasm of a brilliant knight of faith like J G Hamann, but nevertheless declares (Kant, 1781/1964):

> I had to deny knowledge, to make room for faith ...

Within three generations, FW Nietzsche had converted this apparent certainty into the scream and howl of our ineffectual attempt to paste a small measure of order upon the cosmic chaos. Was it that all along?

But, fifthly, above all, Kant's solution to the problem *itself* was/is *staggeringly ambivalent*. Let us look at this.

Kant begins boldly with a radical division between sensation and understanding, intuition and intellect:

> In whatever manner and by whatever means a mode of knowl-edge may relate to objects, *intuition* is that through which it is in immediate relation to them, and to which all thought as a means is directed. But intuition takes place only in so far as the object is given to us. This again is only possible, to man at least, in so far as the mind is affected in a certain way. The capacity (receptivity) for receiving representations through the mode in which we are affected by objects, is entitled *sensibility*. Objects are *given* to us by means of sensibility, and it alone yields us *intuitions*; they are *thought* through the understanding, and from the understand-ing arise *concepts*. But all thought must, directly or indirectly, by way of certain characters relate ultimately to intuitions, and therefore, with us, to sensibility, because in no other way can an object be given to us. The effect of an object upon the faculty of representation, so far as we are affected by it, is *sensation*. That intuition which is in relation to the object through sensation, is entitled *empirical*. The undetermined object of an empirical intuition is entitled *appearance*. [Kant, 1781/1964]

There is a strong body of opinion that Kant took a major step *forward* with this distinction, for example, on the apparently formidable basis that sensory states are *items* whereas concepts are *abilities* (to apply *rules*). For instance, Jonathan Bennett, in *Kant's Analytic*, expresses it as follows:

> Not only Spinoza versus Hume, but also Leibniz versus Locke, as Kant saw; "Leibniz *intellectualised* appearances, just as Locke ... *sensualised* all concepts of the understanding." With the possible exception of the chapter on schematism, the *Critique* is completely free from both rationalist and empiricist forms of the conflation of the sensory with the intellectual. It is not hard to see that being in a sensory state differs from having certain linguistic and other skills; but the insight that the distinction between sensory states and concepts is of this sort was an achievement which cannot be truly appreciated until one has read Kant's predecessors. In them we see how beguiling and, up to a point, how astonishingly serviceable is the view that concepts and sensory states are species of a single genus, differing from one another not at all (Berkeley), or differing only in degree of clarity (Descartes), or reliability (Spinoza), or detailedness (Locke), or vividness (Hume). [Bennett, 1966, p. 55]

It was most important historically to make this distinction, which allowed the processes of experience to be objectified and studied (which makes possible and leads on to Husserl's comprehensive emphasis upon *intentionality*), even if not in the form in which Bennett holds it. Clearly he thinks, or has to think, sensory states are *merely* data, *merely* items which are registered in awareness (and psychology of perception an empirical matter), whilst concepts are functions of what Kant would call synthesis.

But some of us would see the distinction in a different way, rather like our earlier distinction between *means of evocation/characterisation*, and the *function* of it in a given instance. Thus *we* would equally see *perception*, with conceptualisation, as an *ability*, which comprehensively is involved in the organisation of experience, and of course, conversely, a thought can be, in context, an historic event, an item ("a thought occurred to me", equally with "an image came into my head", or "I caught a glimpse of him"). We would, then, see the distinction *more in terms of the domains, or the modes, of abilities and psychological potentialities*, and we would see the breakdown of the literal version of the "concepts versus intuitions" distinction as inevitable. And we would see this reflected and developed in the entirety of the role given by Kant to "imaginative synthesis"—which Bennett, with Strawson, dismisses.

Virtually from the outset Kant hints at qualification of the very sharp distinction:

> By way of introduction or anticipation we need only say that there are two stems of human knowledge, namely, *sensibility* and *understanding*, which perhaps spring from a common, but to us unknown, root. Through the former, objects are given to us; through the latter, they are thought. [Kant, 1781/1964]

Now, Heidegger (1990a) makes a case for thinking that *imagination* is indeed this common root. And in the First Edition *Transcendental Deduction of the Categories* Kant does indeed place it between sensibility and understanding (see also the earlier quoted extract):

> If each representation were completely foreign to every other, standing apart in isolation, no such thing as knowledge would ever arise. For knowledge is [essentially] a whole in which representations stand compared and connected. As sense contains a manifold in its intuition, I ascribe to it a synopsis.
>
> But to such synopsis a synthesis must always correspond; receptivity can make knowledge possible only when combined with spontaneity. Now this spontaneity is the ground of a three-fold synthesis which must necessarily be found in all knowledge; namely, the *apprehension* of representations as modifications of the mind in intuition, their *reproduction* in imagination, and their *recognition* in a concept. These point to three subjective sources of knowledge which make possible the understanding itself—and consequently all experience as its empirical product. [Kant, 1781/1964]

And so, finally, we have imagination as the *mediator* between sense and intellect:

> All consciousness as truly belongs to an all-comprehensive pure apperception, as all sensible intuition, as representation, does to a pure inner intuition, namely, to time. It is this apperception which must be added to pure imagination, in order to render its function intellectual. For since the synthesis of imagination connects the manifold only as it appears in intuition, as, for instance, in the shape of a triangle, it is, though exercised a priori, always in itself sensible. *And while concepts, which belong to the understanding, are brought into play through relation of the manifold to the unity of apperception, it is only by means of the imagination that they can be brought into relation to sensible intuition.* [Kant, 1781/1964, my italics]

Kant, like Freud and Stern, is full of dichotomies, which he then subverts. This of intuition and intellect is one of them. Bennett rightly indicates that the role of imagination in relation to understanding flounders around; indeed it does, but, in its partly confused and unresolved way, it indicates also a crucial *chiasma* where a new recognition and way of understanding opens up.

In some sence, it is difficult for us also, to think outside it, to think outside of incoming data manifesting as the first glimmerings of an experience, on the one hand, and an inherent "already-shapedness" of intellectual form and definition, on the other hand. Somewhere in the middle is the mysterious organisation of the whole, *the multi-modal inner dimensionality of the self*, which is at once replicable, and yet has all the uniqueness of the particular moment, something which actually links one aspect of being, and one being, and another aspect of being and another being, with an "internal relation". Freud revisits this whole set of relations in a profoundly subtle way in *A Note on the Mystic Writing Pad* (1925/1984, c.f., Derrida, 1967/1978), on which we shall touch.

Additionally, it is tangled up with a second antithesis, which we now most associate with Piaget, and psychoanalysis, but which is implicit in Kant, between concrete and formal operations (Piaget, 1953). To verify that this is not identical with that between sensory (as understood by Kant and Bennett!) and intellectual, one needs only think of an organist playing a Bach *Passacaglia and Fugue*, or a pianist playing a Chopin *Ballade*, wherein, in both, and any such graphic examples, the inextricable implication of intellectual reflexivity in the spontaneous sensory outpouring is self-evident.

Further, spatial analogies abound in this conceptual terrain!

There is a further related cluster of distinctions involved, which we need not pursue, but which underlie the important tangle of issues Kant encapsulates in the chapter of the *Critique of Pure Reason* entitled *On the schematism of pure concepts of understanding* but normally just known as the *Schematism*. As Heidegger (1990a) noted (and by implication, negatively, Bennett, see above), this is the only passage of the *Critique* where the reference to imagination is *inherent*, and therefore has not been deleted in the Second Edition.

The miracles and prodigies which Kant's invoked concept of "imagination", then, is called upon by him to perform, arise from all this enormous complexity. And as such it is the proxy or place-holder for our concept of poesis and enactment. It is the *reductio ad absurdum* of the absolute separation of experience and rule-governed conceptualisation, of the objectivisation of experience and the world, that (provisional, as we may think of it) division which saved the objectivised world, for Kant.

It is, in effect, the final abolition of the self as a *thing*, abolition of the objecthood model of the self, and is its replacement, implicitly, by the conception of the self as a *society* and a *temporal multi-modal system*. Now we reach again the connection with Stern's notions of *temporal dynamics* and *lived story*, and his now abandoned, but very useful concept—because it best grasps and pinpoints the energic narrative undulations of experience and emotion—of the "proto-narrative envelope of temporal experience" (Stern, 2004, p. 54).

Yet within the heart of all of this Kant had also grasped—and incorporated into and within the heart of the subjective temporal flux—something absolutely inescapable, which in one way or another all philosophers following him have had to build into their systems, even if only in the form Nietzsche gave it, of very deep-rooted biological reflexes:

*Life no argument*—We have arranged for ourselves a world in which we can live—by positing bodies, lines, planes, causes, motion and rest, form and content; without these articles of faith nobody could now endure life. But that does not prove them. Life is no argument. The conditions of life might include error. [Nietzsche, 1882/2001] [Kant, 1781/1964]

*What Kant grasped is that our circular requirement of these things is indeed that, that they are circular because we cannot think or perceive outside of them, because they are themselves the foundational rules of our thinking, and core perception, that they are the "imaginative" belief-basis of our world.*

Even when Wittgenstein and Nietzsche are attempting to dissolve them, they have paradoxically to appeal to a world which is already "given", and have therefore to posit the perpetration of a fundamental error, *being made by our most basic assumptions*, or by our metaphysical hankering for a founded belief, which then has nothing to contrast itself with, an error therefore infecting even the analysis they themselves are making. Nietzsche is certainly aware of the paradox of this[7]. And Wittgenstein, 1969, implicitly returns to this Kantian realisation of radical and inescapable circularity in *On Certainty*.

Kant had grasped *the unitariness of all intentionality*. He had grasped that, even when we dismember that unitariness, our dismembering it is still unitary. Joyce's *Ulysses* is not the contradiction of Kant; it is his apotheosis! The more the mind colonises the realm of the fragmentary and the dissociated and the indeterminate, the more Kant is vindicated. This is the Kant who leads on to Hegel— and not only Hegel, but Nietzsche, Freud, Jung, Husserl, Bataille, Levinas, Derrida:

> For the mind could never think its identity in the manifold-ness of its representations, and indeed think this identity *a priori*, if it did not *have before its eyes the identity of its act* [my italics], whereby it subordinates all synthesis of apprehension (which is empirical) to a transcendental unity, thereby rendering possible their interconnection according to *a priori* rules.

This is the foundation of Descartes, in the *Meditations*, having recognised that even when he doubts his consciousness, it is his consciousness which is doubting. *But Kant takes it into the root and foundation of identity as such, through its relation to time.*

So, then, following Husserl and Augustine, Heidegger (1990a) connects this threefold synthesis which Kant invokes with the three modes of temporality, and we shall return to this in connection with the three aspects of *precommunicability*, *relational field*, and *text and context*, around which I have organised this book.

*Kant grasps that the very precariousness of consciousness, which I spoke of, presupposes at its heart foundational unitary principles of active self-organisation.* And so Kant connects these, in the *Analogies of Experience*, with the very foundations of scientific inference, above all of causality, permanence, and reciprocity in interactions in the world. We may incline further to postulate that he had glimpsed the necessary basis of interconnection between all identity, and thus, in a new way, takes us back to Leibniz and the interconnection of everything, of every identity with every other (Leibniz, 1714/1998, Whitehead, 1929/1979).

In short, he seems to take us back to that mystery of intentionality and reference *of any kind whatsoever*—how does anything refer *at all?*— even that which is most vividly subjective and "immediate", which Wittgenstein expresses in ironically §386. of Wittgenstein, (1967):

> But I do have confidence in myself—I say without hesitation that I have done this sum in my head, have imagined this colour. The difficulty is not that I doubt whether I really imagined anything red. But it is *this*: that we should be able, just like that, to point out or describe the colour we have imagined, that the translation of the image into reality presents no difficulty at all. Are they then so alike that one might mix them up?—But I can also recognize a man from a drawing straight off.—Well, but can I ask: "What does a correct image of this colour look like?" or "What sort of thing is it?"; can I *learn* this?

Wittgenstein asks with ironic incredulity (Wittgenstein, 1967, §428):

> "This queer thing, thought"—but it does not strike us as queer when we are thinking. Thought does not strike us as mysterious

while we are thinking, but only when we say, as it were retrospectively: "How was that possible?" How was it possible for thought to deal with the very object *itself*? We feel as if by means of it we had caught reality in our net.

But this, "catching reality in our net", the temporal *a priori*, is precisely the Rubicon we have to cross! In effect, Kant identifies imagination as the "referring agency", the inherent "social function", which enables one element in the psyche, or the world, to refer to, or be referred to by, another. Imagination becomes Husserl's *intentionality*, and leads forward to many related concepts.

Kant, himself, to be sure, gripped by the objecthood/substance paradigm, thinks that *what comes from outside, what is data, can only be empirical*, (which taken literally would commit him to solipsism!):

> There are only two possible ways in which synthetic representations and their objects can establish connection, obtain necessary relation to one another, and, as it were, meet one another. Either the object alone must make the representation possible, or the representation alone must make the object possible. In the former case, this relation is only empirical, and the representation is never possible *a priori*. This is true of appearances, as regards that [element] in them which belongs to sensation. In the latter case, representation in itself does not produce its object in so far as *existence* is concerned, for we are not here speaking of its causality by means of the will. None the less the representation is *a priori* determinant of the object, if it be the case that only through the representation is it possible to *know* anything *as an object*. [Kant, 1781/1964]

But this does not annul his insight. As A N Whitehead (the modern Leibniz!) writes (1978) of Kant:

> We have now come to Kant, the great philosopher who first, fully and explicitly, introduced into philosophy *the conception of an act of experience as a constructive functioning, transforming subjectivity into objectivity, objectivity into subjectivity: the order is immaterial in comparison with the general idea* [my italics]. We find

the first beginnings of the notion in Locke and in Hume. Indeed, in Locke, the process is conceived in its correct order, at least in the view of the philosophy of organism. But the whole notion is only vaguely and inadequately conceived. The full sweep of the notion is due to Kant. The second half of the modern period of philosophy is to be dated from Hume and Kant.

In our psychotherapeutic jargon of today, Kant was the first fully full-blooded *process thinker*. Now, his very sober—but yet very radical—account of the structure of experience nevertheless matches what the poets were now discovering; it is indeed no accident that Coleridge turned to Kant to ground himself philosophically. But here, perhaps more accessible, is Keats, writing to Benjamin Bailey in November 1817:

> I am certain of nothing but of the holiness of the Heart's affections and the truth of Imagination—What the imagination seizes as Beauty must be truth—whether it existed before or not—*for I have the same idea of all our passions as of love: they are all, in their sublime, creative of essential beauty.* [my italics] In a word, you may know my favorite speculation by my first book, and the little song I send in my last, which is a representation from the fancy of the probable mode of operating in these matters. *The imagination may be compared to Adam's dream—he awoke and found it truth.* [my italics] I am more zealous in this affair because I have never yet been able to perceive how anything can be known for truth by consecutive reasoning—and yet it must be. Can it be that even the greatest philosopher ever arrived at his goal without putting aside numerous objections? However it may be, O for a life of sensation rather than of thoughts! [Keats, 1817a/1947]

In the italicised phrases, Keats sketches dazzlingly a poetic-symbolic theory of the emotions which had to wait for the psychoanalytic era for fuller formulation. *In our language, enactment and the enactive element is more primary than propositional truth and inference, not negating it but incorporating it.*

And so Kant in effect shows that it actually *follows from* propositional truth and inference, from the very citadel of its apparent opposite. He confirms the poesis conception—by the most unexpected route!

The story of very many major philosophers following Kant, is the recognition, in one form or another, of the *enactive-volitional element* as central to our construction of the world, whether as *will* in Kant, Schopenhauer, Nietzsche, (and Freud and Jung), *spirit* in Hegel, *intentionality* in Husserl, *Care* in Heidegger, *I-Thou encounter* in Buber and Levinas, *actualising process* in Whitehead, *forms of life* in the later Wittgenstein, as the *centrality of action, performance, and force of meaning,* in JL Austin, and *deconstruction as enactment* in Derrida. Even positivistically inclined philosophers like Hume, Russell and Santayana end up with something enacted, like Santayana's "animal faith" (Santayana, 1923), as core postulate. Hume writes: reason is, and ought only to be the salve of the passions (Hume, 1739–40/1978).

If we now return to the question of *technical characterisation* we left hanging from the discussion of Daniel Stern, the first thing we can note is that Stern, probably principally through the great influence of Husserl (and Husserl's *intentionality*) upon him, is clearly also carrying out a thinking agenda in this Kantian territory, for, whatever our divergences in the answers we give, there is, at a much deeper level, what Derrida (1967/1978) calls *a community of the question*. He is in effect exploring the Kantian question of how experience is gathered into wholes; his "present moments", among much else, are "critical mass" moments of the enactive crystallisation of gatherings (the moment of holding of hands, in his example, for instance).

Now, this is what Kant is considering in terms of the organisation of experience by means of *a priori* imaginative synthesis. Kant does not offer us an enactment. He offers us a completely general proposition and analysis. But formal propositions and descriptive analyses can offer us an enactment, by virtue of the fields of awareness they activate. In that sense Kant's concise but wide-embracing vision offers enactment with a vengeance! In the formal sense it is completely and solely a technical characterisation—but it opens the doors to the fecund infinitude of the enactments of the poetic psyche!

Here again is his clearest statement of the threefold cat's cradle of self-organisation we are concerned with:

> As sense contains a manifold in its intuition, I ascribe to it a synopsis.

But to such synopsis a synthesis must always correspond; receptivity can make knowledge possible only when combined with spontaneity. Now this spontaneity is the ground of a three-fold synthesis which must necessarily be found in all knowledge; namely, the *apprehension* of representations as modifications of the mind in intuition, their *reproduction* in imagination, and their *recognition* in a concept. These point to three subjective sources of knowledge which make possible the understanding itself—and consequently all experience as its empirical product. [Kant, 1781/1964]

Kant's imaginative synthesis, staggering in its straddling of the otherwise unbridgeable Kantian divide between data, and the conceptual organisation of self-identity, thus corresponds to Jung's *transcendent function* and other polarity-reconciling "third possibility" concepts (c.f., e.g., Jung, 1957, in Jung, 1960). This reference to Jung, like the reference to Joyce, earlier, reminds us that we are actually in the Freudian realm of the "teeming fecundity" of the psyche, in all its infinite multiplicitousness and cross-referencing.

*The understanding of enactment is the understanding that personhood and volition are correlative to, and bound up with, the infinitude of meaning, of the "textuality" of experience.* (Derrida, 1967/1976, p. 158).

The implicit consequence of the recognition of imaginative synthesis is that "there is no such thing as experience", or intuition, in the Kantian sense; the great Koan of Kant's *"a priori* imaginative synthesis" sweeps up everything in its wake, including the temporality of experience and the specificity of all situational process and experience. There is only experience—this was Heidegger's realisation!—in the sense of something *already temporally organised* and gathered up into a living whole. This is neither deducible from anything in advance—thus it makes room for novelty and "the creative advance" (to use a term of Whitehead, 1929/1979)—but nor is it merely contingent. Ever new wholes are constantly creating further ever new wholes, which succeed one another in a process of "pulses" of catastrophic change, (Freud, 1925/1984), but also in a way which incorporates those circular realisations we cannot think behind or beyond. Each whole is an infinite totality which is simultaneously both event, and *a priori*.

Poetry offers us the most accessible paradigm for these wholes and their, reproducible and iterable, processes of succession, that is, for the "language ... steeped in temporal dynamics" (Stern, 2004). We have a quintessential enactment of this in Marvell's *To His Coy Mistress* (also a seduction!), to which we shall come later.

Kant, as we have already seen, thus also likewise implicitly enacts the deep and challenging claim that the rules of consciousness, being wholes, and driven by imaginative synthesis, can "legislate" for the objective world. But by construing this in terms of imaginative synthesis he takes it on forward into the modern scientific world of reciprocal and social causality.

It is not altogether surprising that both Heidegger and Strawson, otherwise so different, heard this hiddenly as *an objective claim*, concerning, in Heidegger's case, disclosure of *the being of beings*—and this is indeed how Heidegger took him in Heidegger (1990a)—and Strawson too, in *The Bounds of Sense* (1966), sweeps aside his transcendental idealism in favour of a plain proof of ordinary objectivity, "leaving the world as it is", a world safe for commonsense—but it is the same logical step, in Strawson's way, as Heidegger took in his way. But it is more plausible, here, to take Kant as leading us, implicitly, back to Leibniz's recognition, mentioned above in connection with the *Analogies of Experience*, and which is expressed in the passage I quoted in the Heidegger chapter, of the co-relatedness of all things:

> Thus, although each created Monad represents the whole universe, it represents more distinctly the body which specially pertains to it, and of which it is the entelechy; and as this body expresses the whole universe through the connexion of all matter in the plenum, the soul also represents the whole universe in representing this body, which belongs to it in a special way. [Leibniz, 1714/1998]

This may seem, to an objectivising world view, an extravagant supposition, but it is that which is implicit in poetry, and in a developed view of Kant's understanding of imagination.

Next, now, we can test and approach this ontological concept of inherent relationality more cautiously, and indirectly roundabout, through a fuller account of the multi-modal character of the self and psyche.

We have here converged with the point Derrida reaches in his consideration of Freud's *A Note on the Mystic Writing Pad* (1925/1984) in *Freud and the Scene of Writing* (in, Derrida, 1978), where he interweaves Freud's construction of psychic process as *text*, and the human perceptual apparatus as a *writing machine*. The enactive relationship between *person* and *text* (in the above widest sense) is now becoming manifest.

We can now also briefly proceed to sketch the beginnings of an answer to whether it is further possible, within the phenomenological-poetic temporality-based framework, to somewhat reconstruct the psychoanalytic concept of the personality and of human development, using the concept "psychoanalytic" in a broad sense to include: Transactional Analysis, Gestalt, and other para-analytic approaches within the equation.

As already hinted, this approach does indeed offer a way of assimilating the later Freudian metapsychology (Freud, 1923/1984) in a way which moves it away from the remnants of Freud's neuro-anatomical model, and which can bring to life the, as always, immense Freudian insight hidden within the metaphors, if it is assimilated as descriptive-enactive phenomenology.

Likewise, it can illuminate the many later variants on the tri-modal conception which Freud pioneered. Klein (arguably), Fairbairn, Lacan, Berne, Karpman, Perls and Goodman, and Bowlby, are some well-known names; I think it is possible to add Jung, though that is a longer discussion!

It is so far from being the case that the Freudian structural model is a dead duck, that it is well-nigh the default model in the humanistic-integrative and relational psychoanalytic sectors of the narrative-relational psychotherapies' community (and arguably Cognitive-Behavioural Therapy as well, c.f., Wilkinson, 2003c), not to mention the self-help culture, and to "overcome (the effects of) introjects/negative internal messages" is seen substantially as the primary task of psychotherapy ("re-parenting", "healing relationship". "the cure by love not insight", "corrective emotional experience", etc.).

The approach I am pursuing brings to life the phenomenological-hermeneutic bases of what Freud has crystallised into a quasi-anatomical model.

The three differentiated modes, which Freud labelled "It", "I", and "Over-I", are realised as metaphoric evocations of *mixed modes* of action and thought, combining enactment-dimensions with knowledge-founding dimensions, within the total expression of the psyche. To give an account of such differentiations within the psyche is to give an account of *intentional potentials* of the psyche, possible patterns of behaviour, impulse, feeling, action, belief, and so on. We have already seen such a conception emerging gradually from Kant's account of imaginative synthesis. The form the differentiations within the psyche take is connected with their reflexive metaphorical self-conceptualisations (the self-superseding spatial metaphoricity of "I", "Over-I", and "It"), which, in poesic mode, *are* the form the psyche takes in its self-manifestation, and therefore primally enable us to apprehend the psyche as aboriginally *poetic* in nature, forged reflexively out of primary bodily modes (Jaynes, 1990, Derrida, 1967/1978), as Freud indeed half-grasped, from *The Interpretation of Dreams* (Freud, 1900/1991) onwards (including his throw-away remark in *The Ego and the Id*, 1923/1984, that the ego is first and foremost a body ego). The self is constituted and enacted, then, irreducibly as metaphor; we are made of words and images, but words and images not merely subjective, but which evoke the infinite world-whole.

Now, these three dimensions/modes, and their metaphoric roots, can be grounded and contextualised within the three dimensions of *pre-communicability*, *relational field*, and *text and context*, which we have identified earlier. When this is done, there emerges a differentiation, which is a kind of *category difference* between the modes, and which does not appear as such in the ordinary accounts of the relations between conscious and unconscious (etc).

This "category difference", as already hinted, is connected with the relationship the different modes have with *human temporality* (c.f., especially, Augustine, 1963, Kant, 1781/1964, Husserl, 1964, Derrida, 1967/1973, Heidegger, 1990, Stern, 2004); even though there is nothing neat in all of this, to make the cross-connection with temporality enables us to substantially account for the category difference we dimly sense is involved here.

The above mentioned very significant writers about it have all, in their own way, grasped the peculiar connection between modes of temporality, and different modes or dimensions of psychic manifestation. Within the psychotherapies, these connections are also made, in partial fashion, particularly by Lacan, and by the Transactional Analysis and Gestalt traditions (though both of these adhere to a pre-Husserlian/Heideggerian concept of time; but Lacan is more complex). It is now well-known what a strong sense of affinity Stern himself has come to have with the Gestalt community (Spagnuolo-Lobb and Amandt-Lyon, 2003).

We can also consider this in the light of the Kantian recognition of the three *Analogies of Experience*, which might, with something of a stretch, be labelled, Permanence=Background ("It", Pre-Communicability); Causal Succession=Change (Over-I, Text and Context, the constitution of the future); and Reciprocity=Relation ("I", Relational Field). This is not an exact fit but it is a hint that there is something relevant in this. The flipping between past and future turns out to be a correlativity.

Again, the "category difference" is connected with the *conceptual* structure of intentionality. This also gives us a kind of Piagetian conceptual criterion of the developmental status, and degree of archaism of the mode in question (Searles, 1965/1993). Here is a connection with the Freud of the concept of the developmental layers of the psyche, who is implicated in the later structural model, but we get a different light on it all by means of the wider context of temporality we are exploring, a difference which has gradually emerged in psychoanalysis, certainly since Klein, with her greater emphasis on "positions" as opposed to "stages". This integrates the enquiry with the developmental insights of both Piaget and Bowlby (c.f., Searles, 1965/1993). The "stages" versus "positions" difference ceases to be as great a one.

I now sketch briefly the (prima facie controversial) correlations:

i. Precommunicability, the "It", the incommunicable immediacy or ground of experience, correlates with the *present*;

ii. The Relational Field, implicated in the "I", the reciprocal, correlates with the *past* (it is the whole mesh we invoke under the rubric of *transference and countertransference*; the master and prototypical analyst of this, and of its conceptual pastness—see below—is Hegel, 1807/1977);

iii. Text and Context, implicated in the "Over-I", the background of *intentional meaning*, the basis of causality and causal inference in the larger sense, correlates with the *future* (in theological terms, the eschatological).

The full working out of these correlations would certainly involve some (hopefully not overly simple-minded, but virtually unavoidable) version of the distinction, drawn in effect by all existential philosophers (including Buber) and psychotherapists (such as Winnicott, 1960, for instance), between an inauthentic relation to experience, and an authentic one. It is doubtful this would be achieved in terms of, for instance, any simply prioritising of one tense or another, or a simple classification of approaches in terms of which tense they favour (Stern, as we have seen indirectly here, is, interestingly, very substantially wedded to this approach, Stern, 2004). The total working out will involve complex relationships of all three tenses.

Figure 1. A generic three-aspect model of the psychotherapy field.

One might *start* with something like the following provisional and speculative analysis, and then see how it breaks down and take it further. I try to take this far enough to give something of the flavour of it, but I do not claim it as definitive, merely suggestive!

DH Lawrence (1921/2007), in the autobiographical character of Birkin in *Women in Love*, in a brief caustic exchange with the Bertrand Russell figure, Sir Joshua Mattheson, nevertheless enunciates an important positive concept:

> "Knowledge is, of course, liberty," said Mattheson.
>
> "In compressed tabloids," said Birkin, looking at the dry, stiff little body of the Baronet. Immediately Gudrun saw the famous sociologist as a flat bottle, containing tabloids of compressed liberty. That pleased her. Sir Joshua was labelled and placed forever in her mind.
>
> "What does that mean, Rupert?" sang Hermione, in a calm snub.
>
> "You can only have knowledge, strictly," he replied, "of things concluded, in the past. It's like bottling the liberty of last summer in the bottled gooseberries."
>
> "Can one have knowledge only of the past?" asked the Baronet, pointedly. "Could we call our knowledge of the laws of gravitation for instance, knowledge of the past?"
>
> "Yes," said Birkin.
>
> Obviously Lawrence, though brilliantly philosophically intuitive, was not the kind of man who would be interested in pursuing the philosophical argument, but one could defend his position by saying that knowledge of scientific laws is causal inference, and thus essentially based upon experience in the past. Hume, (1739–40/1978), Book One, part III, *Of Knowledge and Probability*, is the locus classicus on this, e.g., section vi:
>
> "Tis therefore by EXPERIENCE only, that we can infer the existence of one object from that of another. The nature of experience is this. We remember to have had frequent instances of the existence of one species of objects; and also remember, that the individuals of another species of objects have always attended them, and have existed in a regular order of contiguity and succession with regard to them. Thus we remember,

to have seen that species of object we call flame, and to have felt that species of sensation we call heat. We likewise call to mind their constant conjunction in all past instances. Without any farther ceremony, we call the one cause and the other effect, and infer the existence of the one from that of the other. In all those instances, from which we learn the conjunction of particular causes and effects, both the causes and effects have been perceiv'd by the senses, and are remembered. *But in all cases, wherein we reason concerning them, there is only one perceiv'd or remembered, and the other is supply'd in conformity to our past experience."* [my italics]

Starting dogmatically from this assumption, then what is our relation to present and future? Our whole known and constructed relational world is either actual or putative knowledge of the past—script, in Transactional Analysis terms—or projection from it. We would then *never* conceptually *know* the present as such (and the possibility of immediate unreflective *participation* in an infinite present in mystical experience would simply confirm this). Our *reflexive* awareness of "now" would be a *combination* of the past, and future projection. A striking illustration of this is our Escher picture, which emblematicises any situation, any "culture immune" (Pirsig, 1992) organisation of experience, which we construct utterly inexorably, and reflexly out of awareness—and that includes *all perception*—in accord with past experience and programming! Which also neatly illustrates Kant's "reproduction in imagination":

So, on that assumption, then what would be our relation to the present? In Freudian/Groddeckian terms, the full present (as opposed to the reflexive past-based "I" of which we have just spoken) is "It", which means it is not a subject of experience, but that it is a inference about experience, and an *emergent drive* within experience. Suddenly we get a possible glimpse of what Freud may have been reaching after, *not* the traditional view of the opacity of drive as sheer *impulse*, but the inherent non-experience-ability of drive as the immediate present emergence (which Lacan, e.g., 2004, accordingly relates to the irretrievably *linguistic* forms of realisation of the drives).

When we feel we are in touch with our core in some way, whether in passion or in tranquillity, this is a reflective awareness, though a non-intrusive and contented one. Our relation to immediacy is one—if I may cut through by being permitted the kind of paradox most philosophers wrestling with these issues *do* permit themselves!—of *immediate inference*. This is reflected in the final words of Andrew Marvell's (1681/1984) great, ostensibly anti-eschatological, poem, and affirmation of the here and now (to which we shall return), *To His Coy Mistress*:

> Thus, though we cannot make our sun
> Stand still, yet we will make him run.

That is, we cannot be in the "infinite moment" of the *nunc stans* of the sun standing still, but we can be in the immediacy of living from the energic emerging "now" of living in the moment.

This *is* how we are in touch with our primary emerging "It", our pre-personal being, and *in conceptualising it we give it the conceptual pastness of the "I"*.

Groddeck writes:

> I hold the view that man is animated by the unknown, that there is within him an "Es", an "It", some wondrous force which directs both what he himself does, and what happens to him. The affirmation "I live" is only conditionally correct, it expresses only a small and superficial part of the fundamental principle, "Man is lived by the It". [Groddeck, 1961]

*This, of course, is also our principle of enactment. But we are also lived equally and correlatively by the "texts" and "relational field" we are enacting!*

Freud's "compartmentalisation" of the "It", which, superficially conceived, turned the "It" into a segment, rather than, in a sense, the whole, gave rise to contention between him and Groddeck (Groddeck, 1988, Freud, 1923/1984), but it is by no means as concrete a compartmentalisation as Groddeck perhaps thought, as is confirmed by the extraordinary aphorism (Groddeckian in spirit, and which Lacan considered comparable to the aphorisms of the Pre-Socratics) which is the penultimate sentence of Lecture 31 of the New Introductory Lectures (Freud, 1933/1995):

Wo es war, soll ich werden.

(An approximate translation of this untranslateable sentence might be: "Where It would have been, shall I come into being ...")

"I" is here conceived of in Kantian fashion as a conceptual *process*, not a thing, or a fixed existent. And it is in a fluent reciprocal relation with "It" (which is, further, not reified, not given the definite article, by Freud). So, on this conception of the *New Introductory Lectures* aphorism, "It" is clearly not a wholly irrational reservoir of impulse that has no intrinsic relation to "I", or relationality, as on the caricature understanding of the later metapsychology in, arguably, Fairbairn, for instance (1952/1994), who contrasts the pleasure-seeking, discharge seeking, concept, of his understanding or version of Freud, with his own view that intentionality is object-seeking (relational). I am not, in fairness, saying there is nothing which supports this caricature in Freud, whose position on this oscillates, as it frequently does. But "It" is what it becomes in Groddeck (op. cit.), and also DH Lawrence (e.g., 1921/2007), a kind of non self-reflexive but nevertheless intelligent "subject" or self which is profoundly "embodied".

*So the past in its pastness is conceptual, for us, and the present is an immediate inference based in an embodied grounded feeling.*

A striking confirmation of this is what can be called Proustian memory, on the model of Proust's account of the immediacy of non-intellectual memory, when for instance the "petit madeleine" cake dipped in his tea brings back in an instant the whole world of his childhood (I give the original, then Scott Moncrieff's version):

Et dès que j'eus reconnu le goût du morceau de madeleine trempé dans le tilleul que me donnait ma tante (quoique je ne susse pas encore et dusse remettre à bien plus tard de découvrir pourquoi ce souvenir me rendait si heureux), aussitôt la vieille maison grise sur la rue, où était sa chambre, vint comme un décor de théâtre s'appliquer au petit pavillon, donnant sur le jardin, qu'on avait construit pour mes parents sur ses derrières (ce pan tronqué que seul j'avais revu jusque là) ; et avec la maison, la ville, depuis le matin jusqu'au soir et par tous les temps, la Place où on m'envoyait avant déjeuner, les rues où j'allais faire des courses, les chemins qu'on prenait si le temps était beau. Et comme dans ce jeu où les Japonais s'amusent à tremper dans un bol de porcelaine rempli d'eau, de petits morceaux de papier jusque-là indistincts qui, à peine y sont-ils plongés s'étirent, se contournent, se colorent, se différencient, deviennent des fleurs, des maisons, des personnages consistants et reconnaissables, de même maintenant toutes les fleurs de notre jardin et celles du parc de M. Swann, et les nymphéas de la Vivonne, et les bonnes gens du village et leurs petits logis et l'église et tout Combray et ses environs, tout cela qui prend forme et solidité, est sorti, ville et jardins, de ma tasse de thé. (Proust)

And once I had recognized the taste of the crumb of madeleine soaked in her decoction of lime-flowers which my aunt used to give me (although I did not yet know and must long postpone the discovery of why this memory made me so happy) immediately the old grey house upon the street, where her room was, rose up like the scenery of a theatre to attach itself to the little pavilion, opening on to the garden, which had been built out behind it for my parents (the isolated panel which until that moment had been all that I could see); and with the house the town, from morning to night and in all weathers, the Square where I was sent before luncheon, the streets along which I used to run errands, the country roads we took when it was fine. And just as the Japanese amuse themselves by filling a porcelain bowl with water and steeping in it little crumbs of paper which until then are without character or form, but, the moment they become wet, stretch themselves and bend, take on colour and distinctive shape, become flowers or houses or people, permanent and recognisable, so in that moment all the flowers in our garden and in M. Swann's park, and the water-lilies on the Vivonne and the good folk of the village and their little dwellings and the parish church and the whole of Combray and of its surroundings, taking their proper shapes and growing solid, sprang into being, town and gardens alike, from my cup of tea. (Proust/Scott Moncrieff)

In the moment of Proustian memory—before reflection sets in!—the experience is of the *present*. But in the recollecting reconstruction the presentness has become an *immediate inference* conjoined with the judgement that it is of the past, and at that point it is known again in the mode of reflection.

This is further confirmed by Shakespeare's Sonnet 30, from which Proust's translator Scott Moncrieff felicitously took the English title of *A la recherché du temps perdu*; (I italicise the sentences which bear the point out):

When to the sessions of sweet silent thought
I summon up remembrance of things past,
I sigh the lack of many a thing I sought,
And *with old woes new wail* my dear time's waste;
Then can I *drown an eye, unused to flow*,
For precious friends hid in death's dateless night,
And *weep afresh love's long-since-cancelled woe*,
And moan th' expense of many a vanished sight;
Then can I grieve at grievances foregone,
And heavily from woe to woe tell o'er
The sad account of fore-bemoanèd moan,
*Which I new pay as if not paid before.*
But if the while I think on thee, dear friend,
All losses are restored and sorrows end.
   (Shakespeare, 2005, *Sonnet* 30)

But *Proust's* "recherché" means, not the remembrance, but the actual "recall", the making present, the immediate inference, of the past. I have said enough on this.

But what of the future? And why associate that with Freud's "Over-I", which surely so patently is repetitional script and introjections, derived from the past?

It is the capacity *to be genuinely be open to the future*, which is connected with the capacity for reflexive conceptualisation, which is our implicit developmental criterion. But in so doing it collides with the traumatisation of the past, which re-enacts itself endlessly in the eternal alienated present of recall without reflection. The psychotherapeutic skill of working with trauma is *to enable it to become past*, and thereby be *forgotten*, through connecting it with the possibility of reflection and of metaphorisation (Searles, 1965/1993). The figures associated with those traumatisations are recalled also in an immediate present.

Or rather they are not *recalled*; they remain in the background; they are *other*, and it is the element of "over" or "beyond" of their otherness which makes them so hypnotic, so persecutory, and so endlessly avoided and recoiled from. When they are genuinely recalled, in the Proustian sense, then reflection can ensue, and the experience can become past, and hence concept. This is the valid element in "catharsis" in psychotherapy; more often a partial process of recall and blockage occurs, because of embedded distress, and then "catharsis" is in danger of becoming retraumatisation. From Freud's later letters to Fliess (Freud, 1986), onwards most approaches have realised, on something like this basis, "catharsis is not enough, and sometimes does harm".

What would further need to be accounted for, which there is not the space for here, is the peculiar status of the *transferential* "other", which oscillates on the boundary between the repetitional present, and the unassimilated (refused) unknown, but seeking to be known, "past" (which is not "past"). But note that, classically understood, work in the transference *is the bringing of the repressed, external-situation, past of the client, into the living relational here-and-now of the therapy encounter*, inviting its dissolution from the present/pastness of the transferential, to the neutral just-presentness of the ordinary. It is immediate inference, in the sense I have indicated. This relates to the Lacanian reconstruction of the Subject = Uber-Ich (e.g., Lacan, 1975/1988).

This all relates to the crucial Freudian concepts, (correlated with that of *repression*—*Verdrängung*—which literally means "driving away" or "out"—refusal), of *Verspätung* (delay, deferral, postponement, retardation), and *Nachtraglichkeit* (deferred effect), whose exploration reaches its apotheosis in *Beyond the Pleasure Principle*

(Freud, 1920/1984), and which is so central to the understandings, and cultural concepts and analyses, of Lacan and Derrida (e.g., Derrida, 1967/1978). It connects also, as indicated earlier, in ways which the full concept of future-intentionality would illuminate, with the concrete/metaphorical (reflexive) continuum (Searles, 1965/1993).

The aspirational-intentional process which makes all this possible is the intentionality involved in our grasp of the future. The unconceptualised future to which we are open is the future which is receptive to the emerging present reaching towards it. *Because the future is literally* **not yet**, *it is never conceptualised; and yet it is the foundation of all conceptualisation (which therefore makes possible all knowledge— knowledge inherently of the past, if all this is even partly right).* (This is the basis of the tentative connection with the Second Analogy of Experience, Causal Succession.)

It is involved in something as simple now as anticipating the end of this sentence even as I begin to write it—without which it would be impossible to write it! Kant expresses it, in the remark we have already encountered, in his usual very general and abstract—but dazzlingly clairvoyant!—terms thus:

> For the mind could never think its identity in the manifoldness
> of its representations, and indeed think this identity *a priori*, if
> it did not have before its eyes the identity of its act, whereby it
> subordinates all synthesis of apprehension (which is empirical)
> to a transcendental unity, thereby rendering possible their inter-
> connection according to *a priori* rules. [Kant, 1781/1964]

In the phrase, *"if it did not have before its eyes the identity of its act"*, we immediately grasp that the maintenance of the anticipatory unity is a *future-projective* activity, and that the inherently never-fully-conceptualisable (but also inherently conceptual) future is fundamentally associated with the emergence from the unconceptualisable present, without both of which, the past as past could not be known. Therefore the anticipatory unity of the apprehended future is an inherently *guiding* and textually "infinite" background, to what is accessible from the past, and in the light of the present. These very condensed remarks will have to suffice to convey a glimpse of

*how the future makes possible the guiding function of the "Over-I", even*
*when this is normally manifest in an alienated and past-projected form.*

This third modality is that also of Text and Context. We now
see that there is a deep inner linkage between this, and the
Pre-Communicable as ground, which makes them both together
constitute *enactment* (textual enactment) as we have explored it.
So, here is what Heidegger (1990a, pp. 127–8) says in relation to all
this—not in the most dazzlingly transparent prose!—in *Kant and the*
*Problem of Metaphysics*:

> As empirical, however, this exploring, advancing, synthesis
> of identification necessarily supposes a pure identification.
> That is to say: just as a pure *reproduction* forms the possibility
> of a bringing-forth-again, so correspondingly must pure *rec-*
> *ognition* present the possibility for something like identifying.
> [my italics] But if this pure synthesis reconnoitres, then at the
> same time that says, it does not explore a being which it can
> hold before itself as self-same. Rather, it explores the horizon
> of being-able-to-hold-something-before-us [*Vorhaltbarheit*] in
> general. As pure, its exploring is the original forming of this
> preliminary attaching [*Vorhaften*], i.e., the future. Thus the third
> mode of synthesis also proves to be one which is essentially
> time-forming. Insofar as Kant allocates the modes of taking a
> likeness, reproduction, and prefiguration [*Ab-, Nach- und Vor-*
> *bildung*] to the empirical imagination, *then the forming of the pre-*
> *liminary attaching as such, the pure pre-paration, is an act of the pure*
> *power of the imagination.* [my italics]
>
> Although at the outset it appeared hopeless, even absurd,
> to elucidate the inner formation of the pure concepts as essen-
> tially determined by time, now not only has the time-character
> of the third mode of synthesis beeen brought to light, but also
> this mode of pure pre-paration, according to its inner structure,
> even exhibits a priority over the other two, with which at the
> same time it essentially belongs together. In this Kantian analy-
> sis of pure synthesis in concepts, which is apparently completely
> aloof from time, when exactly does the most original essence ot
> time, i.e., that it is developed primarily from the future, come
> to the fore?

Be that as it may, the task of proving the inner time-character of the transcendental power of imagination, which was undecided, has been accomplished. If the transcendental power of imagination, as the pure, forming faculty in itself forms time—i.e., allows time to spring forth—*then we cannot avoid the thesis stated above: the transcendental power of imagination is original time.* [my italics]

The peculiar and paradoxical three-way aspect of time we have just considered is illustrated, as in an absolute epiphany, by the poem I have quoted, Marvell's (1681/1984) *To His Coy Mistress*. In this poem the three parts (which also have a very Kant-like syllogistic logic to them, yet combined with a sustained systematic ambiguity which expresses the body-soul ambiguity, and which runs all the way through the poem, something which we have seen manifest in Stern's culminating image also, above) express relations to the three modes of temporality as we have been considering them.

The hypothetical eschatological first part is the (eschatological, framework creating, inscribing) future and (in a benign form) the "Over-I". The shock of the remembrance of death in the second part returns us to our "I", and our script-ishly thwarted erotic hankering for relation, and the irreversibility of the past, and to the savage imperatives of the script of eros and thanatos. And the "It" of the body in its urgent emergent, immediately inferred, present, is the last part. One cannot quote less than the whole poem without missing the point:

*To His Coy Mistress*
Had we but world enough, and time,
This coyness, Lady, were no crime
We would sit down and think which way
To walk and pass our long love's day.
Thou by the Indian Ganges' side
Shouldst rubies find: I by the tide
Of Humber would complain. I would
Love you ten years before the Flood,
And you should, if you please, refuse
Till the conversion of the Jews.
My vegetable love should grow
Vaster than empires, and more slow;

An hundred years should go to praise
Thine eyes and on thy forehead gaze;
Two hundred to adore each breast,
But thirty thousand to the rest;
An age at least to every part,
And the last age should show your heart.
For, Lady, you deserve this state,
Nor would I love at lower rate.
But at my back I always hear
Time's wingèd chariot hurrying near;
And yonder all before us lie
Deserts of vast eternity.
Thy beauty shall no more be found,
Nor, in thy marble vault, shall sound
My echoing song: then worms shall try
That long preserved virginity,
And your quaint honour turn to dust,
And into ashes all my lust:
The grave's a fine and private place,
But none, I think, do there embrace.
Now therefore, while the youthful hue
Sits on thy skin like morning dew,
And while thy willing soul transpires
At every pore with instant fires,
Now let us sport us while we may,
And now, like amorous birds of prey,
Rather at once our time devour
Than languish in his slow-chapt power.
Let us roll all our strength and all
Our sweetness up into one ball,
And tear our pleasures with rough strife
Thorough the iron gates of life:
Thus, though we cannot make our sun
Stand still, yet we will make him run. (Marvell, 1681/1984)

The combination of the exploration of self here with an eschatological note is not an accident. As we consider the way in which one mode of the self may be dominant, and another dependent, and yet all of these being aspects of the economy of the total self, we further still glimpse the potential conception of the self as a kind of *conversation* with itself (or even, with a nod to Derrida, as writing, and perhaps *failing to deliver*, a letter, or even a *postcard*, to itself! c.f., Derrida, 1980/1987).

In the human economy this can take on a form which is an exaggeration or extreme of ordinary human possibilities, but perhaps we can begin to consider whether this exaggeration is the exaggeration of a set of possibilities which is *heuristically* perfection-based for human beings, i.e., something which extends a human internal self-*ideal*.

And with this, to end with, we glimpse a startling connection with the Christian doctrine of the Trinity (and perhaps its analogues in other religions, such as Buddhism). I cannot pursue this much further here, but many familiar things, which are foreign bodies otherwise, make sense in the light of this analogy—such as the metaphor and script of omnipotence, self-expected/imposed omnipotence, not possessed omnipotence; omnipotence we experience as an "Over-I" requirement (!), which comes up so often in our work! Tertullian argued that the soul is naturally Christian: *anima naturaliter Christiana*. Perhaps we now, through psychotherapy, have a modern clue to the significance of this.

In short, just as Christian theologians such as Karl Barth construe secular pagan thinkers like Schopenhauer, Nietzsche, Heidegger, and Sartre, as covertly *theistic*, so we may also explore the possibilities, that, if the human psyche may be covertly divine, also the postulated divine psyche may be covertly *human* (the later Barth talked more and more inclusively of "the humanity of God"), and, indeed, that the divine and human may be correlated, in some sense, in the cosmic co-existence. And then come before us, either the radical *anthropocentricity* of the concepts of God and the Incarnation in, for instance, Schleiermacher and Pannenburg, or the radical *modalism* of Karl Barth's doctrine of the Trinity, in which the three persons of the Trinity are construed as *modes* of God, rather as we have conceived the three aspects as modes of a person. I shall illustrate from the latter, Karl Barth, as a more radical expression of what I am saying.

Our sense of the structural analysis of the person widens out from where Freud left it, to include the kind of analysis we get from Hegel, Husserl, or Heidegger, in whom the quasi-divinity or specialness, of the form of human existence in the world, is taken to give us the structural basis for a kind of secular divinisation of the human—or at least an analysis of human existence from which it is ostensibly possible to make sense of, or provide an analogue for, the belief in God.

Can we now mediate by invoking the three mode conception of human experience? The "I" as the medium of relation, and the intentionality of relation (the "Son"); the "It" as the dimension of pre-communicability and the ground of existence (the "Holy Spirit"); and the "Over-I" as the realm of meaning, of text, law, injunction, rationality, intelligibility and so on ("the Father"): does this work? I think it is arguable this does work as a comprehensive account in terms of an existential-phenomenological paradigm, and it does create a context in which the narrower framework of Freud's more concrete analysis can be assimilated.

Now, there is a hint of a solution in the element Karl Barth, (I think) partly misses in the logic of the Trinity (Barth, 1932/1936), since his insistence is to move the differences he identifies back towards an absolute identity (on the basis of God's complete autonomy of being), which will be seen at the end of the passage I am about to quote. For what he misses is the divine parallel to the human modal solution, which does emerge in terms of the Freudian analysis, and which is that *because of temporality, the modes are structurally, ontologically, different, asymmetrical, different in relation to intentionality, and that is what makes it possible for them to be in relation.* If there is an identity, it is in this difference. This, in turn, as we have seen, connects with the irreducibility and irreversibility of human temporal intentionality. Here, also, is the link across between Freud's analysis, and my existential extension of it. When we allow the metaphors to emerge, we realise that we need an existential-phenomenological temporality-based *grounding of the differences*. Does that perhaps connect with the heuristic infinitisation also?

Here is one of Barth's formulations of his modal analysis of the modes of being within God as three in one and one in three; a long quotation is necessary to get the long-spanned stride of Barth's thinking (Barth, 1932/1936, p. 418):

> Of course, God's real modes of existence cannot be read off
> from the varieties in content, of these and similar conceptual

ternaries. For everything here distinct in content must be thought of as being in its variety sublimated once more to the unity of the divine essence. But they can certainly be read off from the *regularly recurring mutual relations of the three concepts respectively*, as they are most simply to be found between the concepts Father, Son, and Holy Spirit themselves. On these relations is founded God's threeness in oneness. This three-ness consist in the fact that in the essence or act in which God is God there is first a pure origin and then two different issues, the first of which is to be attributed solely to the ori-gin, the second, different in kind, to the origin and likewise to the first issue. According to Scripture, God is manifest, He is God, in such a way that he is Himself in these relation-ships to Himself. He is His own producer and he is in a dou-ble and quite distinct respect His own product. He possesses Himself as Father, i.e., as pure Giver; as Son, i.e., as Receiver and Giver; as Spirit, i.e., as pure Receiver. He is the begin-ning, without which there is no Middle and no End; the Mid-dle, which can only exist by starting from the Beginning and without which there would be no End; the End, which starts absolutely and utterly from the Beginning. He is the Speaker, without which there is no Word and no Meaning; the Word which is the Speaker's Word and the bearer of the Meaning; the Meaning which is as much the Meaning of the Speaker as of His Word. But let us be on our guard against the zone of *vestigia trinitatis* on which we have already almost trespassed. The *alius-alius-alius* representable in such different ternaries does not signify an *aliud-aliud-aliud*; One and the Same may be This and That in the truly corresponding determinations of these original relations, without ceasing to be the One and the Same; and each of these original relations as such is at the same time the One in whom these relations occur—to these facts there are no analogies, this is the unique divine three-ness in the unique divine oneness.

Barth could probably not allow such an irreversible differentiation, without violating his sense of the unity and the perfection of God? Be that as it may, *we* are free to play with the suggestion it contains.

And of course he does manage anyway to include an element of irreversibility in his account!

In what follows I am going to briefly talk about God in "real existence" language without indicating the "As if" dimension—however, I am still suspending judgement; I am just permitting myself to explore freely without inhibiting my use of language and concept, and then appraise the implications of what emerges. I do not have space here to explore the full implications of the "human-divine" concept that emerges[8].

God is right here now. In us. *We* are God. But God is also our absolute Otherness to ourselves. We are *each other*—in the mode of *difference*. We are in touch with the totality resource of the entire universe. But we neither own God nor ourselves. Humility is part of the deal—an axiom (though one our narcissism makes it hard to sustain). God is It (Holy Spirit), God is I (Christ), God is Over-I (God the Father). And I am It, I am I, I am Over-I[9].

The implication could, then, as a first effort, be put that *modal relation is God*. Primordial Relation in *this* sense encompasses also pre-communicability and text and context—all three dimensions of human being-and-time. God is not outside, but is, or is at least the correlate of, the totality of the relational whole. *This is what Barth is saying in relation to God as Trinity* (although man is asymmetrically excluded in Barth's concept), and in this respect, although he does not unequivocally articulate the asymmetry within the reciprocal identity, *he is on the edge of the recognition of intrinsic relation*. He also includes time in God, but (unlike Whitehead, 1979) he does not go so far as to include God in time!

The three aspects of relation are, together, the divinity of relation, including the nothingness and alienation of relation, and its incompleteness as it addresses the future. Metaphoricity, textuality, is revealed as the correlate of relation and personhood, and as intrinsic to its articulation; constructivism, considered as a derivative of relation (i.e., a mere correlate of relation, merely relativity), is objectively false, but constructivism, *as intrinsic to the self-articulation of the related psyche*, is true; we are self-constructs, actualisations, of ourselves! Relation encompasses both veiling and unveiling; truth and falsehood; light and shadow and darkness, and also is intrinsically implicated in the temporal. Here we fringe onto the territory of Jung's Gnostic challenge to Christian orthodoxy, and that of Heidegger's account of the intrinsic absence (or, ambiguously, self-absenting!) of the divine, and, again, that of Buddhism's "no self" doctrine (and Hume's, 1739–40/1978); and at that tantalising point I shall end this essay.

This articulation of the social-modal self, with its radical relational implications, is only one instance of many potential applications of this psychotherapeutic implication of the enactive role we have identified with poetry in human existence.

We can end with Shelley's bold, and both rather Heideggerian and very Nietzschean, claims for poetry, but nevertheless well exemplified in the account I have given of Shakespeare, *in which the future's summoning the present and past is held to be the very essence of what constitutes poetry* (Shelley, 1840/2004):

> The most unfailing herald, companion and follower of the awakening of a great people to work a beneficial change in opinion or institution, is Poetry. At such periods there is an accumulation of the power of communicating and receiving intense and impassioned conceptions respecting man and nature. The persons in whom this power resides, may often as far as regards many portions of their nature have little apparent correspondence with that spirit of good of which they are the ministers. But even whilst they deny and abjure, they are yet compelled to serve, the Power which is seated on the throne of their own soul. It is impossible to read the compositions of the most celebrated writers of the present day without being startled with the electric life which burns within their words. They measure the circumference and sound the depths of human nature with a comprehensive and all penetrating spirit, and they are themselves perhaps the most sincerely astonished at its manifestations, for it is less their spirit than the spirit of the age. Poets are the hierophants of an unapprehended inspiration, *the mirrors of the gigantic shadows which futurity casts upon the present* [my italics], the words which express what they understand not, the trumpets which sing to battle and feel not what they inspire: the influence which is moved not, but moves. Poets are the unacknowledged legislators of the World.

## Notes

1 Including in my view, Husserl, Heidegger, Sartre, Merleau-Ponty, the later Wittgenstein, and the positivist-empiricists, such as Russell, AJ Ayer, and WVO Quine, and also AN Whitehead. The position of people who *apparently* repudiate phenomenalism in favour of commonsense, such as GE Moore, PF Strawson and JL Austin, is difficult to ascertain; I would myself argue that, even in them, there is a covert idealism which does not get named or fully articulated. But that must remain an opinion.

2 What is the difference between a rock and a stone? We find some *huge stones* on Dartmoor, whilst the children were throwing *small rocks* at the fat boy on his way home from school. The subtle difference is not solely a matter of size! There is some hint about stones being a bit more detached or detachable than rocks. Stones have entered the human world a little more than rocks. We throw *stones* on to someone's coffin when they are buried, not *rocks*. So by bringing them both in Wordsworth is at any rate invoking the spectrum between the less human and more elemental, and the more human and less simply elemental. So there is some differentiation amidst the duplication. This is just a start. I believe that the more we worked at this choice of words, the more we would discover.

3 A most powerful example is in De Quincey's analysis (1823), in which he "reverses" the conventional judgement of the matter under discussion, of *On the Knocking on the Gate in Macbeth*:

Or, if the reader has ever been present in a vast metropolis, on the day when some great national idol was carried in funeral pomp to his grave, and chancing to walk near the course through which it passed, has felt powerfully in the silence and desertion of the streets, and in the stagnation of ordinary business, the deep interest which at that moment was possessing the heart of man—if all at once he should hear the death-like stillness broken up by the sound of wheels rattling away from the scene, and making known that the transitory vision was dissolved, he will be aware that at no moment was his sense of the complete suspension and pause in ordinary human concerns so full and affecting, as at that moment when the suspension ceases, and the goings-on of human life are suddenly resumed. All action in any direction is best expounded, measured, and made apprehensible, by reaction. Now apply this to the case in Macbeth. Here, as I have said, the retiring of the human heart, and the entrance of the fiendish heart was to be expressed and made sensible. Another world has stepped in; and the murderers are taken out of the region of human things, human purposes, human desires. They are transfigured: Lady

Macbeth is "unsexed;" Macbeth has forgotten that he was born of woman; both are conformed to the image of devils; and the world of devils is suddenly revealed. But how shall this be conveyed and made palpable? In order that a new world may step in, this world must for a time disappear. The murderers, and the murder must be insulated—cut off by an immeasurable gulf from the ordinary tide and succession of human affairs—locked up and sequestered in some deep recess; we must be made sensible that the world of ordinary life is suddenly arrested—laid asleep—tranced—racked into a dread armistice; time must be annihilated; relation to things without abolished; and all must pass self-withdrawn into a deep syncope and suspension of earthly passion. Hence it is, that when the deed is done, when the work of darkness is perfect, then the world of darkness passes away like a pageantry in the clouds: the knocking at the gate is heard; and it makes known audibly that the reaction has commenced; the human has made its reflux upon the fiendish; the pulses of life are beginning to beat again; and the re-establishment of the goings-on of the world in which we live, first makes us profoundly sensible of the awful parenthesis that had suspended them.

O mighty poet! Thy works are not as those of other men, simply and merely great works of art; but are also like the phenomena of nature, like the sun and the sea, the stars and the flowers; like frost and snow, rain and dew, hail-storm and thunder, which are to be studied with entire submission of our own faculties, and in the perfect faith that in them there can be no too much or too little, nothing useless or inert—but that, the farther we press in our discoveries, the more we shall see proofs of design and self-supporting arrangement where the careless eye had seen nothing but accident!

4 Compare a similar system of assumptions when Wittgenstein, in §244/5 of *Philosophical Investigations* (PI, hereafter) writes:

How do words refer to sensations?—There doesn't seem to be any problem here; don't we talk about sensations every day, and give them names? But how is the connection between the name and the thing named set up? This question is the same as: how does a human being learn the meaning of the names of sensations?—of the word "pain" for example? Here is one possibility: words are connected with the primitive, the natural, expressions of the sensation and used in their place. A child has hurt himself and he cries; and then adults talk to him and teach him exclamations and, later, sentences. They teach the child new pain behaviour.

"So you are saying that the word "pain" really means crying?—On the contrary: the verbal expression of pain replaces crying and does not describe it."

5 Shakespeare, *Macbeth*, Act I, Sc. 7.

6 Mel Gibson's film *Apocalypto* about Aztec or Mayan imperialism graphically features a total eclipse of the sun as the miracle moment which results in the hero being spared from human sacrifice.

7 For example, *The Gay Science* (Nietzsche, 1974) §54.

> *The consciousness of appearance.*— How wonderful and new and yet how gruesome and ironic I find my position vis-à-vis the whole of existence in the light of my insight! I have *discovered* for myself that the human and animal past, indeed the whole primal age and past of all sentient being continues in me to invent, to love, to hate, and to infer—I suddenly woke up in the midst of this dream, but only to the consciousness that I am dreaming and that I *must* go on dreaming lest I perish: as a somnambulist must go on dreaming lest he fall. What is "appearance" for me now! Certainly not the opposite of some essence—what could I say about any essence except to name the attributes of its appearance! Certainly not a dead mask that one could place on an unknown X or remove from it! Appearance is for me that which lives and is effective and goes so far in its self-mockery that it makes me feel that this is appearance and will-o'-the-wisp and a dance of spirits and nothing more—that among all these dreamers, I, too, the "knower," am dancing my dance, that the knower is a means for prolonging the earthly dance and thus belongs to the masters of ceremony of existence, and that the sublime consistency and interrelatedness of all knowledge perhaps is and will be the highest means to *preserve* [*aufrecht zu erhalten*] the universality of dreaming and the mutual comprehension of all dreamers and thus also *the continuation of the dream*.

8 Charles Hartshorne, in *The Divine Relativity* (1964) fleshes out a relational-personal conception of God most fully. I personally think we do need a concept of the divine, for many reasons, but that Spinoza was right in thinking in terms of the God our reason leads us to is impersonal—and non-moral—in a variety of ways. This is not to deny more active "God" or "gods" elements in the cosmos at a subsidiary level.

9 C.f., Heinlein's *Stranger in a Strange Land* (2007).

# CHAPTER SIX

# Epilogue: The Poetry and Politics of Psychotherapy

This book has certainly been as much about poetry and literature, and philosophy, as it has been about psychotherapy.

Some might wonder why I have not presented a great deal of detailed material from therapy sessions, which would corroborate my claim in detail. The quick answer is that I would not have got this book written in five years if I had pursued this path! Having attained a degree of clarity, I wanted to get the cardinal principles out into the field quickly, and this the book as it stands achieves. This is certainly something I would like to do at a later point, or which others can do.

But, as a matter of principle, nor, I believe, would it actually bring the key insights into view. It would have been an implicit concession to empiricism in the way of presenting evidence, and my point, precisely, is that we can grasp the poetic paradigm of therapy as a matter of principle and understanding, without a mass of empirical data.

It is not like showing that, for instance, depression is always triggered by rejection. The latter, implicit in Freud's *Mourning and Melancholia* (1917/1984), is to be corroborated, to the extent that it can be, by a mixed methodology of hermeneutic elucidation and understanding of the introjective process, and corroboration by means of masses of empirical data. But the connection *could be elucidated at the level of meaning* in a single case, if we remain at the level of a personal experience of meaning, as Freud indeed discovered in his Case Histories. And from that, secondarily, we can form social science hypotheses.

Showing that we *can* elucidate a psychotherapeutic process in terms of the poetic paradigm is enough in itself; it is a purely hermeneutic claim and not an empirical one. To demonstrate it on a mass of data would certainly amplify the claim, and would give it a richness and detail which would strengthen it as a methodology. But it would only do that. It is to be *established* by *examples* and this I have done.

I have also taken a large, extended, psychotherapeutic-literary, detour through Heidegger and Shakespeare, before returning to the fundamental philosophical articulation of poesis as enactment in the fifth chapter. I enter their world-envisagement within their own frameworks of reference, deconstructively, in order firstly to reveal the "literary-interpretative order", the textual order, implicit in Heidegger, and then secondly to reveal how thinking about Shakespeare, in enough depth, dissolves the traditional antithesis between text and world, in favour of an *enactment* in which both the author, and we as enquirers, are inescapably implicated.

Finally I, in effect, returned to psychotherapy by showing, or trying to show, that by elucidating the nature of textual enactment philosophically, passing through Kant's philosophical conception of imagination, we eventually reach the recognition of an existential-cosmological conception of the temporal self in its severalfoldness, which draws developmental psychology, as traditionally conceived, into itself, within the framework of an existential conception of the self as totality. This at the same time encompasses the range of psychoanalytic insights as a reservoir of valuable frameworks.

The poetic conception is a Koan, which leads on through Kant's world-creating imagination as a Koan, to the threefold temporal self as a Koan! It is as rich, and as chargedly multiplex, in its own way, though abstract, as Joycean enactment (Joyce, 1922/2000):

> and the sentry in front of the governors house with the thing
> round his white helmet poor devil half roasted and the
> Spanish girls laughing in their shawls and their tall combs

and the auctions in the morning the Greeks and the jews and the Arabs and the devil knows who else from all the ends of Europe and Duke street and the fowl market all clucking outside Larby Sharans and the poor donkeys slipping half asleep and the vague fellows in the cloaks asleep in the shade on the steps and the big wheels of the carts of the bulls and the old castle thousands of years old yes and those handsome Moors all in white and turbans like kings asking you to sit down in their little bit of a shop and Ronda with the old windows of the posadas glancing eyes a lattice hid for her lover to kiss the iron and the wineshops half open at night and the castanets and the night we missed the boat at Algeciras the watchman going about serene with his lamp and O that awful deepdown torrent O and the sea the sea crimson sometimes like fire and the glorious sunsets and the figtrees in the Alameda gardens yes and all the queer little streets and pink and blue and yellow houses and the rosegardens and the jessamine and geraniums and cactuses and Gibraltar as a girl where I was a Flower of the mountain yes when I put the rose in my hair like the Andalusian girls used or shall I wear a red yes and how he kissed me under the Moorish wall and I thought well as well him as another and then I asked him with my eyes to ask again yes and then he asked me would I yes to say yes my mountain flower and first I put my arms around him yes and drew him down to me so he could feel my breasts all perfume yes and his heart was going like mad and yes I said yes I will Yes.

This is a vision which does not reduce psychotherapy to philosophy or to literature, but nor does it reduce philosophy or reduce literature; *it is a vision of an interconnected whole*. It is incommunicable unless one has already apprehended it, but *if one has*, or if the penny / dime drops, it can be elucidated and articulated, which is what I have tried to do, both at the level of specific meaning and that of meta-level principle.

*Because it does not give psychotherapy or psychology primacy*, it makes it possible to reduce (though hardly eliminate) in our work the patronising diagnostical evangelism which pervades so much of psychotherapy and counselling, and which is strongly, though not entirely, associated with a scientistic and (in a narrow sense) evidence-preoccupied approach to the field.

Because it has no one "knowledge-centre" it reduces our clutching at the security of some positive foundation or another, and it seriously places an unknowing, and a scepticism about itself, and its own basis for praxis at the heart of our work, which makes it possible—sometimes! Occasionally!—to *notice the very difficult to notice*, and *that which will not be noticed without the humility to be open to the unexpected.*

But also, by drawing psychotherapy into relation with deeply traditional creative arts, it legitimises psychotherapy as a melting pot of creativity and transformative incubation, which can be applied in an indefinitely wider context, without becoming totatilitarian (Wilkinson, 2002).

At this point, I wanted originally to say something at some length about the political implications of this approach, and I shall still do so briefly, and somewhat dogmatically.

Over the last twenty years I have supported and assisted the efforts of what is now the United Kingdom Council for Psychotherapy (UKCP), to generate a process which would move the Profession of Psychotherapy towards Statutory Regulation. In contrast to the political beliefs of our colleagues in the Independent Practitioners' Network (c.f., e.g., Mowbray, 1995, Postle, 2007), whose *values* in many ways I share and honour, I have pursued this, not because I think it will bring the greater good in some Utopian way, but because it is the lesser evil, in my view.

I believe that the concerted effort which has been made, by what is now UKCP, for over twenty five years, to protect and legitimise, on a pluralistic basis, the whole range of the psychotherapies and of psychopractice, has resulted in a healthy increase in both tolerance and scepticism and multi-disciplinary enquiry within the profession as a whole. I believe it has created a culture within the profession at large, where the more absurd psychotherapeutic and psychoanalytic dogmatisms and cultisms are not quite as easy to mount as they used to be, and where it is more possible to be thoughtfully reflective, in a psychotherapeutically informed way, than it used to be, without being dismissed out of hand by what one might call the

"Paxman" tendency (in the UK, Jeremy Paxman being a notoriously stand-and-deliver interviewer of politicians) in public commentators and interviewers. Of course, it is partly offset by a new conformism and correct-ism, but I also believe it has raised the profile and the general awareness of the Profession, in a way which is, on balance, helpful.

In our Statist world, I do not myself believe we would be able to achieve that kind of influence without working towards legitimising ourselves in the State's eyes. I think that a much more restrictive alternative would have come to pass, upon the basis of a fully medical paradigm and institutional foundation, which would have eliminated official recognition of a whole multitude of rich practices which it has proved almost certainly possible to protect and nurture. I believe that the movement within the non-medical care professions, and indeed the professions generally, towards regulation, has been too powerful and pervasive in our world, for it to be practicable to ignore it.

So, for me, its really a matter of, if you cant *stop* 'em, join 'em!

I don't believe the form of regulation which is likely to come to pass will by any means achieve all that we would have wished from it, but I believe that, as it beds down, it will preserve, we will preserve, sufficient of the diversity we would want to maintain, that non-reductive psychotherapy practice will be able to continue.

I also now think that, as a result of the concerted work which has been over the years, my current endeavour of *posing an alternative paradigm for psychotherapy based in poetry and the arts, not in the sciences*, is not as absurd seeming or quixotic as it once would have seemed. Of course the powerful movement to scientise psychotherapy will continue, and the advances in neuroscience and similar fields will buttress that. But, as Daniel Stern's work, and Allan Schore's work, in particular, illustrates (whatever my theoretical arguments with Stern himself), *the awareness of the richer phenomenology of human selfhood is ever-increasing*, and is having to be taken into account in the neuroscientific investigations which are going ahead.

In such a climate, the emphasis on the poetry of human selfhood and human creativity will be indispensable.

How does your patient, doctor?

DOCTOR: Not so sick, my lord,
As she is troubled with thick-coming fancies,
That keep her from her rest.

MACBETH: Cure her of that.
Canst thou not minister to a mind diseased,
Pluck from the memory a rooted sorrow,
Raze out the written troubles of the brain,
And with some sweet oblivious antidote
Cleanse the stuff'd bosom of that perilous stuff
Which weighs upon the heart?

DOCTOR: Therein the patient
Must minister to himself. (*Macbeth*, V, 3)

No longer! for Asclepios is the son of Apollo!

It is indeed timely to turn to poetry now, to correct the one-sidednesses of medicine, to correct the one-sided ministrations of psychological science, but also because, thus, we can enjoy a psychotherapy which is a creative servant of life and laughter and love.

# BIBLIOGRAPHY

Ackroyd, P. (2005). *Shakespeare: The Biography*. London: Chatto and Windus.

Anderson, M. (2005). *"Shakespeare" by Another Name: The Life of Edward De Vere, Earl of Oxford, the Man Who Was Shakespeare*. New York: Gotham Books/Penguin Groups, USA.

Andersen, H.C. (1837/2004). *The Emperor's New Clothes*. Boston: Houghton Mifflin Company.

Anonymous (1605). *The True Chronicle History of King Leir and His Three Daughters*. Available online at *Elizabethan Authors*: http://www.elizabethanauthors.com/king-leir-1605-1-16.htm>

Armourer's Hall Website, online at:
http://www.armourersandbrasiers.co.uk/history_hall.htm

Aron, L. (1996). *A Meeting of Minds: Mutuality in Psychoanalysis*. New York: Analytic Press.

Asimov, I. (1996). *The Robots of Dawn*, New York: Harper Collins.

Asimov, I. (1982). *Foundation's Edge*. London: Grafton.

Asimov, I. (1986). *Robots and Empire*. London: Grafton.

Ashcroft, P. (unknown date). *BBC Television Interview* of unknown date.

237

Augustine (unknown date/1963). *Confessions*. Trans. R Warner. New York: Penguin.

Austin, J.L. (1961). A Plea for Excuses. In: J.O. Urmson & G.J. Warnock (Eds.), *Philosophical Papers*. London: Oxford University Press.

Austin, J.L. (1962a). *How to do Things with Words*. London: Oxford University Press.

Austin, J.L. (1962b). *Sense and Sensibilia*. London: Oxford University Press.

Ayer, A.J. (1948). Phenomenalism. *Proceedings of the Aristotelian Society*, 47:163–196.

Ayer, A.J. (1954). *Philosophical Essays*. London: Macmillan.

Bacon, F. Francis Bacon website, online at: http://home.hiwaay.net/~paul/shakspere/evidence1.html

Barrell, C.W. (1941–2). *"Shake-speare's" Own Secret Drama: Discovery of Hidden Facts in the Private Life of Edward de Vere, Proves Him Author of the Bard's Sonnets*. First published in Shakespeare Fellowship Newsletter, 1941–2. Online in Shakespeare Authorship Sourcebook at: http://www.sourcetext.com/sourcebook/library/barrell/05Sonnets1.htm

Barrell, C.W. (1944). *Matinee at the Swan: A Topical Interlude in Oxford-Shakespeare Research*. First published in the Shakespeare Fellowship Quarterly. Published online in *The Shakespeare Authorship Sourcebook* at: http://www.sourcetext.com/sourcebook/library/barrell/21–40/21swan.htm

Barth, K. (1932/1936). *Church Dogmatics Vol I. 1. Prologemena to Church Dogmatics, The Doctrine of the Word of God*. Trans. G.T. Thomson. Edinburgh: T. and T. Clark.

Bateson, G. (1979). *Mind and Nature: A Necessary Unity*. Cresskill: Hampton Press.

Beckett, S. (1953). *Waiting for Godot*. London: Faber and Faber.

Berlin, I. (2000). *Three Critics of the Enlightenment: Vico, Hamann, Herder*. London: Pimlico.

Berney, C.V. (2007). *Listening to The Winter's Tale:* Presented as the keynote address at the Fourth Dutch Shakespeare Authorship Conference, Utrecht, the Netherlands, 8 June 2007.

Biesser, A. (1970). Paradoxical Theory of Change. In: J. Fagan & I.L. Shepherd (Eds.), *Gestalt Therapy Now*. New York: Harper Colophon Books.

Bion, W.R. (1970). *Attention and Interpretation*. Tavistock Publications.

Blake, W. (1977). *Complete Poems of William Blake*. London: Penguin.

Bloom, H. (1998/1999). *Shakespeare: The Invention of the Human*. London: Fourth Estate.

Bowen, G. (1965). *Hackney, Harsnett, and the Devils in Lear*. First published in *Shakespearean Authorship Review*, online in *Shakespeare Authorship Sourcebook* at: http://www.sourcetext.com/sourcebook/library/bowen/16hackney.htm

Bowen, G. (1966). *Sir Edward de Vere and His Mother Anne Vavasour*. First published in *Shakespearean Authorship Review*, online in *Shakespeare Authorship Sourcebook* at: http://www.sourcetext.com/sourcebook/library/bowen/17vavasor.htm

Boswell, J. (1791/1998). *Life of Johnson*. Oxford: Oxford University Press.

Brin, D. (2000). *Foundation's Triumph*. New York: Harper Collins.

Buber, M. (1923/1958). *I and Thou*. Edinburgh: T. and T. Clark.

Carlyle, T. (1838/1999). *Sartor Resartus*. Oxford: Oxford University Press.

Chambers, E.K. (1930/1989). *William Shakespeare: A Study of Facts and Problems*. London: Oxford University Press.

Chambers, E.K. (1945). *English Literature at the Close of the Middle Ages*. London: Oxford University Press.

Chomsky, N. (1957). *Syntactic Structures*. The Hague/Paris: Mouton.

Clark, R. (1994). Asimov's Laws of Robotics: Implications for Information Technology, Internet Site: http://www.anu.edu.au/people/Roger.Clarke/SOS/Asimov.html#Zeroth

Coleman, D. (2005). *The Poetics of Psychoanalysis: Freudian Theory Meets Drama and Storytelling*. Tarentum: Word Association Publishers.

Coleridge, S.T. (1817/1983). *Biographia Literaria*. Edited by J. Engell, and W. Jackson Bate. Princeton: Princeton University Press.

Danby, J. (1949). *Shakespeare's Doctrine of Nature: 'King Lear'*. London: Faber and Faber.

De Quincey, T. (1823/2006). *On the Knocking at the Gate in Macbeth*. In: R. Morrison (Ed.), *On Murder*. Oxford: Oxford University Press.

Derrida, J. (1967/1973). *Speech and Phenomena and Other Essays on Husserl's Theory of Signs*. Evanston: North Western University Press.

Derrida, J. (1967/1976). *Of Grammatology*. Trans. G.C. Spivak. Baltimore: Johns Hopkins University Press.

Derrida, J. (1967/1978). *Writing and Difference*. London: Routledge.

Derrida, J. (1972/1983). *Dissemination*. Trans. B. Johnson. Chicago: University of Chicago Press.

Derrida, J. (1980/1987). *The Postcard: from Socrates to Freud*. Trans. A Bass. Chicago: University of Chicago Press.

Derrida, J. (1988). *Limited Inc.* Evanston: Northwestern University Press.

Derrida, J. (1987/1989). *Of Spirit: Heidegger and the Question*. Trans. G. Bennington and R. Bowlby. Chicago: University of Chicago Press.

de Vere, (1571). *Letter of Introduction to Bartholomew Clerke's Translation of Castiglione's The Courtier.*

Elizabethan Authors website: http://www.elizabethanauthors.com/vere106.htm (30th October, 1584) *Letter from Oxford to Lord Burghley*, online at: Oxford Authorship Site: http://www.oxford-shakespeare.com/oxfordsletters1-44.html#15 (27th April, 1603) *Oxford's letter to Robert Cecil on the death of Elizabeth (27th April 1603)*, online at: Oxford Authorship Site, found at: http://www.oxford-shakespeare.com/oxfordsletters1-44.html#42

Dickens, C. (1854/1994). *Hard Times*. London: Penguin.

Dickens, C. (1857/2003). *Little Dorrit*, London: Penguin.

Donne, J. (1941). *Complete Poetry and Selected Prose*. London: Nonesuch Press; New York: Random House.

Dostoievski, F.M. (1880/2003). *The Brothers Karamazov*. Trans. D. McDuff. London: Penguin.

Dover Wilson, J. (1932). *The Essential Shakespeare: A Biographical Adventure*. Cambridge: Cambridge University Press.

Dryden, J. (1668). *An Essay of Dramatick Poesy*, edited by J. Lynch, online: http://andromeda.rutgers.edu~jlynch/Texts/drampoet.html

Durkheim, E. (1995). *The Elementary Forms of the Religious Life*. London: Simon & Schuster.

Ekeland, T.-J. (1997). The healing context and efficacy in psychotherapy: psychotherapy and the placebo phenomenon. *International Journal of Psychotherapy*, 2 (1): 77–87.

Eliot, T.S. (1921/1932). The Metaphysical Poets. In: *Selected Essays*. London: Faber and Faber.

Eliot, T.S. (2004). *Complete Poems and Plays*. London: Faber and Faber.

Eliot, T.S. (1920/1932). Tradition and the Individual Talent. In: *Selected Essays*. London: Faber and Faber.

Fairbairn, W.D.R. (1952/1994). *Psychoanalytic Studies of the Personality*. London: Routledge.

Farias, V. (1989). *Heidegger and Nazism*. Philadelphia: Temple University Press.

Freud, S. (1900/1991). *Interpretation of Dreams*. London: Penguin.

Freud, S. (1913/1990). The Theme of the Three Casket. In: *Art and Literature*, Penguin Freud Library Vol. 14. London: Penguin.

Freud, S. (1917/1984). Mourning and Melancholia. In: *Papers on Metapsychology*, Penguin Freud Library Vol. 11. London: Penguin.

Freud, S. (1920/1984). Beyond the Pleasure Principle. In: *Papers on Metapsychology*, Penguin Freud Library Vol. 11. London: Penguin.

Freud, S. (1923/1984). The Ego and the Id. In: *Papers on Metapsychology*, Penguin Freud Library Vol. 11. London: Penguin.

Freud, S. (1925/1984). A Note on the Mystic Writing Pad. In: *Papers on Metapsychology*. London: Penguin.

Freud, S. (1933/1995). *New Introductory Lectures on Psychoanalysis*. New York: W.W. Norton.

Freud, S. (1939/1967). *Moses and Monotheism*. London: Tavistock Press.

Freud, S. (1986). *The Complete Letters of Sigmund Freud to Wilhelm Fliess, 1887–1904*. Edited by J.M. Masson. Cambridge: Harvard University Press.

Finley, M.I. (1999). *The Ancient Economy*, 2nd Edition. Berkeley: University of California Press.

Gardner, Sir L. (1999). In The Realm of the Ring Lords. In: *Nexus Magazine*, Volume 6, Number 6 (October November 1999), http://www.nexusmagazine.com/articles/ringlords2.html

Gendlin, E. (1997). *Experiencing and the Creation of Meaning*. Evanston: Northwestern University Press.

Girard, R. (1987). *Things Hidden Since the Foundation of the World*. Stanford: Stanford University Press.

*Geneva Bible* (1560/1599/2007). White Hall: Tolle Lege Press.

Green, Nina *Phaeton*, Private (by invitation) Email Forum.

Greene, R. (1592). *Groatsworth of Wit Bought with a Million of Repentance*, published online in *The Oxford Authorship Site*: http://www.oxford-shakespeare.com/groatsworth.html

Groddeck, G. (1961). *The Book of the It*. Edited by L. Durrell. New York: Vintage.

Groddeck, G. (1988). *The Meaning of Illness: Selected Psychoanalytic Writings, including Correspondence with Sigmund Freud*. Edited by G. Mander. London: Karnac Books.

Grunbaum, A. (1992). *The Foundations of Psychoanalysis: A Philosophical Critique*. Berkeley: University of California Press.

Harris, F. (2004). *The Man Shakespeare and His Tragic Story*. Boston: Adamant Media Corporation.

Hartshorne, C. (1964). *The Divine Relativity: A Social Conception of God*. New Haven: Yale University Press.

Harvey, G. (1580). *Speculum Tuscanismi*. Available at Harvey on Elizabethan Authors website: http://www.elizabethanauthors.com/harvey101.htm

Hegel, G.W.F. (1807/1977). *Phenomenology of Mind*. Trans. A.V. Miller, with commentary by J.N. Findlay. Oxford: Clarendon Press.

Hegel, G.W.F. (1840/1955). *Lectures on the History of Philosophy*. London: Routledge and Kegan Paul.

Heidegger, M. (1927/1967). *Being and Time*. Trans. J. Macquarrie & E. Robinson. Oxford: Blackwell.

Heidegger, M. (1981). *Basic Problems of Phenomenology (Studies in Phenomenology and Existential Philosophy)*. Trans. A. Hofstadter. Bloomington and Indianapolis: University of Indiana Press.

Heidegger, M. (1982). *The Question concerning Technology and other Essays*. New York: HarperCollins Publishers.

Heidegger, M. (1990a). *Kant and the Problem of Metaphysics (Sudies in Continental Thought)*. Trans. R. Taft. Bloomington and Indianapolis: Indiana University Press.

Heidegger, M. (1990b). *Nietzsche: Vols 3 and 4*. New York: HarperCollins Publishers.

Heidegger, M. (1931/1995). *Aristotle's Metaphysics 1–3. On the Essence and Actuality of Force*. Bloomington and Indianapolis: Indiana University Press.

Heidegger, M. (2001). The Origin of the Work of Art. In: *Poetry, Language, Thought*. New York: HarperCollins Publishers.

Heidegger, M. (2005). *Sojourns: The Journey to Greece*. New York: State University of New York Press.

Heinlein, R. (2007). *Stranger in a Strange Land*. London: Hodder and Stoughton.

Heron, J. (2001). *Helping the Client: A Creative-Practical Guide*. London, Sage Books.

Hess, L.R. (2002). *The Dark Side of Shakespeare: An Elizabethan Courtier, Diplomat, Spymaster, & Epic Hero*. New York: Writers Club Press.

Hobson, R.F. (1988). *Forms of Feeling: the Heart of Psychotherapy*. London: Routledge.

Honigmann, E.A.J. (1985). *Shakespeare: The Lost Years*. Manchester: Manchester University Press.

Hopkins, G.M. (1948). *Poems of Gerard Manley Hopkins. Third Edition*, edited by W.H. Gardner. London: Oxford University Press.

Hume, D. (1739–40/1978). A Treatise of Human Nature. In: J. Selby-Bigge (Ed.). Oxford, Oxford University Press.

Hume, D. (1748/2007). Of Miracles. In: S. Buckle (Ed.), *An Enquiry Concerning Human Understanding and Other Writings*. Cambridge: Cambridge University Press.

Hunt, R.T. (2007). *Merchant of Venice is not attacking usury*, personal communication.

Husserl, E. (1964). *The Phenomenology of Internal Time Consciousness*. Trans. J.S. Churchill. Bloomington: University of Indiana Press.

Husserl, E. (1977). *Cartesian Meditations: An Introduction to Phenomenology*. Norwell and Dordrecht: Kluwer Academic Press.

Jaynes, J. (1990). *The Origins of Consciousness in the Breakdown of the Bicameral Mind*. London: Penguin.

Johnson, S. (1759/2007). In: P. Goring (Ed.), *The History of Rasselas, Prince of Abyssinia*. London: Penguin.

Johnson, S. (1765/1958). Preface to Shakespeare. In: W. Raleigh (Ed.), *Johnson on Shakespeare*. London: Oxford University Press.

Jonson, B. (1623/1981). *To the Memory of My Beloved, The Author Mr William Shakespeare: and What He Hath Left Us*. In: G. Parfitt (Ed.), *Ben Jonson, The Complete Poems*. London: Penguin.

Joseph, B. (1989). *Psychic Equilibrium and Psychic Change: Selected Papers*. Edited by M. Feldman and E. Bott-Spillius. London: Routledge.

*Journal of Poetry Therapy*. London: Taylor and Francis. http://www.tandf.co.uk/journals/titles/08893675.asp

Joyce, J. (1922/2000). *Ulysses*. London: Penguin.

Jung, C.G. (1956). *Symbols of Transformation,*. London: Routledge and Kegan Paul.

Jung, C.G. (1957/1960). On Psychic Energy. The Transcendent Function. A Review of the Complex Theory, in *The Structure and Dynamics of the Psyche*. London: Routledge.

Kant, I. (1788/1997). *Critique of Practical Reason*. Edited and translated by M.J. Gregor. Cambridge: Cambridge University Press.

Kant, I. (1781/1964). *Critique of Pure Reason*. Trans. N. Kemp Smith. London: Macmillan.

Keats, J. (1817a/1947). Saturday, 22nd Nov., 1817 Letter 31. To Benjamin Bailey. In: M.B. Forman (1947 Ed.), *The Letters of John Keats* (p. 72). London: Oxford University Press.

Keats, J. (1817b/1947). Sunday, 21 Dec., Letter 32. To G. and T. Keats. In: M.B. Forman (1947 Ed.), *The Letters of John Keats* (p. 72). London: Oxford University Press.

Keats, J. (1818/1977). On Sitting Down To Read King Lear Once Again. In: *The Complete Poems of John Keats*. London: Penguin.

Keats, J. (1818/1947). Tuesday, 27th October, 1818. Letter to Richard Woodhouse, (1947 Ed.). *The Letters of John Keats* (p. 227–8). London: Oxford University Press.

Keats, J. (1819a/1947). Friday, 19th March, 1819, Letter 123, to George and Georgiana Keats, (1947 Ed.). *The Letters of John Keats* (p. 316). London: Oxford University Press.

Keats, J. (1819b/1947). Wednesday, 9th June, 1819, Letter 128, to Miss Jeffrey, (1947 Ed.). *The Letters of John Keats* (p. 347). London: Oxford University Press.

Keynes, J.M. (1946). Newton the Man. Lecture given posthumously to the Royal Society for Science, London, in 1946. Available online at: http://www-groups.dcs.st-and.ac.uk/~history/Extras/Keynes_Newton.html

Köchele, H. (2004). Seminar on the Evidence for Psychoanalytic Method. Oral Presentation at the Meeting of European Association for Psychoanalytic Psychotherapy, Llubljana, Slovenia. October, 2004.

Koestler, A. (1959). *The Sleepwalkers: A Study of Man's Changing Vision of the Universe*. London: Penguin.

Kuhn, T. (1962). *The Structure of Scientific Revolutions*. Chicago: The University of Chicago Press.

Lawrence, D.H. (1990). *Studies in Classic American Literature*. London: Penguin.

Lawrence, D.H. (1997). *Twilight in Italy*. London: Penguin.

Lawrence, D.H. (1921/2007). *Women in Love*. London: Penguin.

Lacan, J. (1975/1988). *Seminar on Freud's Papers on Technique, 1953–54*. Edited by J.-A. Miller. Trans. J. Forrester. Cambridge: Cambridge University Press.

Lacan, J. (2004). *Four Fundamental Concepts of Psychoanalysis*, Edited by J.-A. Miller. London: Karnac Books.

Leavis, F.R. (1948). *The Great Tradition*. London: Chatto and Windus.

Leavis, F.R. (1962). *Two Cultures? The Significance of C P Snow*. London: Chatto and Windus.

Leavis, F.R. (1969). *English Literature in our Time and the University*. London: Chatto and Windus.

Leavis, F.R. (1975). *The Living Principle: 'English' as a Discipline of Thought*. London: Chatto and Windus.

Leavis, F.R. (1948/1972). *The Great Tradition*. London: Penguin.

Leavis, F.R. (1995). *Essays and Documents*. Edited by MacKillop, I.D., & Storer, R. Sheffield: Continuum International Publishing Group.

Leavis, F.R., & Leavis, Q.D. (1970). *Dickens the Novelist*. London: Chatto and Windus.

Leibniz, G.W. (1714/1998). Monadology. In: *G.W. Leibniz: Philosophical Texts*. Oxford: Oxford University Press.

Lévi-Strauss, C. (1966). *The Savage Mind*. Chicago: University of Chicago Press.

Ligon, K.C. (2006). Useful Article on King Lear, posted online on Shakespeare Fellowship Discussion forum: http://www.shakespearefellowship.org

Looney, J.T. (1920). *"Shakespeare" identified in Edward de Vere, the seventeenth Earl of Oxford*. London: C. Palmer.

Looney, J.T. (1921). *The Poems of Edward de Vere*. Jennings, La.: Minos Pub. Co.

MacDougall, J. (1986). *Theatres of the Mind: Illusion and Truth in the Psychoanalytic Stage*. London: Free Association Books.

Maguire, K. (2002). Working with Survivors of Torture and Extreme Experiences. *Journal of Critical Psychology, Counselling, and Psychotherapy*, 2 (4): 247–260.

Mair, M. (1989). *Between Psychology and Psychotherapy: A New Poetics of Experience*. London: Routledge.

Malan, D.H. (1979/1995). *Individual Psychotherapy and the Science of Psychodynamics*. London: Hodder Arnold.

Manningham, J. (1976), *The Diary of John Manningham of the Middle Temple 1602–1603*. Edited by R.B. Sorlien. Hanover (NH): University Press of New England.

Margison, F. (1999). *Obituary of Robert Hobson*. The Guardian, November 29th, 1999 at: http://www.guardian.co.uk/obituaries/story/ 0,3604,252220,00.html

Marks, R.G. (1995). *Cordelia, King Lear, and His Fool*. Online at: http://users.bigpond.net.au/catchus/chapters.html

Marvell, A. (1681/1984). *To His Coy Mistress* in *Complete Poems*. London: JM Dent and Sons.

Mason, H.A. (1967). King Lear: Radical Incoherence, part III. *The Cambridge Quarterly*, II (3): 212–235.

May, S. (1980). The poems of Edward de Vere, seventeenth Earl of Oxford and of Robert Devereux, second Earl of Essex. In *Studies in Philology*, 77: 1–132. Chapel Hill: University of North Carolina Press.

Melville, H. (1986). *Billy Budd and Other Stories*. London: Penguin.

Moore, G.E. (1939). Proof of an External World. *Proceedings of the British Academy* 25: 273–300. Reprinted in, (1959), *Philosophical Papers*. London: George Allen and Unwin.

Mowbray, R. (1995). *The Case Against Psychotherapy Registration: A Conservation Issue for the Human Potential Movement*. London: Transmarginal Press.

Mulhall, S. (2005). *Heidegger and Being and Time*. New York: Routledge.

Mystica Encyclopaedia, (no date) *Entry on Horned Celtic god Cernunnous*, online at: http://www.themystica.com/mystica/articles/c/cernunnous.html

Nelson, A. (2003). *Monstrous Adversary: The Life of Edward de Vere, 17th Earl of Oxford*. Liverpool: University of Liverpool Press.

Nelson, A. (undated). *Oxford the Deadbeat Dad*, on Alan Nelson's website: http://socrates.berkeley.edu/~ahnelson/oxdad.html

Nietzsche, F.W. (1872/1999). *The Birth of Tragedy and Other Writings*. Edited by R. Geuss and R. Speirs. Cambridge: Cambridge University Press.

Nietzsche, F.W. (1983/2006). *Thus Spake Zarathustra*, Trans. A Del Caro. Cambridge: Cambridge University Press.

Nietzsche, F.W. (1882/2001). *The Gay Science*, Edited by B. Williams, Trans by J. Nauckhoff and A. Del Caro, Cambridge: Cambridge University Press.

Nietzsche, F.W. (various/2005). *The Anti-Christ, Ecce Homo, Twilight of the Idols, and other writings*. Edited by. A Ridley and J. Norman. Trans. J. Norman. Cambridge: Cambridge University Press.

Nietzsche, F.W. (1952/In Press). *My Sister and I*. Los Angeles: AMOK Books.

Nissim-Sabat, M. (2005). Book Review of: *The Present Moment in Psychotherapy and Everyday Life*, by Daniel N. Stern, Retrieved 22nd October 2007: http://mentalhelp.net/poc/view_doc.php?id= 2540&type=book&cn=28

Ogburn, C. (1988). *The Mystery of William Shakespeare*. London: Cardinal.

Orwell, G. (1990). *Nineteen Eighty Four*. London: Penguin.

Oxford Authorship Site, (Nina Green), found at: http://www.oxford-shakespeare.com/

Piaget, J. (1953). *The Origins of Intelligence in Children*. London: Routledge and Kegan Paul.

Pirsig, R. (1974). *Zen and the Art of Motorcycle Maintenance*. London: The Bodley Head.

Pirsig, R. (1992). *Lila: An Enquiry into Morals*. London: Bantam Press.

Popper, K. (1935/2002), *The Logic of Scientific Discovery*. London: Routledge.

Postle, D. (2007). *Regulating the Psychological Therapies—From Taxonomy to Taxidermy*. Ross-on-Wye: PCCS Books.

Pottle, F. (1950). Introduction to *Boswell's London Journal 1762–1763*. London: Heinemann.

Prechter, Robert R. (2005). The Sonnets Dedication Puzzle. *Shakespeare Matters: The Voice of the Shakespeare Fellowship*, 4 (3): 1–2.

Presley, E. (1956). *Heartbreak Hotel*, Words & music by Mae B. Axton, Tommy Durden, Elvis Presley.

Price, D. (2001). *Shakespeare's Unorthodox Biography: New Evidence of an Authorship Problem*. London: Greenwood Press.

Proust, M. (1922). *Remembrance of Things Past*. Trans. CK Scott Moncrieff. London: Chatto and Windus.

Quine, W.V.O. (1951/1961). On What There Is. III in, *Aristotelian Society Supplementary Volume*, 25: 149–160. Third part of Freedom, Reality, and Language: Aristotelian Society and The Mind Association joint session at Edinburgh, July 6–8, 1951 symposium on On What There Is with Peter Geach (pp. 125–136) and A.J. Ayer (pp. 137–148), reprinted in *From a Logical Point of View*. (1961), Cambridge: Harvard University Press.

Quine, W.V.O. (1969). On Austin's Method. In: *Symposium on J.L. Austin*, Ed. K.T. Fann. London: Routledge, pp. 86–90.

Ricoeur, P. (1970). *Freud and Philosophy: An Essay on Interpretation*. New Haven: Yale University Press.

Rilke, R.M. (1990). *The Notebooks of Malte Laurids Brigge*, trans. S. Mitchell. New York: Random House.

Rowan, J. (2001). Therapy as an alchemical process. *International Journal of Psychotherapy*, 6 (3): 273–288.

Rowse, A.L. (1973). *Shakespeare the Man*. London: Macmillan.

Ryle, G. (1963). *The Concept of Mind*. London: Penguin Books.

Sams, E. (1995). *The Real Shakespeare: Retrieving the Early Years*. New Haven and London: Yale University Press.

Santayana, G. (1923). *Scepticism and Animal Faith*. New York: Charles Scribners Sons.

Searles, H.F. (1965/1993). The differentiation between concrete and metaphorical thinking in the recovering schizophrenic patient. In *Collected Papers on Schizophrenia and Related Subjects*. London: Karnac Books.

Shelley, P.B. (1818/1999). Ozymandias. In *The Complete Poetry of Percy Bysshe Shelley*, Edited by D.H. Reiman and N. Fraistat. Baltimore: Johns Hopkins University Press.

Shelley, P.B. (1840/2004). *A Defence of Poetry and Other Essays*. Whitefish: Kessinger Publishing Co.

Shakespeare Fellowship Website, found at: http://www.shakespearefellowship.org/

Shakespeare Authorship Source Page, found at: http://www.source-text.com/sourcebook/index.htm

Shakespeare, W. (2005). *William Shakespeare: The Complete Works*, Edited by S Wells, G Taylor, J Jowett, and W Montgomery. Oxford: Oxford University Press.

*Shakespeare in Love*. (1998). Film directed by John Madden.

Spagnuolo-Lobb, M., Amendt-Lyon, N. (2003). *Creative License: the Art of Gestalt Therapy*. New York: Springer.

Speanser, E. (1589/1924). *Poetical Works of Edmund Spenser*. Edited by J.C. Smith and E. de Selincourt. London: Oxford University Press.

Stern, D.N. (1985). *The Interpersonal World of the Infant*. New York: Basic Books.

Stern, D.N. (1995). *The Motherhood Constellation: A Unified View of Parent-Infant Psychotherapy*. London: Karnac.

Stern, D.N. (2004). *The Present Moment: in Psychotherapy and Everyday Life*. New York: W.W. Norton.

Stewart, A. (2007). *The Courtier and the Heretic: Leibniz and Spinoza and the Fate of God in the Modern World*. New York: W.W. Norton.

Strawson, P.F. (1959). *Individuals*, London: Methuen.

_____ (1966). *The Bounds of Sense*. London: Methuen.

Thomasson, A.L. (2002). Phenomenology and the Development of Analytic Philosophy. *Southern Journal of Philosophy*, Vol. XL (2002) Supplement: 115–142. (Proceedings of the 2001 Spindel Conference 'Origins: The Common Sources of the Analytic and Phenomenological Traditions').

Trevor-Roper, H. (1962). Article on Shakespeare in *Realites* November 1962, cited in Ogburn 1988.

Trilling, L. (1965/1967). *Beyond Culture: Essays on Literature and Learning*. London: Penguin.

UK Prime Minister's Website (2007) *UK Prime Minister's Guidance on Teaching Intelligent Design Theory*, June 2007, found at: http://www.number-10.gov.uk/output/Page12021.asp

Webbe, E. (1590). *Travels*, excepted at Nina Green's Oxford Authorship website at: http://www.oxford-shakespeare.com/new_files_june_14_04/Webbe_1590_Palermo.pdf

Welsh, A. (2003). A King Lear of the Debtors Prison: Dickens and Shakespeare on Mortal Shame. *Social Research: An International Quarterly of Social Sciences Issue*, 4 (70): 1231–1258.

Whitehead, A.N. (1929/1979). *Process and Reality: An Essay in Cosmology*. Edited by D.R. Griffin & D.W. Shelburne. London: Macmillan, The Free Press.

Wilde, O. (1891/2004). *The Picture of Dorian Gray*. London: Penguin.

Wilkinson, H. (1998). 'Phenomenological causality: and why we avoid examining the nature of causality in psychotherapy: a dialogue'. *International Journal of Psychotherapy*, 3 (2): 165–182.

Wilkinson, H. (1999a). Schizophrenic process, the emergence of consciousness in recent history, and Phenomenological causality: the significance for psychotherapy of Julian Jaynes. *International Journal of Psychotherapy*, 4 (1): 49–66.

Wilkinson, H. (1999b). Psychotherapy, fascism and constitutional history. *International Journal of Psychotherapy*, 4 (2): 117–126.

Wilkinson, H. (1999c). Pluralism as Scientific Method in Psychotherapy'. *International Journal of Psychotherapy*, 4 (3): 313–328.

Wilkinson, H. (2000a). An inspired resurrection of Freudian drive theory: but does Nick Totton's Reichian 'bodymind' concept supersede Cartesian dualism? *International Journal of Psychotherapy*, 5 (2): 153–166.

Wilkinson, H. (2000b). Editorial: To know or not to know: science, beliefs and values in psychotherapy. *International Journal of Psychotherapy*, 5 (2): 93–102.

Wilkinson, H. (2002). Retrieving a Posthumous Text Message: Nietzsche's Fall; the significance of the disputed asylum writing, My Sister and I. *International Journal of Psychotherapy*, 7 (1): 53–68.

Wilkinson, H. (2003a). The shadow of Freud: is Daniel Stern still a psychoanalyst? The creative tension between the present and the past in psychoanalytic and existential psychotherapies. In: *Daniel Stern's The Present Moment, and His Humanistic Existential Partners in Dialogue*. In: M. Spaniolo Lobb, & N. Amendt-Lyon, (Eds.), review article on Daniel Stern's 'The Present Moment: In Psychotherapy and Everyday Life' and 'Creative License: the art of Gestalt Therapy'. *International Journal of Psychotherapy*, 8 (3): 235–254.

Wilkinson, H. (2003b). Review article: Psychoanalysis as finite, psychoanalysis as infinite? Psychoanalysis' religious potential. *International Journal of Psychotherapy*, 8 (2): 147–168.

Wilkinson, H. (2003c). The autonomy of psychotherapy—Why psychotherapy can be subordinate neither to psychology nor psychiatry. *International Journal of Psychotherapy* 8 (1): 9–19.

Wilkinson, H. (2005a). *Episodes and Scenes*. Submission for Metanoia Doctorate.

Wilkinson, H. (2005b). *An Abyss of Alternatives: The Psychodynamics of the Shakespeare Authorship Question*, unpublished paper, available at: http://hewardwilkinson.co.uk/ShakespearePaper.doc

Wilson Knight, G. (1930/1960). *The Wheel of Fire*. London: Methuen.

Wimsatt, W.K., Beardsley, M.C. (1951/1967). *The Verbal Icon: Studies in the Meaning of Poetry*. Lexington: University of Kentucky Press.

Wimsatt, W.K. (1951/1967a). *The Concrete Universal*, in *The Verbal Icon: Studies in the Meaning of Poetry*. Lexington: University of Kentucky Press.

Wimsatt, W.K., Beardsley, M.C. (1951/1967b). The Intentional Fallacy. In: *The Verbal Icon: Studies in the Meaning of Poetry*. Lexington: University of Kentucky Press.

Winnicott, D.W. (1960). "Ego Distortion in Terms of True and False Self". In: *The Maturational Process and the Facilitating Environment: Studies in the Theory of Emotional Development*. New York: International UP Inc.

Wittgenstein, L. (1967). *Philosophical Investigations*. Oxford: Blackwell.

Wittgenstein, L. (1969). *On Certainty*. Oxford: Blackwell.

Wittgenstein, L. (1980). *Culture and Value*. Oxford: Blackwell.

Wood, M. (2003). *Shakespeare*. New York: Basic Books.

Wordsworth, W. (1799/2004). *A Slumber did my Spirit Seal*. In: S. Gill (Ed.), *Selected Poems of William Wordsworth*. London: Penguin.

Yeats, W.B. (1983). *The Poems: A New Edition*. Edited by R.J. Finnerman. London: MacMillan.

Young, J. (1998). *Heidegger Philosophy Nazism*. Cambridge: Cambridge University Press.